HOTEL
Chocolat.
BRITISH COCOA GROWER

A New Way of Cooking with Chocolate

headline

Contents

When I crush roasted cocoa beans...

Introduction by Co-Founder Angus Thirlwell

... over my fried eggs in the morning I often think about Mayan warriors. They could march all day and fight a battle with nothing to eat but a little bag of cocoa beans. They'd win, too. So I figure it's a great way to start the day. I eat them not just because they taste great but also because they are packed with stimulating endorphins and give a cardio boost. We have made it our mission at Hotel Chocolat to restore cocoa to its rightful place.

From the beginning, we wanted Hotel Chocolat to offer pure escapism – as our chocolate melted in your mouth, we would check you into a place of indulgent luxury that existed in your imagination. We didn't know then that just a few years later we would be creating a real hotel on our own cocoa plantation.

The first few years of Hotel Chocolat were all about creating our signature chocolates – a new style of luxury that overturned the traditional chocolate scene. 'More Cocoa, Less Sugar' was our mantra then and still is. We always knew that the magic of chocolate is in the cocoa, not the sugar or any other ingredient. Little did we know that our appreciation of cocoa, through a chocolatier's lens, was about to become a total obsession a few years later, as we discovered its savoury side, too.

You see, man and cocoa go back together 3,000 years in a rich, intertwined history. But only the last 500 years have been about sweet chocolate; the previous 2,500 were focused on the savoury. And for good reason – cocoa is a fabulously tasty ingredient. Don't get me wrong. I love the meltingly hedonistic qualities of chocolate more than anyone else I know. After all, we built a whole business around it. But the story of cocoa as a super ingredient needs to be told and that's what this book is all about. For me, that story began in a field eight years ago.

It was a field in the deep south-west of the Caribbean island of Saint Lucia. I was lost in a reverie, gazing up at the spectacular Piton mountains, when I heard the voice of my business partner Peter Harris, a cautious and careful accountant not exactly famed for his giddy spontaneity. 'We've got to buy this place right now, Angus!' he said excitedly. I knew then that the allure of the Rabot Estate cocoa plantation was irresistible.

We were exploring a beautiful 250-year-old estate, in need of some love and attention but pregnant with possibilities. I was already feeling more than at home there, among the cocoa groves. The scent of the island air took me right back to my childhood, growing up in the West Indies.

Rabot Estate C. 1745

We had sailed over there in the late 1960s, after my dad sold his interest in Mr Whippy and took on the challenge of turning around the Barbados Ice Cream Company. Tasting rum-and-raisin ice cream from the vat at my father's factory is one my earliest food memories. That magical time in my life had never left me, but the memories started coming back vividly after one of our customers sent me a beautiful gift just three months before. It was an old copy of a book called *Cocoa & Chocolate: Their History from Plantation to Consumer*, written in 1920. It was all about the glory days of British chocolate and its link with cocoa farming on steamy West Indian estates.

We were taking the highly unorthodox step of becoming farmers on the other side of the planet.

When I read it I was struck by how intertwined the worlds of farming and luxury chocolate had been 100 years ago, and how different it now was in the modern world, where the two were completely separate. It seemed to me that everyone was losing out from this disconnection, from the foodies who care about the authenticity of what they eat, to the cocoa growers whose efforts and skills are not valued in any way.

After I finished the book, I resolved to change this and started to look for cocoa estates in the Caribbean. Just three months later, we bought Rabot Estate in Saint Lucia and our love affair with cocoa began in earnest. It felt like the beginning of a new adventure. We had built up the Hotel Chocolat brand to be a leader in super premium chocolate, and now we were taking the highly unorthodox step of becoming farmers on the other side of the planet. I will always be grateful to Michele Claire for sending me the book. She and her husband have since planted their own cocoa trees at Rabot Estate for posterity, and we remain in contact today.

The more we learned about cocoa farming, the more it fuelled our imaginations, changing the destiny of our brand. First, we'd create a sustainable model for ethical cocoa-growing, then we'd build a boutique hotel and cocoa cuisine restaurant on the estate, and then we'd bring the concept back to the UK.

As well as exciting our customers, this would highlight the importance of cocoa as a quality ingredient and bring us closer to giving growers some of the respect grape growers receive for top quality wine. We needed to restore the estate, plant out more cocoa, and design and build our hotel-restaurant. Phil Buckley was the man for the job, an 'Indiana Jones of cocoa' with a talent for engineering and a flair for design. He and his wife Judy have made every step possible since then. Phil also began building our Island

---

Page 7: Falling in love with Rabot Estate was easy
Opposite, above: The old Rabot Estate house, 1745
Opposite, below: The Cocoa Research Centre at Rabot, full of fine-flavour young seedlings

Growers programme, an ethical trading partnership with over 160 local cocoa farmers, guaranteeing to buy all of their harvest at a rate far above the world bulk cocoa price. And with no middlemen involved at all, all the cash goes into their pockets.

We chose the name Boucan for our hotel-restaurant. It means 'cocoa-drying shed' in Saint Lucian patois, and the hotel sits on the former site of one. But the real reason we chose it is that it's also the root word for 'boucaneer' or 'buccaneer'. *Faire du boucan* means 'to make a racket' in modern French. Perfect, we thought. Making a noise was exactly what we planned to do with our new restaurant, overturning all expectations of cocoa and chocolate.

I needed a chef. Looking for one near the rainforest on a tiny island didn't fill me with confidence, but we had a stroke of luck. One of the leading lights of the London restaurant scene of the 1990s, Jon Bentham, had made the paradise island his home. Over a few Piton beers we found we had the same ideas and reverence for simple ingredients and authentic flavours. I think I made an impression on him with my passion for cocoa. Jon always says that if you cut my arm, cocoa will flow out, and it's the same with him now.

A few months of experimentation taught us that, much like nose-to-tail cooking, we could use all parts of the cocoa pod in our cuisine; nothing needed to be discarded. The sweet lychee-like pulp surrounding each cocoa bean is perfect for sorbets, ceviches and cocktails. The roasted beans are the most versatile, bringing a fabulously deep and nutty accent and a great texture to meats, fish, salads, breads and cakes. The outer pod casing, like a tough marrow, is mulched down for organic fertiliser, too. No waste.

Jon and I agreed a firm principle at the beginning: cocoa should never be shoehorned into a dish. This was never going to be a gimmick. The cocoa had a role to play, often a subtle one, but always with integrity. The other influences in our cooking are British and West Indian. I think of it as a triangle: Cocoa-British-West Indian.

One of the secrets we quickly learned about this cuisine is that your cocoa must always be freshly roasted. Like ground coffee, cocoa will oxidise and lose its volatile flavours quickly. All our restaurants have on-site daily cocoa roasting. In this book, we show you how to roast your own beans at home and where to get them from. It's quick and easy, and the flavours will astound you.

When I looked at our Boucan menu in the cold light of day, just before the launch, I began to wonder if we had gone too far. Would cocoa cuisine be dismissed as a novelty, or would people get it? It's true that some early guests approached the menu with a degree of trepidation. I could tell what they were thinking: was it all chocolate? But once they tried the food, and the great reviews started flooding in, all concerns fell away. And it wasn't really surprising: all we had done was restore cocoa to the role it had played in our food for 2,500 years.

Opposite, above: Like little, heavy, rugby balls – each cocoa pod holds roughly enough beans to make one bar of chocolate
Opposite, below: The Marcial côte (cocoa grove) at Rabot

CÔTES
MARCIAL

Boucan quickly built a reputation as the culinary hotspot of Saint Lucia, aided by its dramatic, award-winning architecture, open on three sides, with views of the UNESCO World Heritage Piton sea mountains. After the restaurant began drawing diners from as far as Miami and New York, I knew we had to bring this unique cocoa cuisine back to the UK. I needed to find an iconic site. But how could I follow Rabot Estate?

London's famous Borough Market provided the answer. We had set up in the market three years previously with what we described as a cocoa shack, serving cocoa tea, chocolate drinks and single-estate small-batch chocolates.

Every table has freshly roasted cocoa beans to calibrate the palate and unlearn the preconception that cocoa can only ever be sweet.

We had built a good reputation, good enough to secure an upgrade to a larger site in the market. It was a three-storey building, right in the middle, with a projecting open-air terrace and an amazing view – not over the Pitons but over London's oldest food market, a meeting place for the capital's foodies. What better place to bring our cocoa cuisine? Although the glass and steel Shard just around the corner does bear an uncanny resemblance to the Petit Piton…

We named our new London restaurant Rabot 1745, after the date the estate was created. We shipped over some hurricane-felled ironwood from Rabot to make the tables and sideboards. As its name implies, ironwood is hard to cut – so hard that it's impossible in Saint Lucia and needed specialists in the UK – but it was worth bringing over the whole trees as they look fabulous.

It's also the spiritual home of our rare and vintage chocolate range, celebrating our small-batch tree-to-bar creations, which are sold in the little shop underneath the restaurant, as well as online.

Jon created a new menu, using many ingredients from the market. Every table has freshly roasted cocoa beans to calibrate the palate and unlearn the preconception that cocoa can only ever be sweet.

I hope this book of our recipes and stories excites you to explore the possibilities too.

Opposite: The contemporary Boucan architecture by Phil Buckley is drawn from the way little cocoa trees stretch for the sky beneath a canopy of larger shelter trees

The Glossary

Cocoa or Cacao?

The cocoa plant was named *Theobroma cacao* – which means 'Cacao, Food of the Gods' – by the famous Swedish botanist Carl Linnaeus in 1753. The word 'cacao' comes from the old Aztec word '*cacahuatl*'. In Saint Lucia, where we grow it, everyone just calls it cocoa. You can use either name – we'll know what you mean.

Cocoa Butter

The natural vegetable fat within a cocoa bean. The butter is extracted by grinding and pressing the bean. Cocoa butter melts at body temperature, giving chocolate its famously sensuous texture. About 50% of a bean is made up of cocoa butter. It is available at specialist stores and online.

Cocoa Mass (or Cocoa Liquor)

The paste made from finely crushing cocoa nibs. It looks like melted chocolate but in its early stages it's quite bitter and rough.

Cocoa Nib

The small crunchy part at the heart of the roasted cocoa bean, each one is about 50% cocoa butter and 50% cocoa powder. Since they are half cocoa butter, they melt in your mouth after a few chews. You can buy a wide range of freshly roasted nibs directly from Hotel Chocolat, www.hotelchocolat.com. We also have bean roasteries in London (Rabot 1745 at Borough Market and Monmouth Street in Covent Garden), as well as in Leeds. Cocoa nibs are now available at an increasing number of health food outlets and online.

Cocoa Powder

The dark brown part of a cocoa bean – what remains when the butter has been pressed out. The powder is separated from the bean through grinding and pressing, and has all of cocoa's flavour and antioxidants. Make sure to avoid 'Dutched' or alkalised powdered cocoa. Alkalising is a process that darkens the colour and smooths the flavour, often to hide the use of poor quality ingredients. Alkalising also destroys 60–90% of the antioxidants present in chocolate.

Cocoa Shell

The loose covering over the bean, winnowed away after roasting, and usually discarded. It's full of flavour and can be used as an ingredient or for infusions. We use them to make our Cocoa Gin, Cocoa Beer and Cocoa Tea Infusions (see page 206). You can buy cocoa shells online including from Hotel Chocolat or you can even roast your own beans and keep the shells (see page 167).

Cocoa Solids

The total fraction of your chocolate that's made of cocoa. This can be a mixture of cocoa mass and cocoa butter. A 70% dark chocolate is made from 70% cocoa solids and 30% sugar.

Couverture

The technical name for any pure chocolate, used in slabs or filled chocolates.

Criollo

One of the most celebrated fine cocoa varieties, renowned for its delicate flavours.

It's also the most susceptible to disease and one of the hardest to farm successfully. The name is derived from the Spanish for 'native', dating back to when the Spanish first arrived in Central America.

Forastero

Another cocoa variety, most commonly associated with bulk cocoa from West Africa, although the fine cocoa from Ecuador is also a variety of Forastero. Forastero is derived from the Spanish for 'foreigner', as it originated from outside the Central American trading regions.

Ganache

A soft filling made from chocolate mixed with either cream, fruit pulp or alcohol.

Gianduja

A style of super-smooth chocolate made from ground nuts and chocolate.

Hazelnut Paste

Ground roasted hazelnut, available online, or you can make it in a blender.

High-cocoa Chocolate

A term used to distinguish quality chocolate. High-cocoa chocolate replaces sugar with cocoa. We define high-cocoa chocolate as: dark chocolate with a minimum of 70% cocoa, milk chocolate, 40%, and caramel or white chocolates, 35%. Our Supermilk chocolate contains a minimum of 65% cocoa. The average milk chocolate on the high street contains 20–25% cocoa.

House Blend/Grade

A deliberate blending of cocoas from different origins to achieve a consistent 'house' flavour, every time. Distinct from our single origin/estate chocolate, whose flavours can vary with each harvest.

Lecithin from Sunflower or Soya

A naturally occurring plant extract that helps to smooth chocolate and let it flow more easily. This makes it easier for the chocolatier to handle when melted.

Praline

A style of filling with a nut paste, typically a mix of chocolate and ground hazelnut.

Single-côte Cocoa

Harvested from a clearly defined single growing area, smaller than a whole estate, and with the same terroir conditions, e.g. the Marcial and Pépinière côtes at Rabot Estate, from which we have made single-côte chocolate (see page 116).

Single-estate Cocoa

Cocoa grown on a single plantation or estate, with distinctive flavours that may vary from harvest to harvest.

Single-origin Cocoa

Cocoa grown in one region or country.

Trinitario

A hybrid of Criollo and Forastero, it's a fine cocoa, combining the excellent flavours of the first with the hardiness of the second. Trinitario was first created in Trinidad in the eighteenth century and is common in the West Indies. It's the dominant cocoa in Saint Lucia and our Rabot Estate plantation.

Truffle

A filled chocolate with a soft centre, typically made with a hard shell, sometimes dusted with cocoa powder.

The Cocoa Factor

Notes to help you get the most out of your cocoa and chocolate

Depending on the kind of cocoa you use, how much you use and how you use it, cocoa and chocolate will have a different effect on the taste and experience of your dishes. In each of our recipes, we'll tell you how much influence it will have, in our Cocoa Factor notes:
Low – a subtle hint, playing a bass note in the harmony of flavours
Medium – a rich interplay of cocoa with other leading ingredients
High – cocoa flavours take the starring role

The Character of Cocoa

The flavour of cocoa and the chocolate it produces varies depending on where the cocoa is grown. Different growing regions have different personalities, each pairing well with other ingredients.

Madagascar, Vietnam
Fruit-led flavours, refreshing in the mouth – perfect with fruits, dark meats and game.

Saint Lucia, Trinidad, Java
Complex and multi-layered, with fruit and roasted flavours jostling for position. Goes with pork, chicken, rums and wines.

Venezuela, Dominican Republic, Peru, Ecuador
Roasted flavours, led by mellow notes of roasted nuts. Ideal with fish, eggs and desserts.

Demystifying Cocoa Percentages

The percentages used on chocolate labels can sometimes seem a bit confusing. A 40% milk chocolate, for example, is not made with 40% milk. The percentage always refers to the amount of cocoa used in the recipe, and the rest will be either all sugar (darks) or milk and sugar (milks/whites).

You'll find higher percentages in dark chocolate recipes, with less in milk, and the least in white. Surprisingly, one of the UK's most famous dark chocolates contains just 39% cocoa, and its milk counterpart only 23%. That means the largest ingredient overall is sugar. We believe this is wrong. We always prefer to use more cocoa in our chocolate for an authentic and satisfying cocoa hit. We put 40–70% cocoa in our milk and Supermilk chocolate, and 70–100% in our dark. Our white chocolate has a much higher cocoa percentage than average, at 36%.

Sugar only costs a tenth of the price of even the cheapest cocoa beans, so it's no wonder that it is tempting for low-quality makers to use too much of it. But in the world of fine chocolate, deciding on whether to use, say, 73% or 75% cocoa in a recipe is the chocolatier's choice and depends on the quality, character and flavour profile of the bean harvest. In many ways, deciding the cocoa percentage is like deciding the alcohol level in a good wine.

How to Melt your Chocolate

In a Bain-marie (recommended)
This traditional method offers a great deal of control. Put your chocolate in a bowl set over a pan of simmering water, ensuring the bowl doesn't actually touch the hot water (or it can burn the chocolate). Heat in the steam for about 2 minutes until fully melted, stirring occasionally.

In a Microwave
Put your chocolate in the microwave on high power for a total of 40–50 seconds, but only in 10-second bursts, stirring in between to ensure it doesn't burn. Stop when fully melted.

Essential Cocoa Nib Know-How

Knowing how to extract the best flavours from your cocoa nibs is essential to many of our recipes. It's easy to buy cocoa nibs these days, but they can be of variable quality. Follow our tips below to make sure you get the most flavour possible from your nibs.

Awakening your Nibs

Often your nibs will have a silver-grey hue to them as they have oxidised around the outside. This is harmless, but we recommend you grind them vigorously in a pestle and mortar for 30 seconds. You'll see the nibs turn a gorgeous mahogany brown, their amazing flavour and aroma awoken at the same time.

Soak them in Water

After awakening, the nibs may still be hard and flinty. Soak them in a little hot water (just enough to cover them) for about 20 minutes which will soften them, the soaking liquid can be set aside as a flavoursome stock.

Storing your Nibs

Just like coffee, roasted nibs should be kept in an airtight container. If you are able to source 'just-roasted' nibs or have made your own (see page 167), you can freeze them in an airtight container until needed, retaining maximum flavour.

Plantation Breakfasts

Start your day with a cocoa boost

Cocoa Banana Smoothie

Cocoa plants need some shade to grow well, and on our plantation in Saint Lucia they thrive under the tender shelter of hundreds of banana trees. This makes it very easy to gather the ingredients for our take on a classic smoothie, substituting pure cocoa nibs for chocolate to give a pleasingly bitter twist. The cocoa is tempered by the milk and yoghurt, so use a very high percentage chocolate – up to 100% cocoa solids – if not using cocoa nibs.

Cocoa Factor: Medium
Origin: Any | 70–100%

Serves 2
1 ripe banana
110g low-fat natural yoghurt
100ml skimmed milk
50g porridge oats
2 teaspoons roasted cocoa nibs
 or dark chocolate, grated
2 teaspoons flaxseeds
1 teaspoon clear honey
4 ice cubes

Place all the ingredients in a blender and blitz until smooth. Pour into a tall glass and serve immediately.

Cocoa Green Tea Blueberry Smoothie

Fantastically fresh and tasty, this smoothie is packed with healthy stimulants and antioxidants. Cocoa plays a subtle role in the flavour but a starring role as a superfood. We don't think there's a better way to start the day.

Cocoa Factor: Low | **Origin:** Any

Serves 4
2 green tea bags
20g roasted cocoa nibs
180ml hot water,
 just off the boil
1½ tablespoons clear honey
300g fresh or frozen blueberries
500g natural yoghurt
10 ice cubes

Put the green tea bags and nibs in a bowl and pour over the hot water. Allow to infuse for 3 minutes. Remove the teabags and stir in the honey.

Add the mixture and the remaining ingredients to a blender and blitz until the ice has broken down completely. Pour into tall glasses and serve immediately.

Release the Mayan Warrior Within You

'Chocolate is the divine drink which builds up resistance and fights fatigue. A cup of this precious drink permits man to walk for a whole day without food.'

Hernán Cortés, Spanish conquistador and conqueror of the Aztec Empire, 1519

Long after Mayan warriors marched all day and won battles on just a small bag of cocoa beans, the seventeenth century London diarist Samuel Pepys was using chocolate as a hangover cure.

People have known for centuries that cocoa and chocolate have a positive effect on our physical and mental health, but research has only recently begun to uncover just how it works.

Above all, it turns out that cocoa is packed with antioxidants. This doesn't mean you should be reaching for a bar of sugary chocolate for breakfast. But if you choose the right chocolate and cocoa products as part of your daily diet, they can release some of the Mayan warrior in you, sustaining you through the day and keeping you stimulated mentally and physically.

Cocoa nibs are like an exceptional spice that can be used in a huge number of ways, and have a unique savoury flavour until you blend them with milk and sugar. Crushed nibs are great on with eggs or mixed in your granola or muesli (see pages 30 or 34). And they make perfect powerhouses of energy in our breakfast bars (see pages 32–33).

Choosing your Chocolate

When it comes to chocolate, you'll always benefit from choosing the best. A good dark chocolate has remarkably simple ingredients: cocoa mass (the technical name for ground cocoa beans) and some sugar, with perhaps a touch of natural emulsifier (usually soya or sunflower lecithin) to keep the chocolate smooth.

This is all you should see in the ingredients for a bar of dark chocolate. So go for dark chocolate, or high-cocoa Supermilk chocolate (40–70% is now available, comparing favourably to the 25% cocoa or less seen in cheap milk chocolate.) As a general rule the higher the cocoa percentage in your chocolate, the less sugar it contains, letting you enjoy the benefits of cocoa while avoiding carbohydrates.

You can educate your palate and learn to enjoy high-cocoa chocolate and cocoa nibs by starting with what you like and slowly increasing the cocoa content. Don't eat something sweet just before eating a high-cocoa chocolate, or it will taste more bitter than it really is. (See page 18 for more information on the character of cocoa.)

Single-origin chocolates have different characters depending on the region in which they're grown. See the Taste-o-Meter on page 90 to find your favourite.

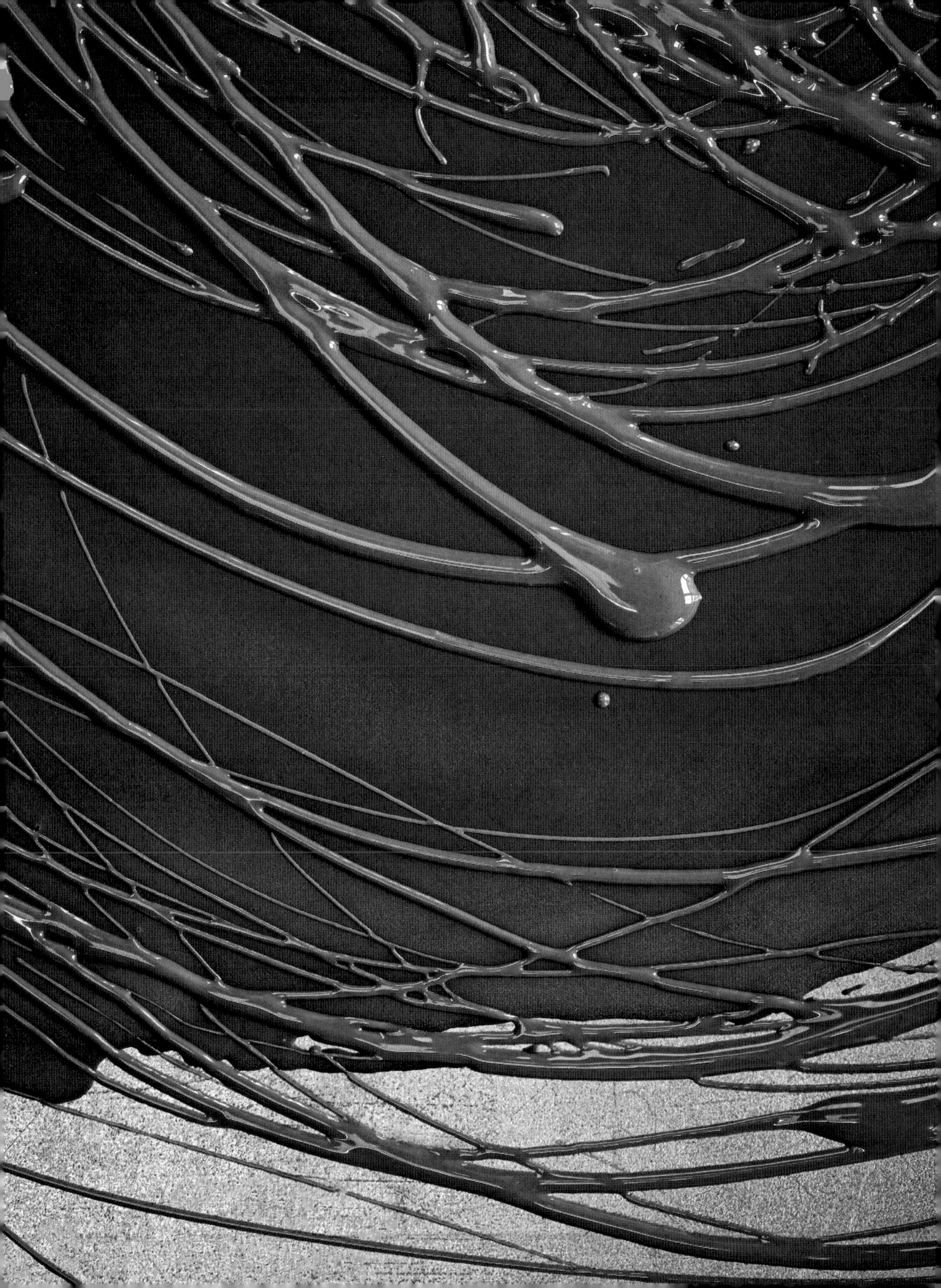

The Power of Cocoa

Cocoa and chocolate contains the following nutrients and compounds, and all of them have amazing effects on your health and wellbeing

Antioxidants

Chocolate is high in antioxidant polyphenols, a group of protective chemicals vital for our general health, including catechins. Catechins are known to protect the cells of the cocoa plant, and research suggests that they may do the same for the human body, as well as inhibiting some cancer cells and mopping up free radicals (molecules that cause cellular damage and can lead to cancer).

Catechins are concentrated in green and oolong tea, raw apples, apricots, nectarines, pears and plums with their skins, raspberries, cranberries, cherries and broad beans. The blackberry is considered the king of catechins, but dark chocolate with 70% cocoa or more has approximately twice the amount (40mg/100g) of catechins found in berries (6–35 mg/100g depending on berry type).

The Food of the Gods

Theobromine is a stimulant found in cocoa and is partly responsible for chocolate's famous feel-good effect. The word theobromine comes from the Greek term 'theobroma', meaning 'food of the gods'. This stimulant drives the production of serotonin, which helps create a positive mood, improves sleep and emotional wellbeing, and promotes a healthy appetite. Decreased levels of serotonin are known to be a factor in cases of depression.

Theobromine is a milder stimulant than caffeine but is found at high levels in chocolate, about 250mg in a 50g bar of dark chocolate.

Following its discovery in the late nineteenth century, theobromine has been used in many medical treatments, mostly for heart and circulation problems, including high blood pressure. So a few squares of dark chocolate really might prolong your life and make you happier in the process!

The Love Drug

Phenylethylamine, or PEA, occurs in small quantities in chocolate, and is thought to trigger the release of endorphins. PEA is a naturally occurring antidepressant that increases when we fall in love. PEA also boosts our dopamine levels, a natural hormone directly associated with pleasure. If you're madly in love and feeling restless with butterflies in your tummy, that'll be the dopamine!

The scientific jury is still out on how strongly chocolate actually delivers PEA into our bodies – some researchers think that it might be metabolised after we eat chocolate and before it has time to affect our mood. It'll take further research to find out, but it's hard to deny chocolate's legendary connection to romance.

The Bliss Effect

Anandamide is an extraordinary chemical known as a cannabinoid, which can be found only in chocolate, the human brain and cannabis. Its name derives from the Sanskrit word '*ananda*', which means 'bliss'. Anandamide produces a feeling of euphoria, and is another reason why some people feel so happy and content when they eat chocolate.

Caffeine

As we all know, caffeine is a natural stimulant that can enhance alertness and decrease tiredness. It can also lift your mood and boost cardiovascular function. Caffeine is generally considered safe and beneficial for most people – up to 300mg per day. Chocolate and cocoa nibs contain a modest amount, with a 50g piece of dark chocolate providing up to 60mg of caffeine compared with a 155ml cup of coffee, which can contain up to 180mg. See page 29 for Angus' Cocoa-Powered Day.

My Cocoa-Powered Day

Hotel Chocolat co-founder and CEO Angus Thirlwell gives a guide to pepping yourself up with cocoa, Mayan warrior-style.

First Thing

I always start the day with a light and detoxing Cocoa Infusion Tea (see page 208). Better than a cup of regular tea to awaken the senses, no question.

Breakfast

Now I need fuel. Bring on the fried eggs, sprinkled with crushed cocoa beans for extra spice and crunch. I'll have this with a hot chocolate – dark chocolate with chilli is my favourite. If I'm in a rush I might whip up a Cocoa Banana Smoothie instead (see page 22).

Mid-morning

I've given myself a good base of cocoa, so now I can boost that with a shot of coffee caffeine: mine's an Americano with a splash of cold milk.

Lunch

A light lunch to keep me nimble: I like an Aubergine Salad with Cocoa Nib Crispbread and Yoghurt for a great cocoa lift (see page 137). After that, I'll take a cocoa tea infusion with peppermint – uplifting and great for digestion.

Teatime

To get out of that mid-afternoon slowdown, I'll hit the accelerator with a chunk of chocolate. I like high-cocoa Supermilk chocolate for the low sugar (less than a dark chocolate, so no blood sugar spike) and the 65% cocoa hit. I'll pair it with a cup of Darjeeling tea.

Apéritif

I love a Rabot 1745 Rum Sour (see page 219) to set me up for dinner: a piquant tang of cocoa bitters offsetting the mellow Chairman's Reserve rum from Saint Lucia.

Dinner

It's hard to choose, but I love fish, and the Chocolate Chilli Crusted Salmon (see page 118) is superb – the bitter bite of dark chocolate pairs perfectly with the rich and naturally sweet salmon, jazzed up with a generous squeeze of lime.

After Dinner

A final cup of cocoa infusion tea with ginger rounds off a perfect cocoa day.

Indulgent Chocolate Granola

Mayan warriors used to munch on cocoa beans as they marched all day to battle, so eating this superfood for breakfast is an excellent idea. Guests at our Boucan plantation hotel in Saint Lucia certainly agree – we make fresh batches of this every morning. As you are serving this with milk, you really need to use a dark chocolate.

Cocoa Factor: Medium | **Origin:** Any | 70–90%

Makes about 900g

400g jumbo porridge oats
115g oat bran or oat germ
115g light muscovado sugar
115g mixed unsalted nuts, chopped
55g desiccated coconut
70g roasted cocoa nibs, or 70g dark chocolate, broken into chunks
85g sunflower seeds
30g sesame seeds
150ml sunflower oil
150ml water
2 tablespoons cocoa powder
½ teaspoon vanilla extract
½ teaspoon salt
200g dark chocolate, chopped into peanut-size pieces

Preheat the oven to 200°C/gas 6. In a large bowl, mix together the oats, oat bran, sugar, nuts, coconut, cocoa nibs (if using, or dark chocolate) and seeds.

In another large bowl, whisk together the oil, water, cocoa powder, vanilla extract and salt until well combined. Stir this into the dry ingredients and mix thoroughly.

Transfer the mixture to large baking trays and spread it out evenly. Bake for 15 minutes, then stir and turn the mixture thoroughly on the trays and bake for a further 15 minutes.

Allow to cool on the trays, then mix in the chopped chocolate. Store in an airtight container for up to 2 weeks. Serve with milk (whole, skimmed, coconut, almond or soya) or yoghurt and sliced bananas or blueberries if you like.

Plantation Power Bars

Cereal bars are a great way to snack when you're on the move or in a hurry, but they are often overloaded with sugars and not very healthy. Here are two no-bake versions for you to try that are quick, easy and enhanced with the power of cocoa. For energy as well as a great taste, choose a dark or a high-percentage milk chocolate, packed with as much cocoa as possible. Once you've tried our versions, customise the recipes with different chocolates, dried fruits, raw nuts and seeds to find your perfect breakfast treat.

Cocoa Factor: Medium | **Origin:** Africa, Ecuador Dark, 70–100%; Milk, 50–75%

Makes 10

140g oats
110g chopped walnuts
220g pitted dates
1 tablespoon flaxseeds
100g chocolate chips
  or chopped chocolate
100g natural almond butter
110g clear honey

Preheat the oven to 180°C/gas 4 and line a 20 x 20cm tin with baking parchment.

Start by toasting the oats and nuts. Spread them on a tray and place in the oven for 12 minutes, stirring halfway through.

Place the dates in a food processor and blend to a thick paste. Scoop out into a mixing bowl along with the toasted oats and nuts, flaxseeds and chocolate. In a small pan, heat the almond butter and honey over a low heat until they start to bubble. Add to the mixing bowl and stir together with the other ingredients to create a sticky dough.

Press the dough firmly into the lined tin and place in the freezer for 15 minutes to firm up. Remove from the freezer and cut into 10 bars measuring 4 x 10cm. Store in an airtight container in the fridge – they will keep for up to 1 week.

Chewy Cocoa-Nut Bar (indulgent)

Cocoa Factor: Medium | **Origin:** Africa, Ecuador | Dark, 70–100%; Milk, 50–75%

Makes 10

50g puffed rice
70g oats
100g chopped roasted nuts,
  (we use 60g almonds
  and 40g hazelnuts)
90g dried cranberries
120g dark chocolate
80g peanut butter or other nut butter
100g clear honey
sunflower oil, for greasing
20g pumpkin seeds, lightly toasted
  (optional)
10g sunflower seeds, lightly toasted
  (optional)

Place the puffed rice, oats, nuts and cranberries in a mixing bowl. Gently heat the chocolate in a microwave, stirring every 10 seconds or so to ensure the chocolate does not burn. Alternatively, you can melt the chocolate in a bowl set over a pan of simmering water, stirring occasionally, for 2 minutes. Make sure the bottom of the bowl doesn't actually touch the hot water. Warm the peanut butter and honey in a pan over a low heat, then stir in the melted chocolate. Now stir the chocolate mixture into the dry ingredients, ensuring everything is coated.

Grease a 20 x 20cm tin with oil. Tip the mixture into the prepared tin and spread evenly. Sprinkle with the toasted seeds (if using) and press it all down tightly – to do this, cover the surface with baking parchment and flatten the mixture using the palm of your hand. Place in the fridge to set for 1½ hours before cutting into 10 slices measuring 4 x 10cm. Store in an airtight container with baking parchment in between each layer.

Superfood Cocoa Muesli

While our Indulgent Chocolate Granola (see page 30) offers a touch of luxury, this recipe unleashes all the power of pure cocoa. The deep, chocolatey notes of cocoa are really drawn out by the seeds. Serve this with any milk you prefer – almond milk adds an extra nutty flavour as well as being dairy-free.

Cocoa Factor: Medium | **Origin:** Any

Serves 5–6
110g malted wheat flakes
1 tablespoon linseeds
1 tablespoon pumpkin seeds
1 tablespoon sunflower seeds
1 tablespoon roasted cocoa nibs
1 tablespoon agave syrup or honey

Preheat the oven to 140°C/gas 1.

In a large bowl, mix together the wheat flakes, seeds and cocoa nibs. Pour over the agave syrup and mix again. Spread out the mixture on a baking tray and bake in the oven for 10 minutes.

Remove from the oven and turn the muesli over with a spoon to mix all the flavours. Allow to cool, then store in an airtight container in a cool place.

Smoked Mackerel, Poached Eggs and Portobello Mushrooms

This is a really great breakfast or brunch dish that ticks all the right boxes. The smoky flavour of the fish works well alongside the meaty mushrooms, while the soft egg yolk provides a rich sauce. White chocolate in the horseradish slightly sweetens the fire with the opulence of cocoa butter replacing the richness of cream.

Cocoa Factor: Low | **Origin:** Any | Butter 70–90%; Ganache, at least 30%

Serves 4

4 portobello mushrooms, wiped clean and stems removed (reserve for a soup or sauce)
20g Cocoa Nib Butter, (see page 234) or regular butter
4 thyme sprigs
1 garlic clove, peeled and finely sliced
1 tablespoon white wine vinegar
4 eggs (as fresh as possible)
4 slices of toasted bread of your choice, to serve
1 quantity of Smoked Mackerel Ganache (see page 228), at room temperature
salt and freshly ground pepper

Preheat the oven to 220°C/gas 7.

Place the mushrooms with the gills upwards on a baking tray. Add 1 teaspoon of butter, 1 sprig of thyme, a few slices of garlic, and salt and pepper to each mushroom. Bake for 25 minutes.

About 10 minutes before the mushrooms are ready, cook the eggs. Bring a medium pan of water to a boil and add a pinch of salt and the white wine vinegar. Turn the heat down to a gentle simmer. Crack an egg into a teacup and then, in one movement, pour the egg into the simmering water. Repeat quickly with the other eggs. For a soft-poached egg, simmer for 2½ minutes; for a firmer egg, simmer for 4 minutes. When cooked to your liking, remove the eggs with a slotted spoon and place on to kitchen paper to drain the excess water.

Start toasting the bread. Place a cooked mushroom on each serving plate, gills up. Using 2 tablespoons, shape a quenelle of Smoked Mackerel Ganache alongside (dip the spoons in hot water if you're having trouble achieving a nice clean shape). Alternatively, just spoon the ganache into a ramekin and place on the plate. Place a poached egg on to a slice of toast, season with salt and pepper, and serve.

Jon's Brilliant Banana Bread

At Hotel Chocolat we still remember the epic 'Battle of the Banana Breads', fought between Angus and Jon to decide which recipe would be served in our restaurants. They're both excellent, but different. Why not try both and do a banana bread taste-off? (See Angus' recipe opposite.) The blackened bananas give this a rich, sticky texture with the cocoa nibs playing the crunchy contrasting role normally given to walnuts.

Cocoa Factor: Medium | **Origin:** Caribbean, Latin America

Makes a 1kg loaf

115g butter, at room temperature, plus extra for greasing
280g plain flour, plus extra for dredging
½ teaspoon salt
1 teaspoon bicarbonate of soda
30g roasted cocoa nibs
2 eggs
½ teaspoon vanilla extract
225g caster sugar
3 very ripe, almost blackened bananas, peeled and mashed with a fork

Preheat the oven to 180°C/gas 4 and butter a 1kg loaf tin. Dredge the greased tin with flour then shake out the excess, leaving just a coating.

In a large bowl mix together the flour, salt, bicarbonate of soda and cocoa nibs. Beat the eggs and vanilla extract in a separate bowl. In a mixer, cream the butter and sugar together until light and fluffy. Gradually add the egg mixture while the machine is still running. Add the mashed bananas and beat for a couple more minutes. Remove the bowl from the mixer and use a rubber spatula to fold in the dry ingredients until just combined – do not overbeat.

Pour the mixture into the prepared tin and bake in the oven for 25 minutes. After this time, remove the loaf from the oven, loosely cover it with foil and return it to the oven for a further 20 minutes. To test if the loaf is ready, insert a skewer into the middle and pull it out. If there is still raw dough on the skewer, return the loaf to the oven for a further 5 minutes.

Allow the loaf to cool in the tin. Once cold, turn the bread out and wrap it in baking parchment, then store either in the fridge or in a cool place. This banana bread is best eaten the day after making, slightly warmed, and ideally served with Super Quick Microwave Chocolate Sauce (see page 191) and some whipped cream.

N.B. Jon's bread won.

Angus' Amazing Dairy-free Banana Bread

Angus' recipe is inspired by his childhood growing up in Barbados. Banana breads are hugely popular in the West Indies and you could eat a different one every day – it seems that everyone has their own recipe. This one combines the best of Angus' childhood favourites, using spelt flour for a heavier texture, paired with cocoa nibs, chocolate from the region and traditional West Indian spices.

Cocoa Factor: Medium | **Origin:** Caribbean, Latin America | 70–90%

Makes a 1kg loaf

115g virgin coconut oil (or use butter if you prefer), plus extra for greasing
115g wholemeal spelt flour (or use wheat flour if you prefer),
115g white spelt flour
2 teaspoons baking powder
¼ teaspoon bicarbonate of soda
½ teaspoon salt
½ teaspoon ground cinnamon
½ teaspoon grated nutmeg
40g roasted cocoa nibs
25g muscovado sugar
3 eggs, beaten
4 large or 6 small very ripe bananas, well mashed
½ teaspoon grated lemon zest
20g crushed walnuts (optional)
150g dark chocolate, cut into irregular chunks roughly the size of whole almonds

Preheat the oven to 180°C/gas 4 and grease a 1kg loaf tin with coconut oil or butter.

Mix together the flours, baking powder, bicarbonate of soda, salt, cinnamon and nutmeg in a large bowl and set aside. Soften the cocoa nibs in a little just-boiled water. Steep for 20 minutes then pour away the liquid. Retain the nibs for later.

In a separate bowl, cream together the coconut oil and sugar, and then beat in the eggs. Mix this into the dry ingredients and then fold in the mashed banana. Add the lemon zest, softened cocoa nibs, walnuts (if using) and chocolate, and beat well to combine.

Pour into the prepared tin and leave to stand for 20 minutes. Bake for 45–50 minutes. To test if the loaf is ready, insert a skewer into the middle and pull it out. If there is still raw dough on the skewer, return the loaf to the oven for a further 5 minutes. Allow the loaf to cool in the tin for a few minutes then turn it out to cool completely on a rack. Serve cut into thick slices.

Chocolate Praline Brioche

Perfect for a lazy Sunday with a mug of hot chocolate. You can do most of the preparation the evening before and bake in the morning. Mellow flavours work best here, so pick a good house blend for your chocolate chunks.

Cocoa Factor: Medium | **Origin:** House Blend | Milk, at least 50%; Dark, 70–80%

Makes 10

For the brioche
310g strong white flour
6g salt
30g caster sugar
7g instant dried yeast
4 eggs
160g butter, cut into small cubes, plus extra for greasing
20ml milk, to glaze

For the filling
150g homemade chocolate spread, (see pages 47–53), or Hotel Chocolat Chocolate Spread
extra chocolate chips or broken pieces of chocolate for added indulgence (optional)

Weigh out the flour, salt, sugar and yeast into the bowl of a free-standing mixer. Add in the eggs and mix on a medium speed using a dough hook. The dough will be sticky at first, but keep on mixing to develop the gluten; this will take around 10 minutes. You may need to stop the mixer to scrape down the bowl. Once the dough is ready it will look smooth and will not stick to the sides of the mixing bowl.

Add the butter gradually, making sure each addition is fully incorporated before adding more. The mixture may start to look greasy at this stage, but do not worry; it will eventually form a smooth, soft dough. When all the butter has been added, continue to mix for a few minutes until the dough is smooth and uniform in consistency. Remove the dough from the machine, place it in a clean bowl, cover and leave in a warm place to rest and prove – it should double in size after 30–60 minutes, depending on the room temperature.

Knock the dough back by flipping it over 2 or 3 times with your hands to remove the air.

Place it back in the bowl, cover with cling film and chill in the fridge for a minimum of 4 hours but preferably overnight.

Recipe continues

A note about handling brioche:
The high butter content of brioche and its delicate texture mean you need to work quickly and gently in the next steps or the dough will become soft and sticky. If this starts to happen, don't panic: put it back in the fridge to cool down and then carry on.

When you are ready to cook the brioche, preheat the oven to 200°C/gas 6 and grease 10 holes in a muffin tin with plenty of butter.

Take the dough out of the fridge and knock it back. Roll the dough out into a rectangle measuring roughly 20 x 40cm. Spread a thick layer of chocolate spread on to the dough, leaving a small space around the edges. Scatter over the chocolate chips or chocolate pieces evenly, if using. Starting from one end, roll the dough up to create a tight log. Slice into 5cm pieces and place in the muffin tray, with the swirl pattern facing upwards. Lightly brush the surfaces with milk to glaze. Leave in a warm place to prove for 60–90 minutes, until they have doubled in size.

Bake in the oven for 20–25 minutes, lowering the temperature to 180°C/gas 4 after 15 minutes. The brioche should be golden brown on all sides. Leave to cool a little in the tray.

Cocoa Nib Cob Loaf

The malty flavours of freshly roasted cocoa nibs work fantastically well in this bread, giving it a sourdough-like taste. Soaking the nibs beforehand leaves them nice and tender.

Cocoa Factor: Medium | **Origin:** Any

Makes an 800g loaf
30g roasted cocoa nibs
500g strong white flour,
  plus extra for dusting
10g salt
10g instant dried yeast,
  or 20g fresh yeast
30g butter, softened

First prepare the nibs by placing them in a bowl. Pour in about a mug's worth of freshly boiled water and leave to steep for 20 minutes. Reserving the water, drain the nibs.

Weigh out the flour into a large bowl and add the salt and yeast. Top up the nib water with cold water to 320ml, then add to the bowl along with the softened butter. Using your fingers, mix together to roughly combine the ingredients, forming a tacky dough. Turn the dough out on to an oiled worktop and knead for about 10 minutes, until smooth and elastic. Shape the dough into a ball, put it into a large, clean, oiled bowl, cover and set aside to prove. The dough should double in size after 1–3 hours, or alternatively you can prove it overnight in the fridge.

After the first proving, turn the dough out on to a lightly floured worktop, sprinkle over the softened nibs and fold them into the dough. Knead again for 5 minutes, ensuring the nibs are well incorporated. Shape the dough into a tight ball and place on a lightly floured tray. Cover the dough with oiled cling film and prove in a warm place until doubled in size, about 35–45 minutes.

Preheat the oven to 220°C/gas 7. For a crusty loaf, set a baking tin filled with three mugs of hot water in the bottom of the oven.

After proving, lightly dust the loaf with flour, slash the top and put it straight into the oven. Bake for 40 minutes until crusty and golden. Cool completely on a rack before slicing and eating. It's great with mature Cheddar and our Creole Tomato Chutney (see page 246).

Chocolate Spreads

We all love chocolate spread as children but then start to grow out of it, typically because it's far too sweet. These recipes hold back the sugar and pump up the chocolate for a deeper, more satisfying hit. **See images on pages 50–51.**

Chocolate Hazelnut Spread

This is one of Hotel Chocolat's most popular chocolate spreads. You can buy hazelnut paste in most supermarkets and health food shops. Alternatively, you can blitz hazelnuts in a food processor to your desired consistency.

Cocoa Factor: High | **Origin:** Any | 70–85%

Makes 300g
150g hazelnut paste
50g icing sugar
80g dark chocolate
25ml sunflower oil

In a mixing bowl, mix the hazelnut paste and sugar until smooth.

Melt the chocolate in the microwave in 10-second bursts on medium power for 40–50 seconds. Alternatively, melt the chocolate in a bowl set over a pan of simmering water for 2 minutes. Make sure the bottom of the bowl doesn't actually touch the hot water and stir the chocolate occasionally.

Slowly add the oil to the chocolate in a trickle, beating the chocolate all the time to create a smooth emulsion. Now beat in the mixed nut paste and ensure everything is thoroughly combined. Chill in an airtight container for about 1 hour until set.

This can be kept for up to 2 weeks in the fridge. Soften at room temperature for about 30 minutes before serving.

Coconut Chocolate Spread

We sometimes call this the 'free spread' because it's dairy-free and nut-free. This one lets a good naturally dairy-free dark chocolate take centre stage with nothing obscuring its deep aromas and punchy notes apart from a delicate touch of mellow coconut. And, since coconut trees shelter cocoa trees from the fierce sun around the equator, we think that's OK. Lavish it on some hot toast. You can use a good milk chocolate instead, although it obviously won't be dairy-free. This spread can be kept in your store cupboard or fridge for up to 4 weeks and is best served at room temperature.

Cocoa Factor: High | **Origin:** Any | Dark, 70–85%; Milk, 50–70%

Makes 300g
105g virgin coconut oil
200g dark chocolate,
  broken into small pieces

Place the virgin coconut oil in a bowl and heat in the microwave for 15–20 seconds on high, stirring every 5 seconds or so to prevent it from getting too hot. The oil should be melted, with no lumps. Alternatively, place in a bowl set over a pan of simmering water and warm through for 2 minutes. Make sure the bottom of the bowl doesn't actually touch the hot water and stir occasionally.

In a separate bowl, gently melt the chocolate as above. It should be completely melted and smooth but not too hot.

Pour the coconut oil into the molten chocolate and stir until incorporated; the mixture should be smooth. Pour the mixture into a lidded container and chill in the fridge for 30 minutes, until set. Remove the spread from the fridge and let it come up to room temperature, then smother over your favourite bread.

Crunchy Peanut Chocolate Spread

A milk chocolate of at least 40% cocoa solids marries well with the roasted, salty notes of peanut, making it perfectly spreadable over hot granary bread or warm brioche (see Chocolate Praline Brioche on page 40). If your peanut butter doesn't already contain salt, add a pinch of good sea salt to the mix. You can personalise your spread by using your favourite nut butters and chocolate grades – if you prefer a smoother texture, just use peanut butter without the crunchy bits! Almond butter complements creamy caramel chocolate, and hazelnut butter pairs perfectly with a 50% cocoa milk chocolate or a Supermilk chocolate, like our Peru 75%. Milk chocolate works better in this recipe, as the lower-intensity cocoa and creamier notes produce a gentler, smoother spread that allows the nut flavours to shine through. If you prefer, you can use dark chocolate for a more intense finish. This spread can be kept in your store cupboard or fridge for up to 4 weeks and is best served at room temperature.

Cocoa Factor: Medium | **Origin:** Any | 40–70%

Makes 300g
110g milk chocolate
2 tablespoons sunflower oil
or rapeseed oil
165g crunchy peanut butter
(we use organic, with no additives)

Gently melt the chocolate in a microwave, stirring every 10 seconds or so to ensure the chocolate does not burn. Alternatively, you can melt the chocolate in a bowl set over a pan of simmering water, stirring occasionally, for 2 minutes. Make sure the bottom of the bowl doesn't actually touch the hot water. It should be completely melted and smooth.

Add the sunflower oil, stirring well. Stir in the peanut butter until evenly incorporated into the molten chocolate. Pour into an airtight container and chill in the fridge for 30 minutes, or until set. Remove from the fridge and bring up to room temperature before spreading.

Coconut Chocolate Spread
Chocolate Hazelnut Spread
Crunchy Peanut Chocolate Spread

Chocolate Salted Caramel Spread
Chocolate Salted Caramel and Nut Spread

Caramel Spreads

Caramel chocolate and a dash of salt can make any recipe feel like an indulgent treat. These spreads are great on toast, as a filling for a layered sponge cake (see page 180) or even to share with breadsticks as a dessert. Make sure you use a good quality caramel chocolate made with cocoa butter, caramelised sugar and milk powder.

Chocolate Salted Caramel Spread

Cocoa Factor: Medium | **Origin:** Any | At least 35%

Makes 500g
300g good quality unsalted high-cocoa caramel chocolate, broken into small pieces
150ml whipping cream
large pinch of sea salt

Gently melt the caramel chocolate in a microwave, stirring every 10 seconds or so to ensure it does not burn. Alternatively, you can melt the chocolate in a bowl set over a pan of simmering water, stirring occasionally, for 2 minutes. Make sure the bottom of the bowl doesn't actually touch the hot water.

Measure the cream and sea salt into a saucepan and warm until simmering. Allow to cool for 2 minutes. Pour one-third of the cream into the chocolate and stir. Slowly add more cream, stirring continuously to create a smooth mixture – don't worry if it looks slightly separated at first; it will come together as you stir. Place the cooled mixture in the fridge to set for 2 hours before using. The spread can be stored in an airtight container in the fridge for up to 1 week.

Chocolate Salted Caramel and Nut Spread

Cocoa Factor: Medium | **Origin:** Any | At least 35%

Makes 600g

200g roasted pecans
100g roasted hazelnuts
pinch of sea salt
240g good quality unsalted caramel chocolate, broken into small pieces
2 tablespoons sunflower oil

Put the pecans, hazelnuts and salt in a food processor and blitz until the nuts become a fine powder. Stop and scrape down the sides, then carry on blending until the nuts form a liquid paste – this will take 5–10 minutes.

Set aside 80g of the chocolate and chop it finely. Melt the remaining chocolate. You can do this in 10-second bursts in the microwave, for 40–50 seconds, stirring frequently. Alternatively, melt the chocolate in a bowl set over a pan of simmering water for 2 minutes. Make sure the bottom of the bowl doesn't actually touch the hot water and stir the chocolate occasionally. Ideally the chocolate should be just melted and not hot. Stir in the chopped chocolate. As this melts, the chocolate will cool down and thicken. If the chocolate becomes too thick, gently reheat it for a few seconds and stir thoroughly.

When all the chocolate is melted, stir in the nut paste and sunflower oil, and blend well. Place the cooled mixture in the fridge to set for 1 hour before using. The spread can be stored in an airtight container in the fridge for up to 1 week.

Food for a Jump Up

Starters and party plates, Saint Lucian style

'Jump up' - the Saint Lucian name for an impromptu party after sunset, when friends and neighbours get together in a garden or on a local beach for drinks, food and music.

Black Pepper Cocoa Nib Beef Jerky

In Saint Lucia, French pirates hiding out on Pigeon Island would prepare this kind of jerky for snacking on during their shipping raids on Spanish ships in the Caribbean. This recipe makes a moreishly rich and peppery party snack with the cocoa joining with the soy, Worcestershire sauce and beef to create an umami powerhouse.

Cocoa Factor: Medium | **Origin:** Any

Serves 4

170ml lager
110ml dark soy sauce
25ml Worcestershire sauce
1½ teaspoons whole black peppercorns, lightly crushed
250g beef rump, cut along the grain into 3cm-thick strips
1 teaspoon coarsely ground black pepper
3 teaspoons roasted cocoa nibs

In a large bowl, whisk together the lager, soy sauce, Worcestershire sauce and cracked peppercorns. Take each strip of beef and cut into 5mm-thick slices across the width. Place in the marinade and turn the contents over to mix well. Cover the bowl with cling film and chill in the fridge for between 12 and 18 hours.

Preheat the oven to its lowest setting, or 100°C/gas ¼. Place a wire cooling rack on a baking tray big enough to hold it. Remove the meat from the marinade and shake off any excess liquid. Arrange the beef in a single layer on the rack then sprinkle over the coarsely ground pepper and the cocoa nibs. Place the tray in the oven and bake for at least 4 hours – you want to almost dry the beef out but still keep it a little chewy.

Remove from the oven and allow to cool completely. Store in an airtight container in the fridge – it will keep for up to 4 days.

Opposite: Boucanier II, one of the hotel's boats, doing the pirate run up the Saint Lucian coast

Boucanier II

Chocolate-Covered Rum-Soaked Raisins

Watch out: these pack a punch! Rum, raisin and chocolate sing together in perfect harmony. Customise our recipe by changing the origins of your chocolate and rum to subtly introduce different flavours. We find that rum pairs best with a robust dark chocolate or a high-cocoa milk chocolate but we tend to avoid fruity dark chocolates, such as those from Madagascar. Try adding different spices to the alcohol before soaking to create seasonal specials – for example, add a little cinnamon, nutmeg and clove for a Christmas version. Or, for an alternative, try the Amaretto and almond version opposite. These are great served after dinner with coffee.

Cocoa Factor: High | **Origin:** West Africa, Ecuador, Caribbean | Dark, 65–75%; Milk, 50–65%

Makes about 30 clusters
350g raisins
250ml golden rum
210g chocolate, finely chopped

Put the raisins in a bowl and pour over the rum, making sure all the raisins are completely covered. Cover the bowl with cling film and leave in the fridge for 24–48 hours. When the raisins have soaked, drain off the liquid and dry the raisins using kitchen paper.

Weigh out 140g of the chocolate, reserving 70g. Melt the larger amount in 10-second bursts in the microwave, stirring frequently until melted but not too hot. Alternatively, melt the chocolate in a bowl set over a pan of simmering water for 2 minutes. Make sure the bottom of the bowl doesn't actually touch the hot water and stir the chocolate occasionally. Keep a close eye on it: ideally the chocolate should be just melted. Remove from the heat and stir in the remaining 70g of chocolate. This will lower the temperature of the chocolate and it will thicken, but if the chocolate starts to set too much, warm it up for a few seconds and continue stirring until it has all melted.

Add the raisins to the chocolate and stir through so they are all coated. (Make sure the raisins are at room temperature – if they are too cold the chocolate will set too quickly.) Using a teaspoon, place bite-size clusters of raisins on to a tray lined with baking parchment. Place in the fridge to set.

Amaretto-Sultana and Almond Clusters

Cocoa Factor: High | **Origin:** Columbia, Ecuador | 50–65%

Makes about 30 clusters
350g raisins
250ml Amaretto liqueur
240g almonds, roughly chopped
360g high-cocoa milk chocolate

Follow the method for Chocolate-Covered Rum-Soaked Raisins opposite, replacing the rum with Amaretto and mixing the almonds in with the drained raisins before coating with chocolate.

Not-So-Scotch Egg

The classic Scottish recipe is reborn with a crunchy cocoa nib and breadcrumb crust over a cloak of softened pearl barley.

Cocoa Factor: Medium | **Origin:** Any

Serves 4

1 garlic bulb, cloves separated but skin left on
2 tablespoons olive oil
20g dried ceps or wild mushrooms
2 teaspoons butter
1 leek, cleaned and finely sliced
100g pearl barley
2 thyme sprigs, leaves picked and chopped
300ml vegetable stock
100ml boiling water
5 eggs
100ml whole milk
150g dry breadcrumbs
20g roasted cocoa nibs
50g plain flour
salt and freshly ground pepper
sunflower oil, for deep-frying

Preheat the oven to 190°C/gas 5.

Roast the garlic in 1 tablespoon of olive oil for 20 minutes in the oven. Remove, allow the garlic to cool, then peel and roughly chop.

Soak the dried mushrooms in tepid water to soften for 10 minutes, then squeeze the mushrooms – keep the liquid – and roughly chop them. Pour the remaining olive oil into a pan over a medium heat and cook the mushrooms until softened but not coloured. Add the butter and sliced leek, and continue cooking until the liquid evaporates.

Rinse the pearl barley in a fine sieve under a cold tap, then add this to the leek and mushroom mix, along with the thyme, roast garlic, vegetable stock, the saved mushroom water and the boiling water. Bring to a boil then turn down the heat to a gentle simmer. Cook for 20–30 minutes, stirring often, until the pearl barley is soft but still with a little bite. Add salt and pepper to taste, and leave to cool completely.

Now cook 4 of the eggs. Put them into a large pan of boiling water, turn the heat down slightly and gently boil for 7 minutes. When the time is up, run the eggs under a cold tap to stop the cooking, then peel them.

When everything is cool, shape a thin layer of the pearl barley around each egg – you want to keep the egg shape as much as possible – then place in the fridge to cool after handling.

Beat the remaining egg together with the milk in a separate bowl. Mix the breadcrumbs and the nibs together. Take the eggs from the fridge and dust in the plain flour. Fully coat the floured eggs in the beaten egg mixture, then shake off any excess liquid and finally coat them in the breadcrumb mix. To achieve a really crispy coating, dip the eggs again in the egg and milk mixture, and coat again with the breadcrumbs. The eggs may now be stored in the fridge for up to a couple of days.

To serve, heat a pan of sunflower oil deep enough to submerge and deep-fry 2 eggs at a time. If you have a deep fryer, even better. Whichever pan you use, please ensure the oil comes up to halfway or below. Heat the oil to 165°C. (If you don't have a thermometer, drop a grain of rice in the oil. If it pops back up straightaway and starts to cook, it's hot enough.) Gently lower in 2 eggs using a spoon and deep-fry for 6 minutes or until golden brown. Remove with a slotted spoon and place on kitchen paper. Repeat with the remaining eggs. Leave to cool for a minute before serving.

Beetroot Carpaccio

The cocoa marinade in this recipe gently softens the raw beetroot and injects a sweet-sour flavour. We use our own cocoa balsamic vinegar, as the cocoa has a mellowing effect on the vinegar (see the recipe below to make your own). This is perfect with a walnut and crumbled goats' cheese salad, and you can use the marinade to dress your salad leaves. It also pairs brilliantly with roast game.

Cocoa Factor: Low | **Origin:** Any

Serves 4

2 raw beetroots
50ml olive oil
50ml sunflower oil
2 tablespoons Cocoa Balsamic Vinegar (see below) or any good quality balsamic vinegar
2 tablespoons clear honey
1 tablespoon caster sugar
1 teaspoon thyme leaves (lemon thyme is lovely here)
salt and freshly ground pepper

Peel the beetroots and then slice them as thinly as possible – a mandolin is good for this. Place them in a large stainless steel bowl – plastic bowls will colour red.

Mix together the oils, vinegar, honey and sugar until well combined. Pour the marinade over the sliced beetroot. Add the thyme leaves and season with salt and pepper. Cover the bowl with cling film and chill in the fridge for a minimum of 12 hours, turning the beetroot slices in the marinade a couple of times. It can be made up to 2 days in advance. Serve with some of the juices spooned over the top.

Cocoa Balsamic Vinegar

100g roasted cocoa nibs
250ml balsamic vinegar

Tip the cocoa nibs into a sterilised 500ml bottle with a screw top or cork. Top with the vinegar. Leave in a warm place for at least 3 days, gently turning the bottle a few times each day. It will keep for up to 1 month and the flavours will deepen over time.

Creating a New Kind of Cocoa Cuisine

When we first became cocoa farmers at Rabot Estate in Saint Lucia in 2006, it soon dawned on us that there was a little known aspect of cocoa that needed to be shared with the world.

'We would drink unsweetened cocoa tea made from the latest harvest and munch on the roasted beans without a grain of sugar,' says Angus Thirlwell. 'The flavours were unbelievable – nutty, dark, earthy, peppery – and when I began crushing them on to my fried eggs, I noticed how much energy I started to have.' In fact, for more than 2,500 years people enjoyed cocoa as a savoury ingredient, and it is only in the past 500 years that we have all come to know it in only its sweet form.

Of course, we enjoyed darker chocolate and had some experience of using it in savoury cooking, but this was a totally new kind of cocoa cuisine. And with each kitchen experiment came more proof that there was a whole lot more to this little bean.

We set to work with some expert chefs: first, David Demaison, a disciple of Alain Ducasse, who developed some wonderful pairings (spinach and cocoa is still one of Angus' favourites), and then Jon Bentham, who, having led some of the UK's finest

Michelin-starred restaurants, had uprooted to Saint Lucia in 2001.

Together, we soon realised just how much the cocoa pod had to offer. The fresh white pulp around the beans had a sweet, fruity flavour that tasted great in everything from ceviche to sorbets, ice cream and martinis. The freshly roasted cocoa nibs, crunchy and rich in umami flavours, made wonderful crusts and garnishes, and when we marinated scallops or beef in them, the nibs brought in entirely new spiced-oak flavours that were simply amazing. Even the shells around the cocoa nibs were packed with goodness, bringing rich depth to stocks and infusions. We put them into the blender and powdered them to mix with ingredients like smoked paprika, creole and Cajun spices, adding a deep bass note to partner the hot flavours. And then, of course, there was the chocolate. The soul of the menu we were piecing together was a single spice, cocoa, but it had endless possibilities.

We began to explore combining these exciting new flavour discoveries with classic British recipes, and we also incorporated some of the local Saint Lucian traditions – recipes like Roast Yard Bird (see page 80) and Caribbean Fish Run Down (see page 108) soon found their place alongside Yorkshire Nib Puddings (see page 249) and Not-So-Scotch Eggs (see page 60). We drew inspiration from all around us, all with a cocoa twist.

Working with cocoa in this way taught us all about its nuances. We were respectful

Left: The traditional way to dry cocoa beans is to lightly toast them in the equatorial sun. They need to be quickly carried under cover when the rain comes

of the flavours from the different beans. Just like chillies, with their habañero, Scotch bonnet and jalapeño variants, cocoa beans have dramatically different flavour profiles influenced by the regional character of where they're grown. From the Caribbean to Ecuador, Madagascar and Vietnam, we began to discover the subtleties and complexities of each region's cocoa and how it can influence and change a dish.

We developed our own Taste-o-Meter, which provides a simple guide to identifying complementary flavours from different cocoa-producing regions around the world – see pages 90–91 for more information on flavour matching. And the Cocoa Factor that accompanies each recipe tells you a little more about the ideal chocolate to use.

Left, top: Ironwood dining table at Rabot 1745, Borough Market, London
Left, middle: Cocoa Calibration: nibbling on freshly roasted cocoa tunes our diners' taste buds to the savoury delights of cocoa
Left, below, and opposite: Nightfall at Boucan's open-air dining room, Saint Lucia

Cocoa-Spiced Beef Satay

Ingredients that grow well together commonly go well together on a plate. Peanuts, coconuts, citrus, ginger, chilli and cocoa all grow in our garden in the Caribbean and this recipe uses all of them in a superb twist on a classic chocolate-chilli combination. You can also make this using chicken or pork instead of beef.

Cocoa Factor: Medium | **Origin:** Any | 70–100%

Makes 16 skewers

600g beef fillet or flank steak, cut into 8–9cm-long, 2cm-thick strips
1½ tablespoons Spiced Chilli Chocolate Glaze (see page 245)
lime wedges, to serve

For the marinade

1½ teaspoons finely chopped shallots
1 teaspoon finely grated garlic
2 teaspoons brown sugar
70g smooth peanut butter
30ml sunflower oil
25g freshly grated coconut
30ml coconut milk

For the satay sauce

½ teaspoon grated garlic
1 teaspoon grated fresh ginger
1 teaspoon caster sugar
70g smooth peanut butter
80ml water
2 teaspoons hot chilli sauce
1½ teaspoons fresh lime juice
½ teaspoon dark soy sauce
½ teaspoon sesame oil

You'll need 16 x 25–30cm bamboo skewers, soaked in water to prevent burning.

Blend all the ingredients for the marinade in a food processor. Place the meat in a large bowl and cover it with the marinade, turning the meat over to coat it. Cover with cling film and chill in the fridge for 12 hours.

To make the satay sauce, blend all the ingredients together until smooth. If the sauce is thicker than you'd like, add a little more water.

When ready to cook, preheat your barbecue or grill to high. Thread a strip of meat on to each skewer, using its full length. Cook for about 2 minutes on each side. (Chicken and pork should be cooked for a minute or so longer until cooked through.) While the meat is still hot, brush it on all sides with the Spiced Chilli Chocolate Glaze. Do not put the skewers back on the heat or the chocolate will burn.

Serve alongside a small dipping pot of the satay sauce, lime wedges and a fresh green salad.

Salmon with White Chocolate Horseradish Open Sandwich

This dish is inspired by frequent visits to Hotel Chocolat's stores in stylish Copenhagen, where the classic Danish *smørrebrød* (an open rye sandwich) is very popular. There are hundreds of varieties available but traditional toppings include smoked fish, pickles or thinly sliced cheese and mountains of fresh dill and crisp red onion. Our version makes a quick and easy lunch, or you can use blinis instead of rye bread to create canapés. Try experimenting with different flavour combinations: this lush and tangy horseradish also pairs perfectly with rare roast beef.

Cocoa Factor: Low | **Origin:** Any | At least 30%

Serves 2
4 slices of rye bread
2–3 teaspoons White Chocolate Horseradish (see page 231)
handful of watercress
4–6 slices of smoked salmon (try experimenting with other fish, e.g. rollmop herrings)
½ red onion, peeled and finely sliced
2 tablespoons chopped fresh dill

Spread the rye bread liberally with the White Chocolate Horseradish. Top with the watercress and the salmon, then scatter over the red onion and dill. Serve immediately.

Dark & Meaty

Mains with a savoury cocoa twist

Rump Steak Burger with Cocoa Beer-Braised Onions

Roasted cocoa is rich in the flavour notes of umami – that elusive but delicious savoury taste. Blending it into beef delivers deeper flavours, a satisfying texture and some real cocoa power. Ask your butcher to mince your rump steak for you (or you can just chop it by hand very finely) and, while you're at it, ask him to pop the bone marrow out of the bone – this will give the burger a good ratio of meat to fat, resulting in a really juicy burger. If you can't find bone marrow, an equal weight of beef suet works as well.

Cocoa Factor: Medium | **Origin:** Latin American, Caribbean

Serves 4

150g bone marrow or shredded beef suet
500g rump steak, minced once (or see method)
1 egg, beaten
50g roasted cocoa nibs, finely chopped
salt and freshly ground pepper
sunflower oil, for frying

To serve
4 burger buns
1 quantity of Cocoa Beer-Braised Onions (see page 76)
150g Spiced Chilli Chocolate Glaze (see page 245)
cheese, bacon or toppings of your choice
Creole Tomato Chutney (see page 246)

If you are using bone marrow, mix 1 litre of cold water with 2 tablespoons of salt to make a brine. Add the bone marrow, cover with cling film and chill for 1 hour.

If your rump steak isn't minced, place a wet tissue or cloth underneath a large chopping board to keep it steady. Cut the meat into 2cm strips along the length of the steak, then dice into 2cm pieces. Gather the dice together and chop finely so it resembles mince. Place the meat in a large bowl, add the egg and cocoa nibs, and season with salt and pepper.

Drain the brine from the bone marrow, if using, and chop to the size of hazelnuts. Add to the meat. Alternatively, add the suet. Using your hands, gently massage all the ingredients together until well combined. Do not overwork the mixture as the bone marrow will break down and melt.

Heat a little oil in a small frying pan and fry a small amount of the burger mixture (about the size of a large coin) for about 1 minute on each side. Taste and check the seasoning, adjusting if necessary.

Now shape the mixture into 4 patties, patting rather than squeezing them into shape. Place on a tray, cover with cling film and chill for at least 1 hour.

Recipe continues

When ready to cook, heat 2 tablespoons of oil in large frying pan or griddle pan over a high heat. When the oil begins to shimmer, lower the heat to medium. Carefully place the burgers in the pan and cook for about 3 minutes on one side, until golden brown and slightly charred. Flip over the burgers and cook for a further 4 minutes for medium-rare – or to your desired degree of doneness.

To assemble, split the buns in half and place a spoonful of the braised onion on the base of each one. Top with a burger and brush with the Spiced Chilli Chocolate Glaze, then add cheese, bacon and whatever other toppings you like. Serve with Creole Tomato Chutney on the side.

Cocoa Beer-Braised Onions

If you wish to make a cocoa-infused beer of your own, simply soak 2 tablespoons of nibs in your pale ale or other beer, being careful to awaken the flavours of your nibs first using our quick technique on page 19. Leave to infuse for at least 4 hours and up to 2 days if possible.

Serves 4–6
20g butter
1 large onion, peeled and thinly sliced
225ml cocoa beer, bitter or pale ale
1 teaspoon caster sugar
salt and freshly ground pepper

In a large pan, melt the butter gently over a medium heat. Add the sliced onion and stir gently, keeping the heat low to medium. Cook until soft and tender but do not let it colour.

Add 200ml of the beer, the sugar and a pinch of salt, and cook over a medium heat for 15–18 minutes, until the beer is absorbed and the onion is turning golden. Add the remaining beer and simmer for 2 minutes. Check the seasoning.

Cocoa and Herb-Crusted Fillet of Pork with Garlic and Olive Oil Mashed Potatoes and Cocoa Mint Sauce

The nibs in the crust add extra crunch and provide a slightly bitter savoury flavour, which contrasts subtly with the natural sweetness of the pork. We think pork and cocoa are perfect partners. With the sauce, we play on the timeless combination of mint and chocolate, making it seem as though it was always meant to be paired with savoury dishes.

Cocoa Factor: Medium | **Origin:** Any | 70–90%

Serves 4

For the cocoa and herb-crusted fillet of pork

1 tablespoon freshly chopped mint
1 tablespoon freshly chopped parsley
1 teaspoon freshly chopped tarragon
125g Cocoa Nib Breadcrumbs, (see page 244)
4 x 200g pork fillets
2 tablespoons olive oil
1 tablespoon Chocolate Grain Mustard, (see page 243)
1 quantity of Cocoa Mint Sauce, (see page 237)

For the garlic and olive oil mashed potatoes

6 fat garlic cloves, unpeeled
3 tablespoons olive oil
1 thyme sprig
500g Desiree potatoes, peeled and cut into quarters
30–50ml liquid from the potatoes
1 tablespoon freshly chopped parsley
salt and freshly ground pepper

Preheat the oven to 160°C/gas 2.

Toss the garlic cloves with 2 tablespoons of the olive oil. Lay them on a 25 x 25cm sheet of foil. Season with salt and pepper, scatter over the thyme and seal the foil to make a loose bag. Place in the oven on a baking tray and cook for 40 minutes. Sealing the foil will capture all the sweet flavours of the roasting garlic and thyme.

Once cooked, remove the tray from the oven, keep the foil sealed and allow to cool for 20 minutes. Increase the oven temperature to 230°C/gas 8.

While the garlic is cooling, prepare the mashed potatoes. Cook the quartered potatoes in a large pan of salted boiling water until soft but not breaking apart – about 20 minutes.

Recipe continues

TEL

Meanwhile, start preparing the pork. Mix the chopped herbs with the Cocoa Nib Breadcrumbs to combine. Season the pork with 3 pinches of salt and a good few twists of pepper. Add the olive oil to a non-stick frying pan over a medium-to-high heat and carefully place in the pork fillets. Seal the pork on all sides to a light caramel colour – this will take about 5 minutes.

Remove the pork from the pan to a plate and leave to rest for 4 minutes. Wipe the pork gently with kitchen paper, then brush the Chocolate Grain Mustard all over the fillets and roll them in the breadcrumbs, coating all sides thoroughly. Place on a non-stick baking tray and into the oven. Immediately lower the oven temperature to 190°C/gas 5 and continue to cook the pork for 12 minutes.

While the pork is in the oven, squeeze the garlic from its skin into a small bowl and mash with a fork to a smooth paste. Drain the potatoes, saving 50ml of the cooking water. While the potatoes are still warm, add the garlic paste and the remaining tablespoon of olive oil, plus the oil from the roasted garlic. Add some of the reserved cooking water and start to mash to a smooth purée, adding more liquid if needed. Taste for salt and pepper and fold in the chopped parsley.

Remove the pork from the oven to a plate, cover very loosely with foil and allow the meat to rest for 5 minutes. This helps tenderise and relax the meat, and redistributes the moisture throughout the fillet.

Divide the mashed potatoes between 4 serving plates. Slice the pork into 4 equal slices per fillet and place on the mashed potatoes. Drizzle the Cocoa Mint Sauce over and around the meat and serve with your favourite vegetables.

Left: Soufrière town, just down the road from Rabot Estate and, at one time, the capital of Saint Lucia

Roast Yard Bird

Yard bird – or chicken – is a real treat in the West Indies. The light, gamey flavours harmonise beautifully with roast cocoa. Chicken gravy can be a little thin on flavour sometimes, and cocoa adds some delicious depth. We use Saint Lucian cocoa nibs to connect this recipe to its place of origin.

Cocoa Factor: Medium | **Origin:** Any | 70–90%

Serves 4

1 x 1.8kg free-range chicken
80g Cocoa Nib Butter,
 (see page 234)
110g butter, at room temperature
salt and freshly ground pepper
juice of 1 orange, keeping the halves
3 sprigs each of thyme, parsley and tarragon
2 garlic cloves, peeled and crushed

Preheat the oven to 230°C/gas 8. Loosen the skin from the breast of the chicken by simply working your finger between the skin and flesh. Slice the Cocoa Nib Butter into 1cm-thick slices and push it under the skin on either side of the bird. Now rub all over the outside of the bird with the regular butter.

Place the bird in a large roasting tin, season with salt and pepper, and pour over the orange juice. Stuff the herbs, garlic and orange halves in the cavity of the chicken, then place it in the hot oven and cook for 12 minutes.

Remove the chicken from the oven and lower the temperature to 190°C/gas 5. Spoon the fat in the tray over the chicken to baste it with flavour and moisture. Return the chicken to the oven and cook for another 15 minutes, then baste it again. Repeat twice more before removing from the oven. Insert a sharp knife into the thickest part of the meat and check that the juices run clear. If they are at all pink, cook for 10 minutes longer and check again.

Leave the bird to rest uncovered for 10 minutes before carving to allow all the flavours to settle and keep the bird moist.

In the bottom of the roasting tray you will have a tasty mixture of chocolate nibs, orange and chicken juices. To make a simple gravy just add 150ml hot water to the roasting tin and use a wooden spoon to scrape and loosen all the bits at the bottom. Pour this into a pan and bring to a boil. Pass the gravy through a fine sieve and return it to the pan. Reduce the heat and whisk until combined, then stir until the gravy has reduced by one-third.

Choc au Vin

Dark and slightly bitter chocolate enriches the earthy red wine in this version of the classic French staple, giving the whole dish richness and warmth. It also thickens the sauce a little. Great with White Chocolate Mash (see page 149).

Cocoa Factor: Medium | **Origin:** Caribbean, Latin America | 65–85%

Serves 4

3 tablespoons sunflower oil
120g unsmoked thick bacon, diced
1 x 2kg free-range chicken, jointed, legs and breasts halved
200g carrots, peeled and cut diagonally in 2cm-thick slices
1 onion, peeled and finely sliced
2 garlic cloves, peeled and finely chopped
4 tablespoons good brandy
375ml dry red wine
250ml chicken stock
10 thyme sprigs
30g butter, at room temperature
1½ tablespoons plain flour
220g small whole onions, peeled
225g cremini or button mushrooms, stems removed, sliced
100g dark chocolate, broken into small pieces
salt and freshly ground pepper

Preheat the oven to 130°C/gas ½.

Heat the sunflower oil in a large casserole over a medium heat. Add the bacon and cook for 8 minutes, or until lightly browned, then transfer to a plate. Pat the chicken pieces dry with kitchen paper and season all over with salt and pepper. Brown the chicken pieces in single-layer batches in the casserole for about 5 minutes, until they turn a golden colour, then transfer to a plate.

Add the carrots, sliced onion, 2 teaspoons of salt and 1 teaspoon of pepper to the casserole, and cook over a medium heat for 10–12 minutes, stirring occasionally, until all the vegetables are lightly browned. Add the garlic, stir and cook for 1 minute. Add the brandy, bacon, chicken and any juices from the plate. Add the wine, chicken stock and thyme, and bring to a boil. Turn the heat down to a simmer and skim off any foam that rises to the top with a ladle. Cover the casserole with the lid and place in the oven for 40 minutes.

After this time, remove from the oven and place on top of the stove over a medium heat. Now mix half the butter together with the flour to make a paste and stir it into the stew. Add the small onions. In a medium sauté pan, melt the remaining butter and cook the mushrooms over a medium-low heat for 5–10 minutes, until browned. Add to the stew. Bring the stew to a simmer, add the chocolate and cook for another 10 minutes. Check for seasoning before serving.

Cocoa Brine Roast Turkey

This marinade can be used for brining pork, veal, chicken or chops. It helps meats that can tend towards dryness to remain moist and tender. The nibs in this recipe give the brine a rich flavour and colour while also imparting a little savoury bitterness.

Cocoa Factor: Low | **Origin:** Any

Serves 8–10

1 x 5kg fresh turkey
120g butter
juice and zest of 1 lemon
1 teaspoon freshly chopped thyme leaves
large bunch of thyme
1 lemon, halved
1 onion, peeled and quartered
1 garlic bulb, halved crosswise
sea salt
freshly ground pepper

For the brine
2.5 litres water
50g coarse sea salt
3 tablespoons caster sugar
2 bay leaves
2 whole cloves
1 cinnamon stick
2 teaspoons black peppercorns
1 garlic clove, crushed
30g roasted cocoa nibs

To make the brine, bring the water, salt and sugar to a boil. Add the remaining ingredients and simmer for 5 minutes. Remove from the heat and cool the liquid as quickly as possible by placing the pan in a sink and filling the sink with cold water to halfway up the outside of the pan. In a large container, big enough to hold the turkey and brine but that will fit in the fridge, submerge the turkey in the liquid. Put this in the fridge for 12 hours, turning the turkey 3 times.

Preheat the oven to 180°C/gas 4. Melt the butter in a small pan. Add the zest and juice of the lemon and the chopped thyme leaves and set aside.

Take the turkey out of the brine and wash it under cold running water inside and out. Remove any leftover pin feathers and pat the outside dry. Place the turkey in a large roasting tray. Liberally season the inside of the turkey with salt and pepper. Stuff the cavity with the bunch of thyme, halved lemon, quartered onion and garlic. Brush the outside of the turkey with the butter mixture and sprinkle with salt and pepper. Tie the legs together with string and tuck the wing tips under the body.

Roast the turkey for 2½ hours, until the juices run clear when you cut between the leg and thigh. Transfer the turkey to a board, keeping the juices in the pan for a gravy (see page 248), and cover with foil. Leave to rest for 20 minutes. Serve with Garlic and Olive Oil Mashed Potatoes (see page 77) and White Chocolate Parsnips (see page 130).

Chocolate Balsamic Glazed Pork Ribs

Dark, rich chocolate in a sweet and sour glaze adds another dimension to the flavours of rich and meltingly tender pork. Just perfect for barbecuing, it's fabulous as a thick glaze, dipping sauce or salad dressing, and can be used with other cuts of pork, venison or chicken.

Cocoa Factor: Medium | **Origin:** Any | 70%

Serves 6

2 x 1kg racks of meaty pork ribs (ask the butcher to cut each rack into 3 sections)
250ml pineapple juice
salt and freshly ground pepper

For the chocolate balsamic glaze
40ml balsamic vinegar
70g clear honey
35g brown sugar
20ml light soy sauce
2 garlic cloves, peeled and crushed
1 rosemary sprig
50g dark chocolate

First make the glaze. Blend or whisk together the balsamic vinegar, honey, sugar and soy sauce until the sugar has dissolved. Add the liquid to a bowl along with the garlic and rosemary. Cover and leave at room temperature for 1 hour or overnight in the fridge.

Pour the mixture into a pan and bring to a gentle simmer. Reduce the heat to low and cook until it has a honey-like consistency – about 10 minutes. Add the chocolate and stir to melt. Pass through a fine sieve and leave to cool. When it is cool test the thickness – it should be like single cream; if it is too thick, stir in 1 tablespoon of warm water.

When you're ready to cook the ribs, preheat the oven to 120°C/gas ½. In a roasting tray large enough to hold the ribs in a single layer, lay a sheet of foil on the bottom with a little overlap at the sides. You may need to use 2 trays.

Season the ribs well with salt and pepper, then gently place them in the tray, taking care not to tear the foil. Pour the pineapple juice around the ribs.

Take another sheet of foil to cover the tray, lay it on top of the ribs and gather the ends around the tray, twisting the foil to form a seal all around. Place in the oven and cook for 2¾ hours. Remove from the oven and leave to cool at room temperature for

1 hour without opening the foil. Then remove the ribs and place on a plate, cover them with cling film, and chill until needed. Pass the juices from the roasting tray through a fine sieve into a bowl.

Preheat the grill and place the ribs on a baking tray lined with foil. Put the ribs on the bottom of the grill furthest away from the heat and cook for 5 minutes, brushing with the roasting juices, then turn over and cook for 5 five minutes further, brushing with the juices until golden brown. Keep a close eye on the ribs as grill heats will vary. Finally brush with plenty of the glaze and return to the grill for 20 seconds each side.

Alternatively, get a barbecue to a medium heat. Cut the ribs into 2-bone pieces and place on the grill, brushing them with the roasting juices to give a golden brown colour. Cook for 5 minutes, then turn over and cook for 5 five minutes further, brushing with the roasting juices. Finally, take the ribs off the heat and brush with plenty of the chocolate balsamic glaze, then return to the grill and cook for 20 seconds on each side. Brush again with the glaze and serve with baked potatoes and some White Chocolate Horseradish (see page 231).

Pulled Pork Pie

This recipe has more of a spiritual connection to our Saint Lucian plantation than a direct link through your taste buds. It requires you to take a step back from life's busyness and throw yourself into the enjoyment of preparing a hearty meal for loved ones. Clear the diary and take your time over crafting pastry from scratch and slow-roasting meat; it'll be worth it. The pastry is superbly light and flaky, the nibs delivering a light cocoa kick and distinctive crunch. We've suggested pulled pork, but beef, lamb or even chicken would be worthy substitutions. It goes well with either White Chocolate Horseradish (see page 231) or Chocolate Grain Mustard (see page 243).

Cocoa Factor: Low | **Origin:** Any | 70–90%

Serves 4

1 medium potato, peeled and quartered
2 new potatoes, cut into 5mm dice
1 tablespoon sunflower oil
1 shallot, peeled and finely chopped
1 tablespoon chopped parsley
1 thyme sprig, leaves picked
2 tablespoons Chocolate Grain Mustard (see page 243)
1 quantity of cocoa nib pastry (see page 144)
butter, for greasing
flour, for dusting
1 egg yolk mixed with a splash of milk, to seal and glaze
salt and freshly ground pepper

For the pulled pork
40g light brown sugar
2 teaspoons hot paprika
1 teaspoon mustard powder
½ teaspoon ground cumin
2 teaspoons vegetable oil
1½–2kg boneless pork shoulder, trimmed of excess fat
100ml apple cider vinegar
3 tablespoons tomato purée
salt and freshly ground pepper

You will need 4 x 10cm tart tins or 1 x 20–23cm tart tin.

Start by preparing the pulled pork. Combine one-third of the brown sugar with the paprika, mustard powder, cumin, 2 teaspoons of salt and half a teaspoon of pepper in a small bowl. Rub this spice mixture all over the pork.

Heat the vegetable oil in a large frying pan. Add the pork and cook, turning, until browned on all sides – about 5 minutes. Remove the pork and transfer to a plate, then whisk 170ml of water into the dripping in the pan.

Transfer the liquid to a large slow cooker. Add the vinegar, tomato purée, the remaining brown sugar and 500ml of water to the slow cooker and whisk to combine. Add the pork, cover and cook on low for 8 hours. If you don't have a slow cooker, use a 3-litre casserole with a tight-fitting lid. Cook in an oven preheated to 140°C/gas 1 for 6–7 hours, basting every so often to keep it moist.

Remove the pork and transfer to a cutting board. Strain the liquid into a pan, bring to a boil and cook until reduced by half – about 10 minutes. Season with salt. Roughly chop the pork and mix in a bowl with 225ml of the reduced cooking liquid. Check the seasoning and add pepper to taste and then set aside to cool.

While it is cooling, prepare the other pie ingredients. Firstly, cook the quartered potato in salted boiling water then remove it with a slotted spoon and dry-mash it – i.e. do not add any liquid. Now cook the diced new potatoes in the same water until just soft. Remove with a slotted spoon and allow to steam-dry on kitchen paper.

Heat the oil in a pan over a medium heat. Cook the shallot for 1 minute, until soft, and then add 220g of the pulled pork. Cook for a couple of minutes then transfer the mixture to a mixing bowl. Add the mashed and diced potatoes, parsley, thyme and Chocolate Grain Mustard, and gently combine. Add salt and pepper to taste, and leave to cool. Preheat the oven to 200°/gas 6.

On a lightly floured surface, roll out two-thirds of the Cocoa Nib Pastry to a thickness of 3mm. Cut into 4 x 13cm circles for individual tart tins or 1 x 28–30cm circle for a large pie. To prevent the pastry from sticking to the counter and to ensure uniform thickness, keep lifting up and turning the pastry a quarter turn as you roll (always roll from the centre of the pastry outwards to get uniform thickness).

Butter and flour the tins or pie dish, then line with the pastry. Cover and chill in the fridge for about 20 minutes. When chilled, trim off the excess pastry from around the edge of the tin(s), making sure the pastry is right up against the edge.

Take the cooled pulled pork mixture and divide it into 4, if making individual pies. Roll each portion into a ball then press into the moulds, keeping a slight dome in the middle of the pie above the rim of the tin(s) but also pushing the mixture right into the corners. For a large pie, do exactly the same but with all of the mixture.

From the remaining pastry, roll out 4 small lids or 1 large one to the same size as before. Using a pastry brush, paint the edges of the pastry with the egg and milk mixture before placing the lid(s) on top. Gently press the pastry together around the edges, then trim them using a small sharp knife. Brush the top of the pastry with more egg wash and prick a couple of times with a fork.

Place the pie(s) on a baking tray and cook for 20–25 minutes for individual pies and 30–35 minutes for a larger pie, or until golden brown. Leave to cool for 8–10 minutes before carefully removing from the tin(s) and serving.

The Cocoa Taste-o-Meter

West Africa

Dominican Republic

Saint Lucia

Trinidad

Chuao, Venezuela

Ecuador

Peru

Our Taste-o-Meter cuts through the jargon and makes it easy to match your taste buds with cocoa regions.

The taste of cocoa is influenced by many factors, from the genotype of the individual plant to local terroir. Flavours can vary wildly from region to region, depending on everything from the soil and climate to where and how farmers ferment and dry their beans.

The most fruity cocoa is famously from Madagascar, but other countries like Vietnam also produce cocoa with powerful red-fruit flavours. We like to use these to match with raspberries and dishes where a refreshing edge is an advantage.

For classically mellow but robust cocoa flavours with low levels of acidity, Ecuador is our first choice, with good quality West African beans close behind. These deliver a straightforward cocoa flavour which is excellent in many dishes.

The most multi-layered and intriguing cocoa flavours come from the Caribbean and across Latin America, typically with notes of red wine, leather, tobacco, roast nuts, spices and sometimes yellow fruit. These are balanced and versatile cocoa varieties, excellent in desserts or for pairing with savoury dishes from the same regions.

Fruit-led Flavours

Refreshing in the mouth.

Complex Flavours

Multi-layered with fruit and roasted flavours jostling for position.

Roasted Flavours

Led by mellow notes of roasted nuts.

Parkin Spiced Beef with Yorkshire Pudding, White Chocolate Mash and Cocoa Red Wine Gravy

The classic Sunday lunch is already so indulgent, but adding chocolate brings an unbelievable intensity to the rich gravy and tender spiced beef. This spiced beef is a fabulous main with the usual roast potatoes, Yorkshire puddings and buttered seasonal vegetables but it is also a great starter on its own. Caribbean or Latin American chocolate is most likely to have the leather, tobacco, red wine and spice notes that work best in the gravy.

Cocoa Factor: Medium | **Origin:** Caribbean, Latin America | 70–90%

Serves 6

For the parkin spiced beef
100g treacle
50ml water
1 teaspoon ground cinnamon
2 pinches of ground ginger
2 pinches of ground pimento (allspice)
400g beef flank or skirt steak
salt and freshly ground pepper

For the cocoa red wine gravy
1 tablespoon sunflower oil
3 shallots, peeled and roughly chopped
2 tablespoons tomato purée
1 rosemary sprig, bashed gently with the back of a knife to release the flavours
2 teaspoons caster sugar
200ml red wine
250ml beef stock
50g dark chocolate, chopped

To serve
1 quantity of White Chocolate Mash (see page 149)
6 Yorkshire Nib Puddings (see page 249)
small bunch of watercress

Mix the treacle, water and spices together well. Pour the mix into a re-sealable bag, big enough to hold the beef. Add the beef and seal the bag. Give the bag a good shake to allow the meat to be fully covered. Place on a tray and leave in the fridge for 24 hours. Turn the bag and meat over 4 times during this period.

To make the Cocoa Red Wine Gravy, heat the tablespoon of sunflower oil in a pan over a medium heat and cook the shallots until soft and tender – around 5 minutes. Do not let them colour. Add the tomato purée, rosemary and sugar. Cook for 2 minutes, then remove the rosemary. Pour in the red wine then reduce to about two-thirds the volume. Add the beef stock and again reduce, until it coats the back of a tablespoon. Add the chopped chocolate and allow to dissolve. Pass the sauce through a fine sieve.

Recipe continues

Take the beef out of the marinade and wipe off the excess marinade with kitchen paper. Heat a large cast-iron frying pan over a high heat. Sprinkle both sides of the steak with salt and pepper. Place the steak in the hot pan. Sear for 2–3 minutes, using tongs to lift it up to see if it is nicely browned. If so, flip on to the other side and sear for 2–3 minutes more. Remove the pan from the heat and let the steak continue to cook for 5–10 minutes in the residual heat of the pan.

Use your fingertips to check for doneness (it should be soft but with some resistance) or insert a meat thermometer into the thickest part of the steak: 49°C for very rare, 51.5°C for rare, or 54.5°C for medium rare. Flank steak should be served rare or medium rare, otherwise it may be too dry. Transfer the steak from the pan to a cutting board and leave to rest for 10 minutes, covered with foil.

Reheat the mash, Yorkshire puddings and gravy. Cut the meat into very thin slices, at an angle, against the grain of the meat (this way you break through the tough long muscle fibres). Spoon some mash on to each serving plate and place a Yorkshire pudding on top. Spoon some mash into the puddings and add the sliced beef on top. Pour over a little of the Cocoa Red Wine Gravy and put the rest of the sauce in a gravy jug so people may help themselves. Garnish the beef with a sprig of watercress.

Dark Chocolate Ragù

A high-percentage chocolate is a must for this recipe, delivering the richest and most satisfying ragù we've ever tasted.

Cocoa Factor: Medium | **Origin:** Any | 70–90%

Serves 6–8

6 tablespoons olive oil
1 onion, peeled and finely chopped
4 fat garlic cloves, peeled and grated
75g good quality pancetta, chopped into 1cm dice
200g minced beef
200g minced pork
100g chicken livers, chopped into 1cm dice
200g chopped tinned tomatoes
200g tomato purée
250ml red wine
bunch of basil, leaves picked and roughly chopped
100g dark chocolate, broken into small pieces
salt and freshly ground pepper

Preheat the oven to 140°C/gas 1.

Pour 2 tablespoons of the olive oil into a large casserole with a tight-fitting lid. Add the onion and garlic, and gently cook over a medium heat until softened but not coloured – about 5–7 minutes. Add the pancetta and cook for a further 5 minutes.

In a large non-stick frying pan over a medium to high heat, brown the minced beef and pork in 2 tablespoons of the olive oil, stirring and loosening the meat as it cooks – this takes about 10 minutes. Transfer the meat from the pan to a colander set over a bowl to drain the excess fat. To the same frying pan add the remaining olive oil and chicken livers and fry over a medium heat for 5 minutes, stirring as they cook.

Combine the minced meat, livers, and the onion and bacon mix in the large casserole. Stir in the tomatoes, tomato purée and red wine. Bring to a boil and add salt and pepper to taste. Reduce to a simmer and cover with the lid, then place in the oven to cook for 4 hours. After this time the ragù should be quite thick. Remove the casserole from the oven, add the chopped basil leaves and stir in the chocolate. Taste again for seasoning.

As this is a very rich ragù only a small amount is needed. Serve with spaghetti or pasta of your choice.

Slow Roast Shoulder of Lamb with Cocoa Gravy

Cooking lamb shoulder this way causes the marbled fat to melt slowly through the meat, giving a soft, delicate texture and a sweet flavour. This is enriched by the dark chocolate, but also cut through with the mild sharpness of balsamic vinegar. Perfect with Garlic and Olive Oil Mashed Potatoes (see page 77) and some buttered carrots.

Cocoa Factor: Medium | **Origin:** Any | 70–90%

Serves 4

1 x 2.5kg shoulder of lamb, boned and rolled (ask your butcher to do this)
4 rosemary sprigs
4 onions, peeled and cut in half through the root
2 tablespoons sunflower oil
8 thyme sprigs
2 whole garlic bulbs, cut in half crosswise
125ml balsamic vinegar
120ml water
100g dark chocolate, broken into pieces
salt and freshly ground pepper

Preheat the oven to 180°C/gas 4.

Season the lamb all over with salt and pepper. With a small sharp knife stab the flesh a few times and push the rosemary into the cuts. Toss the onions in the sunflower oil then place them in a roasting tray large enough to hold the lamb as well. Roast the onions in the oven for about 15 minutes, until they start to colour at the edges, then remove the tray and turn the oven down to 120°C/gas ½.

Add the lamb, thyme and garlic to the roasting tray on top of the onions, cover tightly with foil and cook for 4½ hours.

Taking the tray out of the oven first, remove the onions and garlic, keeping the onions to serve with the roasted lamb and discarding the garlic. Now add the balsamic vinegar and water to the tray and cook the lamb, uncovered, for 1 hour longer, basting it with the juices every 15 minutes. Remove from the oven and cover loosely with foil.

Strain the juices from the roasting tray through a fine sieve into a pan big enough to hold the liquid. With a small ladle or serving spoon, try to remove the excess oil floating on the top. Place the pan over a medium heat and simmer until the sauce has reduced slightly and thickened. Finally, stir in the dark chocolate.

The lamb will be tender and almost falling apart so just serve chunks of the meat with the gravy, plenty of Garlic Mashed Potatoes and buttered carrots.

Cocoa Pork Meatballs

It may seem a little surprising but pigs love chocolate – all the chocolate left over from our factory in Cambridgeshire is used to feed local pigs. This recipe reunites them with the cocoa, enriching the flavours. Avoid fruity chocolates such as those from Madagascar or Vietnam, instead opting for more robust notes from Africa or the Caribbean. These meatballs go perfectly with White Chocolate Mash (see page 149) and Chocolate Grain Mustard (see page 243). If you can't get hold of caul fat, use an extra 100g of breadcrumbs and an additional egg.

Cocoa Factor: Medium | **Origin:** Africa, Caribbean, a good House Blend | 70–85%

Serves 4

500g pork liver, minced
300g pork belly, minced
100g pork caul fat
2 tablespoons sunflower oil
2 onions, peeled and finely chopped
10 sage leaves, finely chopped
2 garlic cloves, peeled and grated
100g dark chocolate, broken into pieces
2 eggs, beaten
120g fresh breadcrumbs
½ teaspoon ground mace
1 quantity of Cocoa Onion Gravy (see page 248)
salt and freshly ground pepper

Preheat the oven to 180°C/gas 4.

Ask your butcher to mince the liver and belly once through the machine, or pulse-chop it at home in a food processor until it reaches the consistency of minced meat. Wash the caul fat under cold running water, then leave it in a bowl of cold water mixed with 1 teaspoon of salt while you prepare the meatballs.

Pour the sunflower oil into a small pan over a medium heat. Add the onions, sage and garlic, and cook slowly until the onion softens but does not colour – about 5–7 minutes. Remove the pan from the heat and add the chocolate. Stir until melted and combined. Transfer the mixture to a bowl and leave to cool at room temperature.

In a large bowl, mix together the minced pork belly, liver, cold onion mixture, eggs, breadcrumbs and mace, and season with salt and pepper. Shape the mix into 8 balls. Drain the caul fat and wrap each meatball with a double layer all around.

Put the meatballs in a roasting tray just big enough to fit them in, so that they touch each other. Place in the oven and roast for 10 minutes. Remove the tray and turn the meatballs over, then return to the oven for a further 10 minutes. Remove and gently tip the excess oil from the tray. Pour over the Cocoa Onion Gravy and bake for a further 25 minutes. Serve with White Chocolate Mash, additional gravy and some Chocolate Grain Mustard on the side.

Cocoa-Glazed Cumberland Sausages

Cocoa nibs add a superb crunch and subtle umami flavour to the tangy balsamic vinegar, honey and robust rosemary in this sweet, sticky glaze. For a fiery kick, try it with spicy Italian sausages instead. You could also use cocktail sausages for a unique canapé – adjust the cooking time accordingly. This is great served with White Chocolate Mash (see page 149) and Cocoa Beer-Braised Onions (see page 76), with the excess glaze drizzled over the top, and a crisp green salad.

Cocoa Factor: Low | **Origin:** Any

Serves 4
2 tablespoons sunflower oil
12 good quality Cumberland sausages

For the cocoa balsamic glaze
40ml balsamic vinegar
70g clear honey
2 tablespoons brown sugar
1½ tablespoons light soy sauce
2 garlic cloves, peeled and crushed
1 rosemary sprig
2 teaspoons roasted cocoa nibs, crushed

First make the glaze. In a bowl, whisk together the balsamic vinegar, honey, sugar and soy sauce until the sugar has dissolved. Add the garlic, rosemary and cocoa nibs, then cover with cling film and leave at room temperature for 1 hour or overnight in the fridge.

Pour into a pan and bring to a gentle simmer, then reduce over a low heat until it has a honey-like consistency – about 10 minutes. Pass through a fine sieve and leave to cool. When it is cool test the thickness – it should be like single cream. If it's too thick stir in a tablespoon of warm water; if it's too thin, return to the heat for a couple of minutes.

Heat the oil in a non-stick pan over a medium heat, and sear the sausages on all sides. Cover the pan with a lid and cook for 6–8 minutes, turning the sausages often, until they are well browned and cooked through. Pour over the balsamic glaze and cook for 2–3 minutes more before serving.

A Good Catch

Fresh fish enhanced with fine cocoa

Cod Fillet One Pot

In villages across Saint Lucia this is the traditional cooking method, capturing all the flavours of the ingredients in a single pot and then serving them as a broth with 'green figs' – young bananas, which have a potato-like texture.

Cocoa Factor: Medium | **Origin:** Vietnam, Java, Madagascar, Caribbean

Serves 6

5 tablespoons sunflower oil
1 onion, peeled and finely chopped
1 leek, washed and finely sliced
1 courgette, trimmed and cut in half lengthways
100g butternut squash, peeled
750g large new potatoes, peeled and cut into 2cm cubes
250g sweet potatoes, peeled and cut into 2cm cubes
2 green figs (green unripe bananas), peeled and sliced into 3mm-thick pieces
2 salted anchovies in oil
175ml white wine
365ml whole milk
200ml double cream
500ml vegetable stock
1kg cod fillet, skinned and boned, cut into 6 equal portions
bunch of spring onions, washed, trimmed and finely sliced
bunch of flat-leaf parsley, roughly chopped
20g roasted cocoa nibs
juice of ½ lime
2 tablespoons olive oil
salt and freshly ground pepper

Add the sunflower oil to a large pan and gently soften the onion and leek over a medium heat for about 5 minutes. Do not let them colour.

Remove the seeds from the courgette and butternut squash using a teaspoon, then grate them both into the pan with the onion and leek. Continue cooking over a gentle heat for 5 minutes. Add the new potatoes, sweet potatoes and green figs to the pan. Stir well then add the anchovies. Turn up the heat to full and add the white wine, then reduce the liquid in the pan by half the volume.

Now add the milk, cream and vegetable stock. Bring this to a boil and skim off the foam that rises to the top using a small ladle. Reduce the heat to a simmer for about 15 minutes, until the potatoes are cooked, then add the cod fillets to the pot and simmer gently for 10 minutes. Taste for seasoning, adding more salt or freshly ground pepper as needed.

Ladle into large soup bowls. Mix the sliced spring onions, chopped parsley, cocoa nibs and lime juice with the olive oil, and add a small amount of this garnish to the top of each bowl.

The Island Growers

Our fight for fairer cocoa

When we told cocoa farmer Laurence Auguste that we wanted to buy his beans at a price far above the world bulk price, every year, he nodded politely. He told us he'd think about it.

To Laurence, the offer sounded like a tale taller than an 80-year-old cocoa tree.

We could hardly blame him for not taking us seriously. In 2006, it was hard for Saint Lucian cocoa farmers to feel optimistic about anything. The island's cocoa economy was in a death spiral.

Every harvest had become a lottery with a meagre jackpot. The island's cocoa was sold via a single export organisation, which worked like this: you left your cocoa at the warehouse and they would try to sell it on your behalf, with no guarantees. If they did, you got the world bulk cocoa price, minus deductions for the middleman. And then you waited six months to get paid.

It was becoming a route into poverty. Growers couldn't afford to risk investing in quality cocoa seedlings. Instead, they were tearing out old cocoa groves and planting crops such as bananas.

You couldn't even taste pure Saint Lucian chocolate; all the local cocoa beans that made it to market were lost in mixed bulk sales and anonymous chocolate blends. Saint Lucia's once-prized variety of Trinitario cocoa was in danger of disappearing into the annals of chocolate history.

We didn't want to let that happen. In 2006, we bought our own cocoa plantation on the island: the 250-year-old Rabot Estate, a beautiful but distressed property dating back to the French colonial era. Our mission: to reconnect luxury chocolate with cocoa agriculture. We were the

first chocolatier to make single-origin Saint Lucian chocolate and we knew that the local cocoa was good enough to bind the two together.

If properly fermented, dried, roasted and conched, Saint Lucian beans can produce chocolate with a dazzling array of tasting notes, ranging from classically rich cocoa to black tea and ripe yellow fruit, grassy olive oil and dry red Burgundy.

We wanted to put Saint Lucian cocoa at the heart of Hotel Chocolat, and we needed local partners who could add their harvests to our own. But there was one slight problem: to find them, we'd have to rejuvenate the island's cocoa economy.

Over the years, none of the schemes that had promised to fix Saint Lucia's ailing cocoa industry had worked, thus increasing the cynicism that prevailed among local farmers. So what could we do?

Our Estates Director, Phil Buckley, never deterred by a seemingly impossible mission, worked with his team on a plan to make it happen. Phil's team travelled up and down the island, meeting groups of ten farmers at a time. They introduced Hotel Chocolat and Rabot Estate and asked farmers to join us as 'Island Growers'.

The Deal

The deal we offered Laurence and other local farmers was this:

- We'll guarantee to buy your whole crop each harvest, so you can be certain it's worth investing money in your farm.
- We'll pay you directly, with no middleman deductions, at a rate that is always substantially higher than world bulk cocoa price, and you'll be paid within a week.
- We'll provide free technical help to improve crop quality and give you access to top quality cocoa seedlings at a highly discounted price.

The condition was that we would only buy their beans 'wet', just after harvesting, and do the fermenting and drying ourselves. We do that so we can keep the process consistent enough to ensure the high flavour quality we need.

It took him three months to be persuaded. Finally, convinced that we meant what we said, Laurence Auguste of the Ti'Delcer plantation joined us as our first Island Grower partner in Saint Lucia.

Laurence stuck with us, inspiring 70 more local farmers to join us in the first year. By 2011 we had 120 cocoa partners, ranging from start-up farmers to well-established estates returning to cocoa. And it paid off. In 2013–2014, we paid our Island Growers US$5.14 per kilo of cocoa, more than twice what they would have been paid on the world bulk cocoa market and with no middleman deduction.

A key part of our plan is helping Island Growers to keep farming. By buying their harvests at a good price, we allow farmers to reinvest in their farms, and with technical support and access to higher quality cocoa, it's a win–win for everyone.

Sadly, Laurence passed away in October 2007, but his wife Angela has held on to the Island Grower partnership that he started with us.

Today, more than 166 Island Grower partners have joined us, and their beans now create some of the finest chocolate in the world. We've won several prestigious awards for chocolates made with Saint Lucian cocoa, including a 2013 Gold Great Taste Award for our Rabot 1745 Saint Lucia Island Growers 70% Milk.

'Hotel Chocolat has breathed new life into cocoa-growing in Saint Lucia,' Laurence once said. 'For the first time we have a fair price, prompt payment and a secure future.' And we're just getting started.

Left, top: Cocoa seedlings under dissipated light to replicate the growing conditions in the rainforest
Left, middle: Careful management of the old and rare Rabot gene types
Left, below: Cocoa blossoms and a baby pod
Opposite: Cuthbert Monroque, who personally leads most of the tree-to-bar experiences at Rabot

HOTEL
Chocolat.

Caribbean Fish Run Down

A best-seller in our Rabot 1745 Borough Market restaurant – a legendary West Indian broth with numerous variations passed from mother to daughter. The name 'run down' refers to the technique of slowly reducing the coconut milk to produce a rich and satisfying sauce. The roasted nibs imbue the dish with their signature earthy nuttiness, which provides a warming contrast to the fresh ginger and a tender and welcome crunch.

Cocoa Factor: Medium | **Origin:** Any

Serves 6

3 tomatoes
2 tablespoons sunflower oil
1 onion, peeled and finely chopped
2 garlic cloves, peeled and grated
3cm piece of fresh ginger, peeled and finely chopped
2 teaspoons curry powder
1 teaspoon ground turmeric
½ teaspoon ground allspice
5 tablespoons roasted cocoa nibs
1 hot red chilli, deseeded and finely chopped
750ml unsweetened coconut milk
350ml water
500g cod fillet (or any fish of your choice), cut into 6 equal pieces
bunch of coriander, leaves picked and chopped
salt and freshly ground pepper

Cut a small cross in the base of each tomato and blanch in boiling water for 10 seconds. Plunge into iced water. Peel off the skin then cut into quarters and remove the seeds.

Pour the sunflower oil into a large pan over a medium heat and add the onion. Cook until soft but not coloured, stirring as you go – about 4 minutes. Add the garlic and ginger and cook for 1 minute only. Add the curry powder, turmeric, allspice and cocoa nibs and cook gently for 1 minute. Add the tomatoes and red chilli and cook for another minute.

Mix the coconut milk and water together to combine, add to the pan and bring to a boil. Skim any foam off the top with a ladle and discard. Lower the heat to a simmer and, stirring every minute, reduce this to two-thirds of its volume – this should take about 10–15 minutes. Taste for salt and pepper and adjust accordingly.

Season the fish all over then bury the fillets in the sauce. Bring to a boil then turn down the heat to a simmer. Cook gently for 2–3 minutes further until the fish is cooked through. Finally sprinkle over the chopped coriander. Serve with rice and a green salad.

Market Fish of the Day with Coconut, Lime and Ginger

A riot of colours and flavours, just like the Saturday market in downtown Soufrière near our cocoa estate in Saint Lucia. This is a traditional 'one pot' style dish, capturing the flavours of land and sea. The cocoa shells give a subtle bass note and rich hue to the classic Caribbean blend of chilli, ginger and lime. You can use cocoa shells that are sold for making tea, or just roast and crack your own (see page 167).

Cocoa Factor: Low | **Origin:** Any

Serves 4

zest and juice of 1 lime
1 red chilli, deseeded and finely chopped
1 garlic clove, peeled and roughly chopped
1 lemongrass stick, roughly chopped
½ small bunch of coriander, stalks and leaves separated, chopped
5cm piece of fresh ginger, peeled and finely chopped
½ teaspoon creole seasoning
3 tablespoons cocoa shells
½ teaspoon ground cumin
2 tablespoons sunflower oil
½ onion, peeled and finely sliced
300g butternut squash, peeled and cut into 1cm dice
200ml vegetable stock
4 x 180g white fish fillets, such as cod, haddock, halibut or turbot, deboned and skinned
400ml unsweetened coconut milk
salt and freshly ground pepper

In a blender, purée the lime zest, chilli, garlic, lemongrass, coriander stalks, ginger, creole seasoning, cocoa shells and cumin to a dry paste. If needed to keep the motor running, add a tablespoon or two of cold water. Remove the paste and discard any stringy pieces.

Heat the oil in a large pan over a medium heat, add the onion and the spice paste and cook gently for 10 minutes, stirring often to stop it sticking. Add the diced squash and vegetable stock and stir well, scraping the bits from the bottom of the pan. Add salt and pepper to taste. Bring to a boil, reduce the heat to a simmer and cover. Cook for 5 minutes then add the fish fillets, pushing each piece into the sauce. Cook for a further 5 minutes until the squash has softened. Add the coconut milk and bring to a boil, then lower the heat and simmer for 5 minutes.

To serve, divide equally between large bowls and sprinkle with the chopped coriander leaves and lime juice. Serve with rice.

Cocoa Creole-Spiced Monkfish, Almond Purée and Jerusalem Artichokes

There is a sensational combination of flavours at work in this dish. Blending the spices with cocoa-shell powder mellows their heat and adds a subtle richness to the monkfish that is utterly delicious. This is complemented by the almond purée and the nutty flavour of the artichokes, all enlivened by fresh, sharp lemon juice. You can use cocoa shells that are sold for making tea, or just roast and crack your own (see page 167).

Cocoa Factor: Low | **Origin:** Any

Serves 4

2 tablespoons creole seasoning
4 tablespoons cocoa shells, blitzed in a blender or ground in a pestle and mortar to a fine powder
4 x 200g monkfish fillets, or any thickly cut fish
500g Jerusalem artichokes (look for evenly sized ones)
1 tablespoon white wine vinegar
50g butter
2 tablespoons sunflower oil
juice of 1 lemon
2 bunches of watercress, thicker stalks trimmed and discarded
salt and freshly ground pepper

For the almond purée
100g flaked almonds
500ml almond milk or whole milk

Mix together the creole seasoning and cocoa shell powder and use to coat the monkfish fillets. Place on a plate, cover with cling film and chill in the fridge for 2–4 hours to allow the fish to absorb the flavours.

To make the almond purée, place the almonds and milk in a small pan and simmer over a low to medium heat, with the lid on, for 1 hour or until the nuts are soft. If the liquid reduces below the level of the nuts, top up with water and continue cooking.

Drain the nuts, reserving the liquid. Place the nuts and half the cooking liquid in a blender and blitz until smooth, adding more liquid if you need to – it should have the consistency of custard. Add salt to taste then scrape into a bowl and leave to cool to room temperature.

Peel the Jerusalem artichokes and place in a bowl of cold water with the white wine vinegar. Bring a pan of salted water to a boil. Add the artichokes and simmer until cooked – about 10–15 minutes. (The cooking time will vary as Jerusalem artichokes are all different sizes and cook unevenly. The best way is to test each one as you cook it –

they should be tender when poked with a sharp knife.) As each is ready, remove and put on a plate to cool.

When you're ready to cook the fish, preheat the oven to 200°C/gas 6. Melt the butter in a large, ovenproof frying pan over a medium to high heat. When foaming, add the sunflower oil and the monkfish. Cook for 2 minutes on each side until golden brown. Squeeze the lemon juice over the fish. Transfer the fillets to a warm plate, lower the heat to medium and add the cooked Jerusalem artichokes to the pan. Cook for 2 minutes, seasoning with salt and pepper to taste. Return the monkfish to the pan, scatter over the watercress and put the pan in the oven for 3–4 minutes, or until the fish is cooked through.

Spoon some almond purée on to each serving plate. Divide the monkfish, Jerusalem artichokes and watercress evenly between the plates, pour the cooking liquid from the pan over the fish and serve.

Baked Fish Escabeche

Escabeche is a dish in which fish is marinated and preserved using vinegar or citrus fruit. Like quite a few dishes from the Caribbean, it is best prepared a day or two before eating. With roots in Latin America, escabeche makes the most of the cocoa, spices and citrus fruits that grow so well in the region and work so wonderfully with chocolate. Serve with a salad and plenty of crusty bread to mop up the juices.

Cocoa Factor: Medium | **Origin:** Caribbean | 75–100%

Serves 4

4 x 180g oily fish fillets, such as mackerel, sardines or red mullet, deboned and skinned
2 tablespoons curry powder
salt and freshly ground pepper
sunflower oil, for frying

For the marinade
40ml sunflower oil
4 shallots, peeled and thinly sliced
2 carrots, peeled and thinly sliced
1 fennel bulb, trimmed and thinly sliced
2 garlic cloves, peeled and thinly sliced
2 bay leaves
2 teaspoons curry powder
1 dried red chilli
100ml white wine
50ml white wine vinegar
½ teaspoon sea salt
1 teaspoon caster sugar
2 tablespoons freshly chopped coriander
50g dark chocolate
20g roasted cocoa nibs
salt and freshly ground pepper

To make the marinade, heat the oil in a pan set over a medium heat. Cook the shallots, carrots and fennel until soft but not coloured – about 7 minutes, stirring often. Stir in the garlic, bay leaves, curry powder and chilli and cook a further 2 minutes. Add the wine, vinegar, sea salt, sugar and coriander and simmer for 5 minutes. Now melt in the chocolate and add the nibs. Taste and season with salt and pepper. Remove from the heat and leave to cool before placing in an airtight container in the fridge for at least 12 hours.

Preheat the oven to 220°C/gas 7. Dust the fish fillets with curry powder and salt and pepper. Heat a little oil in a sauté pan and fry the fish for 1 minute on each side. Remove and leave to cool on a plate. Take 4 pieces of foil about 3 times the size of each fillet. Place a fillet in the centre of each piece of foil and spoon over equal amounts of the marinade. Gather the sides of the foil and seal tightly to form an enclosed package. Place on a large baking sheet and bake for 12–15 minutes, depending on the thickness of the fillets. The fish should be just cooked through and firm to the touch. Serve in their foil parcels – be careful when you unwrap them as the steam will be very hot.

Cocoa Beer Mussels

This classic dish uses beer instead of white wine, in the Belgian style, giving a malty flavour to the sweet mussels. You can make this with pale ale or our Cocoa Beer, which is made using an infusion of cocoa shells left over from making chocolate, adding even more of a rich, earthy flavour to this dish. Serve with warm, crusty French bread and a pot of roasted garlic aioli (see Chocolate Aioli on page 232) for dipping into the mussel broth.

If you wish to make a cocoa-infused beer of your own, simply soak 2 tablespoons of nibs in your pale ale or other beer, being careful to awaken the flavours of your nibs using our quick technique on page 19. Leave to infuse for at least 4 hours and up to 2 days if possible.

Cocoa Factor: Low

Serves 4

65g butter
1 small onion, peeled and finely chopped
3 large shallots, peeled and finely chopped
2 sticks of celery, peeled and finely chopped
150ml cocoa beer or other pale ale
2kg mussels, cleaned and de-bearded (discard any that are open)
3 bay leaves
4 tablespoons crème fraîche
1 tablespoon freshly chopped parsley
1 tablespoon freshly chopped tarragon
salt and freshly ground pepper

Melt the butter in a large pan over a medium heat and add the onion, shallots and celery. Cook until softened but not coloured – about 5 minutes. Pour in the beer and bring to a boil then take off the heat.

Tip the mussels, bay leaves, softened vegetables and beer into a large pan set over a high heat. Cover with a tight-fitting lid and cook for 4–5 minutes, shaking the pan every minute or so.

Set a colander over a clean bowl or pan and strain the mussels, reserving the liquid and throwing away any mussels that haven't opened. Heat the reserved liquid in a pan over a high heat and reduce to one-third of its volume. Stir in the crème fraîche and herbs, and season with salt and pepper.

Spoon the mussels into 4 large bowls and pour equal amounts of sauce over each. Serve immediately.

Cocoa-Marinated Fish Fillet

Marinating fish in cocoa oil imparts a subtle bitterness, delivering a wonderful savoury contrast to the sweet creamy leeks and spiced port sauce in this recipe. Most of the work goes into the preparation, leaving you plenty of time for entertaining guests.

Cocoa Factor: Medium | **Origin:** Any

Serves 4

3 tablespoons sunflower oil
2 tablespoons roasted cocoa nibs
4 x 180g white fish fillets, such as sea bass or halibut, skin on
salt and freshly ground pepper

For the creamed leeks
100g butter
2 leeks, finely sliced
1 garlic clove, peeled and grated
100ml double cream
salt and freshly ground pepper

For the spiced port sauce
1 cinnamon stick
1 star anise
1 teaspoon coriander seeds
1½ teaspoons green cardamom pods
1 teaspoon black peppercorns
250ml red wine
300ml port
1 bay leaf
2 pinches of roasted cocoa nibs
50g butter

First prepare the fish. Mix 2 tablespoons of the sunflower oil together with the nibs in a shallow tray and add the fish fillets, turning to coat them all over. Cover with cling film and leave in the fridge for 3 hours or until needed.

To make the sauce, combine all the ingredients apart from the butter in a small pan and bring to a boil. Turn the heat down to medium and reduce to a thin syrup. Whisk in the butter over a gentle heat until completely incorporated. Pass through a fine sieve.

Melt the butter for the leeks in a large pan over a low heat. Add the leeks and garlic, and cook until very soft, 10–15 minutes – if the leeks start to colour, lower the heat. Drain away any excess fat. Add the cream and bring to a boil. Take off the heat and season to taste.

Remove the fish fillets from the fridge 20 minutes before you're ready to cook them. Add the remaining sunflower oil to a large sauté pan set over a medium to high heat. Season the fish with salt and pepper. Place the fillets skin side down in the pan and lower the heat to medium. Cook for 3 minutes, then turn and cook the other side for a further 3 minutes, depending on the thickness of the fillets. Remove to a warm plate.

Warm through the leeks over a low heat for 5–8 minutes. Also reheat the port sauce. Serve the leeks topped with the fish, skin upwards. Drizzle the spiced port sauce around the side.

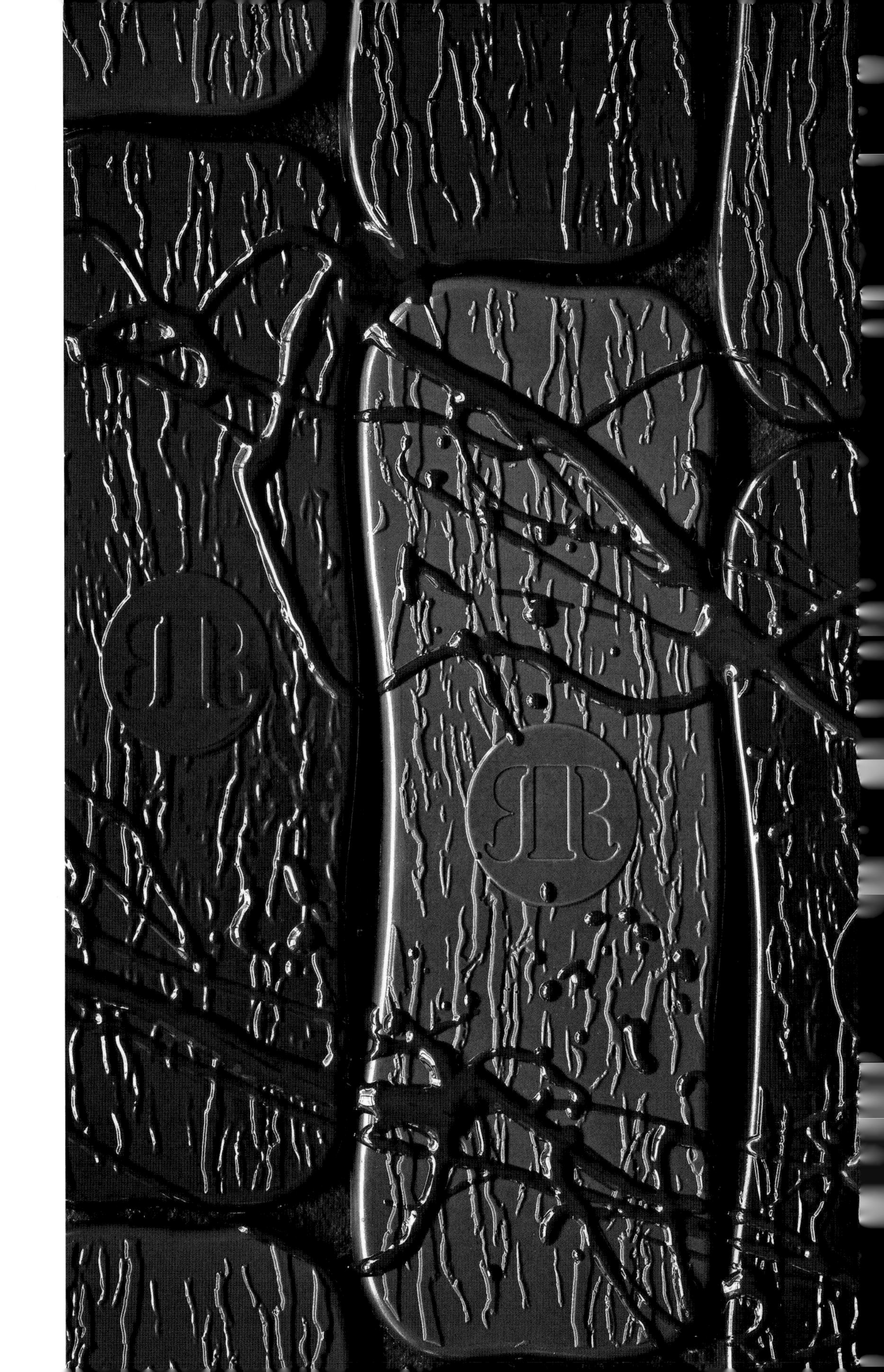

The World's Most Exclusive Chocolate Bar

Cocoa beans are enormously sensitive to the land they grow on, and also pick up flavours when they are dried and fermented (see page 18).

Although harvesting from just a single section of a farming estate occurs among winemakers, we think we're the first to produce a single-côte chocolate bar. It is made from cocoa grown and harvested on just one part of Rabot Estate, our 250-year-old cocoa plantation in Saint Lucia.

The Marcial côte is just one of 16 côtes – or cocoa orchards – at Rabot, bordered by riverbeds on the side of a volcanic basin beneath the spectacular Piton sea mountains, and it is blessed with fabulously rich and fertile soil.

During the harvest seasons of spring and autumn, we collect the ripe pods and take them back to the 'nursery', where their beans are extracted within 24 hours. We then make sure that they're fermented and sun-dried separately from all the other beans on our estate and, depending on the weather, they can be ready to roast within about 2 weeks.

At Hotel Chocolat we've always sought to push the limits of what can be done with cocoa and chocolate, and in 2013 we created our second single-côte chocolate bar, with cocoa harvested from a côte called Pépinière. Although the two côtes are close, the subtle differences in terroir produce remarkably different cocoa personalities. The flavour of our Marcial chocolate is full of red fruits and wine, with a woody, acidic middle and a clean finish, while our Pépinière delivers milder yellow and citrus fruits, with a mellow, sweet and creamy middle and a smoky finish.

Opposite and above: The Rabot Marcial single-côte chocolate bar. Only chocolate made from rare and vintage beans bears the 'double R' emblem of our Rabot Estate

Chocolate Chilli Crusted Salmon

The spicy, slightly bitter chocolate notes in the crust beautifully complement the richness of the salmon. A very quick way to add a bit of excitement to your fish supper.

Cocoa Factor: Medium | **Origin:** Any | 70–100%

Serves 4

1 slice of white bread, crusts removed
1 tablespoon freshly chopped coriander
1 garlic clove, peeled and chopped
juice of ½ lime
1 teaspoon Spiced Chilli Chocolate Glaze (page 245)
55g mayonnaise
4 x 180g salmon fillets, skinned
salt and freshly ground pepper

Preheat the oven to 220°C/gas 7.

In a food processor blend the bread, coriander, garlic, lime juice and Spiced Chilli Chocolate Glaze. When combined, remove to a bowl and fold in the mayonnaise.

Season the salmon with salt and pepper. Divide the bread mixture equally between the 4 salmon fillets, spreading across the top of each one. Place on a baking tray and cook in the oven for 15 minutes. The fish will be a lovely pink colour and should flake when pressed gently with the back of a fork. Serve with a green salad or steamed French beans and boiled new potatoes.

Rare Seared Tuna with Spiced Aubergine Salad and Cocoa, Ginger and Lime Dressing

A quick, wholesome and flavoursome dish, with earthy cocoa, roast cumin and the slight bitterness of the aubergines combining with the freshness of lime and ginger.

Cocoa Factor: Medium | **Origin:** Any

Serves 4

bunch of fresh coriander, leaves picked and finely chopped
2 tablespoons roasted cocoa nibs
½ red chilli, deseeded and sliced
1 teaspoon peeled and grated fresh ginger
1 garlic clove, peeled and grated
juice of 2 limes
3 tablespoons light soy sauce
50ml olive oil
4 x 180g thickly cut tuna steaks
½ quantity of Spiced Aubergine Salad (see page 128), at room temperature
salt and freshly ground pepper

In a large bowl, mix together the coriander, cocoa nibs, chilli, ginger, garlic, lime juice, soy sauce and 2 tablespoons of the olive oil. Add salt and pepper to taste and set aside.

Season the tuna steaks with salt and pepper on both sides. To a large, non-stick frying pan set over a medium to high heat, add half the remaining olive oil. Gently place 2 of the tuna steaks in the pan and sear for 1 minute on each side. Remove from the pan and place on a large plate. Repeat the searing with the remaining oil and 2 tuna steaks then add them to the plate.

Lower the heat under the frying pan and pour in half the coriander mixture to warm through. Stir to catch the caramelised bits on the bottom of the pan, then pour this over the resting tuna steaks.

To serve, place a tuna steak on each serving plate. Add a spoonful of Spiced Aubergine Salad to the side of each steak and drizzle the remaining dressing over the top. Serve with boiled new potatoes, green beans and salad leaves.

Chocolat.
Cocoa GIN
A SMALL BATCH ARTISANAL GIN
Infused with cocoa shells

Cocoa Gin-Cured Salmon

At Rabot 1745 we cure salmon using the traditional salting and spicing method, then add our own Cocoa Gin for a unique flourish. It does its job as a preservative but also, and much more importantly, its botanicals infuse the fish with their subtle flavours. There are high notes of lemon zest, juniper, minneola and angelica, with bass tones of roasted cocoa shells and rich macadamia nuts. If you are making your own cocoa gin, make sure the nibs have had their flavour awakened (see page 19).

Cocoa Factor: Low | **Origin:** Any

Serves 4–6

1 x 500g salmon fillet (ask your fishmonger and scale the fish but leave the skin on)
30ml Cocoa Gin (or 30ml gin mixed with 2 tablespoons crushed roasted cocoa nibs)
2 tablespoons caster sugar
1½ tablespoons coarse sea salt
1 teaspoon freshly ground pepper
1 teaspoon chopped fennel fronds
1 teaspoon freshly chopped dill
3 juniper berries, crushed and finely chopped

Lay the salmon on a piece of foil big enough to wrap the fillet completely. Mix all the remaining ingredients together and massage all over the salmon. Wrap the foil loosely around the salmon and leave it in the fridge for 2 days, turning it occasionally.

When ready to serve, unwrap the salmon, wash off the salt and herb mixture, and pat dry with kitchen paper. Slice the salmon thinly across the grain using a sharp knife. This is great served with a green salad, some sourdough bread and a lemon wedge.

Love Them & Leaf Them

Vegetables and salads

Citrus Salad with White Chocolate Dressing

This recipe came about in response to the abundance of fresh citrus fruits, cocoa and vanilla growing on our estate in Saint Lucia. The contrasting flavours of zingy citrus and soothing white chocolate combine beautifully to create something both unusual and delicious. Try to obtain good quality, not too sweet white chocolate. Check the ingredients are only cocoa butter, milk or cream powder and sugar.

Cocoa Factor: Low | **Origin:** Any | At least 30%

Serves 6

1 plum tomato
2 limes
5 oranges
2 grapefruits
3 lemons
55g caster sugar
2 tablespoons water
80–100g mixed salad leaves
small bunch of chives, chopped
handful of basil leaves, chopped
15g cashew nuts
salt and freshly ground pepper

For the white chocolate dressing
125g white chocolate, broken into small pieces
150ml sunflower oil
pinch of sea salt
juice of ½ lemon
1 teaspoon vanilla extract
2 teaspoons coconut milk

For the dressing, gently warm the chocolate in the microwave at 10-second intervals on medium until liquid. Alternatively, melt the chocolate in a bowl set over a pan of simmering water for about 2 minutes. Make sure the bottom of the bowl doesn't actually touch the hot water and stir the chocolate occasionally.

To make an emulsion, slowly whisk the oil into the chocolate, beating all the time. When completely mixed, whisk in the salt, lemon juice, vanilla and coconut milk. Store in an airtight container in the fridge until needed (it will keep for up to 3 days).

To skin the tomato, make a small cross in the base and put it into a pan of boiling water for 10 seconds, then remove it and plunge into a bowl of iced water. Peel and deseed the tomato and cut it into large dice, about the size of a postage stamp. Peel all the citrus fruits and cut away the white pith so you are left with just the flesh of the fruit. Using a small sharp knife cut in between the segments, keeping any juices in one bowl and the segments in another.

In a pan, cook the sugar and water over a medium heat until the syrup begins to caramelise to the colour of honey. When you reach this colour add the citrus juices. Stir until the sugar has dissolved, but no more – do not reduce. Now pour this syrup on to the citrus fruits but do not stir as it will break up the fruit.

Arrange a few drained citrus segments in the base of 4 shallow serving bowls. Toss the mixed leaves and herbs with the white chocolate dressing and add salt and pepper to taste. Place a small amount of leaves on top of the citrus fruit, and then repeat the layers. Add a few tomato pieces to each salad. Finish with some more citrus fruit and sprinkle with cashew nuts. Finally, drizzle with a little more of the white chocolate dressing.

The Gardener

These amazing vegetarian dishes can be served as starters or as a main course for sharing. The roasted cocoa nibs provide an earthy, peppery spice that pairs perfectly with the likes of aubergine, hummus, olives and pesto, and their nibby texture plays just as important a role. Serve them up with grilled peppers, asparagus or baby artichokes and plenty of warm crusty bread to mop up the juice. **See image overleaf.**

Spiced Aubergine Salad

Cocoa Factor: Low | **Origin:** Any

Serves 6

2 small aubergines, cut into 1cm dice
300g ripe plum tomatoes
1 teaspoon whole cumin seeds
4 tablespoons olive oil
1 onion, peeled and cut into 1cm dice
3 garlic cloves, peeled and grated
1 teaspoon cumin powder
1 teaspoon hot chilli sauce
60g roasted cocoa nibs
1 heaped tablespoon freshly chopped coriander
1 heaped tablespoon freshly chopped mint
salt and freshly ground pepper

Place the aubergine in a bowl and sprinkle with 1 tablespoon of salt. Mix well and cover, then place in the fridge for 1 hour. Remove the aubergine from the fridge. Take small handfuls and gently squeeze out the excess liquid before placing the aubergine dice in a clean bowl. Discard the liquid. To skin the tomatoes, make a small cross in the base of each one and drop into a pan of boiling water for 10 seconds, then remove and plunge into a bowl of iced water. Peel and deseed the tomatoes and chop into small dice.

Dry-fry the cumin seeds in a pan over a medium heat. When the seeds become fragrant and start jumping around the pan, after about 2 minutes, transfer them to a plate. When cool, crush to a fine powder using a pestle and mortar.

Heat the olive oil in a pan over a medium heat, add the onion and cook until soft and turning golden. Add the grated garlic and cook for 1 minute. Add the cumin powder and cook for 30 seconds. Now add the aubergine and stir until the vegetables are all coated. Cook this mixture over a medium heat, stirring occasionally, until the aubergines start to brown, about 10 minutes. Add the diced tomatoes and stir well. Cook gently until the liquid has reduced, leaving a dry mixture.

Remove from the heat. Stir in the chilli sauce, cocoa nibs and herbs. Taste for salt and pepper and adjust as needed. Place in a bowl and leave to cool. When cool, give everything a good stir, cover with cling film and chill for 12–24 hours. Take out of the fridge 1 hour before serving.

Hummus with Chilli Cocoa-Spiced Walnuts

Most recipes use tahini paste, but we prefer the slight nuttiness of peanut butter and cumin, which work well with chickpeas. This recipe is great served with Cocoa Nib Crispbread (see page 226) or thin slices of sourdough.

Cocoa Factor: Low | **Origin:** Any

Serves 6

1 x 450g tin of chickpeas
2 garlic cloves, peeled and finely grated
zest and juice of ½ lemon
1 tablespoon smooth peanut butter
¼ tablespoon ground cumin
1 teaspoon salt
2 tablespoons olive oil
30ml Cocoa Chilli Oil (see page 239)
20g walnut pieces
1 tablespoon freshly chopped parsley

Drain the chickpeas, reserving 3 tablespoons of the liquid. Place all the ingredients apart from the Cocoa Chilli Oil, walnuts and parsley in a food processor and blitz to a smooth purée. Scrape the bowl occasionally to make sure everything is properly combined.

Transfer the mixture to a bowl and drizzle over the Cocoa Chilli Oil. Scatter with the walnuts and chopped parsley.

Cocoa Nib-Infused Kalamata Olives

Cocoa Factor: Low | **Origin:** Any

Serves 6

200g good quality, dry-cured, pitted Kalamata olives
20g roasted cocoa nibs
40ml sunflower oil

Mix the olives and cocoa nibs together. Heat the oil in a pan for 1 minute or so just to warm. Pour the warm oil over the olives and cocoa nibs and cover with cling film. Leave at room temperature for 3–4 hours to allow the flavours to develop. If not using immediately, store in an airtight container in the fridge for up to 2 days.

Hummus with Chilli Cocoa-Spiced Walnuts
Cocoa Nib-Infused Kalamata Olives

Spiced Aubergine Salad

Roasted Rainbow Vegetable Salad with Puy Lentils and Goats' Cheese

Cocoa plays an important role in the flavour, texture and appearance of this hearty dish. Crunchy cocoa nibs add a sultry, nutty edge, while the sharp goats' cheese counterbalances the sweetness of the deep-red beetroot and golden sweet potato. It also pairs well with peppered mackerel.

Cocoa Factor: Medium | **Origin:** Any

Serves 6

2 sweet potatoes, peeled and cut into 2cm cubes
3 large beetroots, peeled and sliced into 5mm-thick circles
6 tablespoons olive oil
1 garlic clove
200g Puy lentils
1 tablespoon vegetable bouillon powder
3 spring onions, trimmed, peeled and sliced finely at an angle
small bunch of parsley, finely chopped
20g shelled walnuts
20g roasted cocoa nibs
100g goats' cheese log, cut into 5mm slices
2 large handfuls of watercress
salt and freshly ground pepper

Preheat the oven to 180°C/gas 4.

Toss the cubed sweet potatoes and beetroot rounds with 3 tablespoons of olive oil, the garlic clove, and a pinch of salt and pepper. Tip into a roasting tray and cook in the oven for 35–40 minutes or until tender but still retaining their texture. Squeeze the roasted garlic flesh from its skin and combine with the vegetables.

Meanhile, cook the lentils. Place them in a pan and fill with enough water to cover the lentils by 2cm. Place the pan over a high heat, cover and bring to a boil. Add the vegetable bouillon powder then reduce the heat and simmer, loosely covered with a lid, for 15–20 minutes or until the lentils are tender (do not overcook). Drain thoroughly, transfer to a large mixing bowl and mix with 1 tablespoon of olive oil, the spring onions and the parsley. Stir through the roasted vegetables, season, then cool to room temperature.

Gently crush the walnuts and cocoa nibs in a pestle and mortar. Combine with a pinch of salt then tip on to a large plate. Roll each slice of goats' cheese into a small ball. Carefully roll the balls over the walnut and nib mixture, pressing the mixture into each one until they are covered entirely.

Spread out the watercress on a large serving plate and spoon over the roasted vegetable and lentil mix. Place the goats' cheese on top and drizzle with the remaining olive oil.

Jewelled Superfood Salad with Cocoa and Ginger Dressing

A vibrant salad bursting with flavour and goodness. The combination of cocoa and ginger works beautifully with the nuttiness of brown rice. Packed full of antioxidant-rich fruit and vegetables, it's perfect for lunch, as a light dinner or a more substantial side.

Cocoa Factor: Low | **Origin:** Any

Serves 4–6

300g long-grain brown rice
1 tablespoon vegetable bouillon powder
1 large head of broccoli, cut into florets
1 tablespoon shelled pistachio nuts
2 tablespoons almonds, soaked overnight in water and rinsed
2 tablespoons pomegranate seeds
2 tablespoons pumpkin seeds, dry roasted
1 red onion, peeled and finely diced
small bunch of coriander, leaves and stalks finely chopped
12 mixed cherry tomatoes, halved
½ cup frozen edamame beans, defrosted
salt and freshly ground pepper

For the cocoa and ginger dressing
1 garlic clove, peeled and grated
2.5cm piece of fresh ginger, peeled and grated
5 tablespoons good quality extra-virgin olive oil
juice of 1 lemon
80ml water
1 tablespoon roasted cocoa nibs

First make the dressing by whizzing together all the ingredients apart from the cocoa nibs and salt and pepper in a blender. When the consistency is fairly smooth, add the cocoa nibs and pulse a few times. The dressing should retain some of the delicious crunch of the cocoa nibs. Season to taste, transfer to a small glass jar and shake well before using.

To make the salad, put the rice in a large pan and cover it with boiling water mixed with the bouillon powder. The water level should be approximately 2cm higher than the rice. Place a lid on top and simmer gently until the rice is tender and the liquid has been absorbed – about 25 minutes (do not overcook).

While the rice is cooking, cook the broccoli florets in a separate pan of boiling water for 2–5 minutes; the florets should still retain their crunch. Drain and plunge into iced water to stop them cooking and ensure they remain a vibrant green. Drain and set aside.

Place the cooked rice in a large bowl while still warm. Mix in the dressing then leave to cool to room temperature. Add the broccoli, pistachios, almonds, pomegranate seeds, pumpkin seeds, red onion, coriander, cherry tomatoes and edamame beans to the rice. Mix together and season with salt and pepper before serving.

Aubergine Salad with Cocoa Nib Crispbread and Cocoa Nib-Infused Yoghurt

Aubergines take on flavours very well. Here, the characteristic bitter tang of the aubergine skin harmonises irresistibly with the warming combination of chocolate and chilli. The cocoa nib-laced yoghurt with coriander and mint provides a soothing contrast to the spice in the salad – it's well worth the effort of making it. And the crispbread rounds it all off with a super crunch. This aubergine salad is a hotter variation on the Spiced Aubergine Salad we serve as part of The Gardener (see page 128), and is made without cocoa nibs.

Cocoa Factor: Medium | **Origin:** Any | 70–100%

Serves 4

For the aubergine salad

2 small aubergines, cut into 1cm cubes
350g ripe red tomatoes
1 teaspoon whole cumin seeds
3 tablespoons olive oil
1 onion, peeled and cut into medium dice
3 garlic cloves, peeled and grated
3 tablespoons Spiced Chilli Chocolate Glaze (see page 245)
1–2 teaspoons hot chilli sauce
1 tablespoon freshly chopped coriander
2 tablespoons freshly chopped mint
salt and freshly ground pepper

For the cocoa nib-infused yoghurt

3 tablespoons roasted cocoa nibs
125ml thick natural Greek yoghurt

To serve

as many crispbreads as you like (see page 226)

Place the aubergine in a bowl and sprinkle with 1 tablespoon of salt. Mix well and cover, then place in the fridge for 1 hour.

To skin the tomatoes, make a small cross in the base of each one and place into a pan of boiling water for 10 seconds, then remove and plunge into a bowl of iced water. Peel and deseed the tomatoes and chop into small dice.

Dry-fry the cumin seeds in a pan over a medium heat. When the seeds become fragrant and start jumping around the pan, after about 2 minutes, transfer them to a plate. When cool, crush to a fine powder using a pestle and mortar.

Remove the aubergine from the fridge. Take small handfuls and gently squeeze out the excess liquid before placing the aubergine dice in a clean bowl. Discard the liquid.

Recipe continues

Heat the olive oil in a pan over a medium heat and fry the onion until soft and pale brown, about 8–10 minutes. Add the grated garlic and cook for 1 minute. Now add the aubergines and cook until they start to brown at the edges. Add the diced tomatoes and cook until the liquid has reduced to create a dry mixture – this should take around 10–15 minutes. Remove from the heat, add the Spiced Chilli Chocolate Glaze and hot chilli sauce, and season to taste with salt and pepper. Allow to cool, then stir in the chopped herbs. Cover and store in the fridge for at least 12 hours to allow the flavours to develop.

To make the Cocoa Nib-Infused Yoghurt, preheat the oven to 120°C/gas ½. Place the nibs on a baking tray and heat in the oven for 10 minutes. Tip the yoghurt into a bowl. Remove the nibs from the oven and tip into the yoghurt. Stir well, cover and chill in the fridge for 2 hours or longer for a better flavour.

Divide the aubergine among 4 plates, serving small pots of yoghurt alongside and a large bowl of crispbreads for everyone to help themselves.

Portobello Mushroom Risotto

Mushrooms help the savoury and umami notes of cocoa stand out in this dish. Combined with the earthy flavours of the cocoa nib stock there is an almost meaty flavour to this great vegetarian dish.

Cocoa Factor: Low | **Origin:** Any

Serves 6

1 tablespoon olive oil
2 small shallots, peeled and finely chopped
1 teaspoon fresh thyme leaves
50g butter
250g portobello mushrooms, peeled and cut into small dice
350g Arborio rice
20g roasted cocoa nibs
250ml white wine
1 litre hot vegetable stock
70g Parmesan, grated
½ bunch of chives, snipped short with sharp scissors
salt and freshly ground pepper

Heat the oil in a large, deep pan and cook the shallots with the thyme over a low heat for about 3 minutes, until soft. Add the butter and diced mushrooms and cook until the mushrooms release their liquid. Carry on cooking until most of the liquid has evaporated. Now add the Arborio rice and cocoa nibs and cook, stirring constantly, coating the rice with the shallots and mushrooms until the rice is translucent.

Add the wine, increasing the heat to medium, and cook until the liquid is completely absorbed. Add 1 ladleful of hot stock and continue cooking, stirring frequently, until the stock has been absorbed. Repeat until all the stock has been used and the rice is cooked. If the rice is still a little undercooked, add some hot water. Stir through the Parmesan and season to taste.

Divide the risotto between bowls and scatter over the chives. Serve with some crusty bread on the side.

Chilli Ravioli

A colourful and flavourful dish that excites every sense. The ravioli are suffused with a warm, teak-brown shade and a taste of cocoa richness that plays perfectly with the heat of the chilli, the earthiness of the mushrooms and the saltiness of the feta. Here they are bathed in a bright red tomato sauce with fresh green herbs. Make sure you use pure cocoa powder. Non-Dutched (non-alkalised) cocoa powder is best as more of the antioxidants are retained during processing.

Cocoa Factor: Medium | **Origin:** Any | 100%

Serves 4

For the pasta dough
400g strong white flour, plus extra for dusting
90g cocoa powder
4 eggs
2 egg yolks
2 tablespoons whole milk
1 tablespoon olive oil

For the filling
200g spinach, thick stalks removed
2 green chillies, deseeded and finely chopped
1 onion, peeled and finely chopped
2 tablespoons sunflower oil
4 portobello mushrooms, peeled and chopped into 1cm dice
100g feta

For the tomato sauce
5 plum tomatoes
1 tablespoon olive oil
1 onion, peeled and finely chopped
3 garlic cloves, peeled and grated
pinch of sugar
1 teaspoon white wine vinegar
50g tomato purée
1 teaspoon lemon thyme leaves
1 teaspoon freshly chopped parsley
1 bay leaf
handful of basil leaves, torn into strips
salt and freshly ground pepper

First make the pasta. Sift the flour and cocoa powder together 3 times into a large bowl. In a separate bowl, beat the eggs, egg yolks, milk and oil together. Mix this into the flour and cocoa – it will create a very stiff dough. Turn the dough out on to a floured surface and use your hands to bring it together. If it feels a little dry add 1 tablespoon or more of milk. Knead the dough for around 10 minutes, until it becomes smooth, shiny and very elastic. Wrap the pasta dough in cling film and place in the fridge for 30 minutes.

While the pasta dough is resting, prepare the filling. Bring a large pan of salted water to a boil and add all the spinach, stirring briefly to separate the leaves. When the leaves start to wilt, after about 1 minute, drain them into a large colander and run under cold water until the spinach is cool enough to handle. Squeeze out the excess water and set to one side.

Fry the green chillies and the onion in half the oil over a medium heat. Cook this gently until the onions begin to turn golden brown at the edges – about 8 minutes. In another pan, fry the mushrooms in the remaining oil until they give up their juices and begin to colour lightly – about 8 minutes.

Chop the spinach roughly and place in a bowl along with the mushrooms and onion mixture, then crumble in the feta. Give everything a good stir and season to taste with salt and pepper. Leave to cool completely before assembling the ravioli.

To assemble the ravioli, roll the pasta dough with a rolling pin to a thickness of 2cm. Cut it into strips about one-third of the width of your pasta machine and run each one through the machine down to the second lowest setting. Lay a sheet of rolled pasta on a floured surface and cut out 20 circles using a 7cm round cutter. Each ravioli will need a bottom and a top piece of pasta. Place 1 teaspoon of the filling in the centre of 10 discs – work quickly as the pasta will dry out around the edges. Lightly brush around the filling with water and place a disc of pasta on top. Seal the ravioli around the whole edge, pushing out any air and making sure the two discs of dough are sealed tight. Place on a tray lined with greaseproof paper. Repeat until the pasta and filling are used up.

To precook the ravioli, drop half of them into a large pan of boiling salted water. Cook for 2 minutes from the point when the water starts to boil again, then drain and refresh in iced water. Repeat with the remaining pasta. Drain the ravioli well before tossing them in a little olive oil. (You can now freeze the ravioli if you wish. Spread in a single layer on a tray, cover with cling film and store in the freezer for up to 2 weeks.)

Now make the sauce. To skin the tomatoes, make a small cross in the base of each one and drop into a pan of boiling water for 10 seconds, then remove and plunge into a bowl of iced water. Peel and deseed the tomatoes and chop into 1cm dice. Heat the olive oil in a pan over a medium heat and add the onion, cooking until softened but not coloured – this will take about 5–6 minutes, stirring every now and then.

Add the garlic and cook for 30 seconds, then add the sugar and vinegar and cook for 1 minute before stirring in the tomato purée and cooking for a further 30 seconds. Next add the diced tomatoes and all the herbs, reserving some basil as a garnish. Cook slowly over a low heat until most of the liquid has evaporated, 12–15 minutes. Season with salt and pepper and taste to check the balance of sweet or sour: if too sweet, add a little vinegar; if too sour, add a little more sugar.

When you are ready to serve, bring a large pan of salted water up to simmering, drop in the blanched ravioli and cook for 2 minutes. Drain and add to the warm tomato sauce, finishing the dish with a few strips of torn basil leaves.

The Delicious Anatomy of Cocoa

1

The Tree

As small as an apple tree and with leaves the size of dinner plates that rustle and sway in the breeze, walking through a cocoa tree grove is a magical experience. Although they like to grow in a belt around the equator (20 degrees either side) they also like to be in the shade of larger protective trees, like banana, mango and coconut. This means that a well-tended cocoa plantation looks like just a piece of jungle from a distance. The only thing giving it away is the spectacular crimson flushes of new cocoa leaves. The trees produce cocoa virtually all year round, with tiny one-month-old baby pods co-existing with six-month-old, fully mature pods. The pods do not drop to the ground when they are ripe, instead needing the intervention of an animal to spread the beans around the forest floor. The cocoa tree is a very environmentally sustainable crop, as it prevents soil erosion, thrives among indigenous flora and fauna, and is low impact in terms of water and nutrients. Cocoa cross-pollinates at an incredible pace, and only now are experts discovering quite how many types of cocoa there are.

2

The Pod

Like a small, heavy rugby ball, the cocoa at Rabot Estate has deep ridges and tapering points. Some are deep purple when ripe, others golden yellow. In other parts of the world, cocoa can have different shapes, sometimes even as round as a melon. One thing they all have in common though is the sweetness of the creamy pulp surrounding the beans, designed to lure monkeys, squirrels and jungle rats so that they can disperse the bitter beans around the jungle at the same time. Known as 'Jungle M&Ms' by the agricultural team at Rabot Estate, sucking the lychee-sweet pulp is an essential initiation for all visitors to our plantation. It is also served in a great cocoa pulp martini at the bar and a refreshing sorbet at the table. And if you're wondering, the pod casing is mulched down into organic fertiliser. No waste.

3

The Bean

When we are not eating the pulp, it is the essential catalyst for the fermentation of cocoa. We pile the wet pulp and beans in deep wooden boxes and cover with banana leaves. The sugars in the pulp heat up naturally and convert to a vinegar. Over about a week, the beans transform from a bitter astringent purple to a nutty, light brown. Still sticky, they are then spread in racks to dry off slowly in the sun, always protected from rain. Hessian sacks are the usual way for the beans to be stored.

4

The Shell

The beans are made up of two parts: the shell and the nib. When cocoa is roasted to develop the characteristic chocolate flavour notes, the thin shell is easily cracked off and separated from the nib. The nib is precious and saved to make chocolate. The shell is traditionally discarded, but not any more. We saw that they were tasty, although flaky, and full of nutrients and antioxidants. Our experiments led us to make an award-winning Cocoa Gin and Cocoa Beer. Undoubtedly the healthiest taste is via our cocoa shell teas, blended with ginger, peppermint and giving a brew similar to a green tea (see page 208). Toasty cocoa flavours, an antioxidant super-fix and zero calories.

5

The Nib

The inside of the bean is the nib and it breaks easily into little pieces. A light roasting is all that's needed to make cocoa nibs taste delicious. Like coffee, they oxidise quickly, so freshness is paramount, otherwise they can taste dull and flat. See page 19 for our tips on getting the most flavour from your nibs. They are heavy and dense in the hand, and packed with 50% cocoa butter and 50% cocoa powder. The seductive melt of chocolate all comes from the butter, melting at exactly blood temperature. The unique flavour of chocolate comes from the other half of the dark brown nib. Simply grinding them vigorously in a pestle and mortar will make a smooth un-sweetened chocolate paste as the friction melts the butter and releases the flavours. See page 166 to make your own chocolate bar.

Mac and Cheese Pie

Mac and cheese is a key element in Sunday lunch on our cocoa estate and all over Saint Lucia. This is the classic version we serve in our restaurants, a deep filling in a dramatic-looking cocoa-nib pastry case. Cocoa plays a subtle role in making the pastry case extra delicious, with bursts of savoury flavour.

Cocoa Factor: Low | **Origin:** Any

Serves 4

For the cocoa nib pastry
250g chilled butter,
  plus extra for greasing
375g plain flour,
  plus extra for dredging
1 teaspoon salt
2 teaspoons roasted cocoa nibs,
  bashed a little to break them down
125ml iced water
1 egg, beaten

For the mac and cheese filling
200g small macaroni
2 leeks
2 tablespoons sunflower oil
200g portobello, or chestnut/button
  mushrooms, wiped clean and sliced thickly
100ml double cream
50g strong Cheddar, grated
4 tablespoons finely chopped chives
salt and freshly ground pepper

You will need 4 x 9cm-wide, 6cm-deep chef rings or individual pie dishes.

First make the pastry. Coarsely grate the butter on to a plate then put it in the freezer to firm up. In a large bowl, mix together the flour, salt and cocoa nibs. Take the butter out of the freezer and gently rub it into the flour mix using your fingertips, working as quickly as possible to prevent the mixture becoming warm.

Carefully measure out the iced water and pour it into the bowl. Use a cold knife to stir until the dough binds together, adding more cold water 1 teaspoon at a time if the mixture is too dry. Turn it out on to a floured surface and bring the dough together, then wrap it in cling film and chill for 30 minutes.

Once the pastry has rested, roll it out on a floured surface to a thickness of 5mm. Cut into the size needed for the moulds with a little extra to overhang. Butter and flour the individual moulds and line with the pastry. Allow these to rest in the fridge uncovered while you preheat the oven to 170°C/gas 3.

Line the pastry cases with greaseproof paper and fill with baking beans. Bake for 15 minutes or until the pastry is a pale golden colour. Remove the baking beans, lightly brush the insides of the pastry cases with a little beaten egg and bake for a further 5 minutes.

Recipe continues

While the pastry cases are in the oven, make the filling. Cook the macaroni in a pan of boiling salted water according to the packet instructions. Drain in a colander and refresh under cold running water. Shake out all the excess water.

Split the leeks in half lengthways and rinse under a cold running tap to get rid of any soil and sand between the layers. Shake out the water and finely slice. Heat the sunflower oil a large pan over a medium heat and add the chopped leeks, then turn the heat down to low. Cover with a lid and gently cook for 10 minutes, checking and stirring every 2 minutes. Do not colour the leeks; if the heat is too high, turn it down, so that the leeks basically melt over a low heat. Add the mushrooms to the pan, cover with the lid and cook slowly for a further 5 minutes, or until the vegetables are soft. Add the cooked macaroni and stir well. Add the cream and turn the heat up to medium. As soon as the mixture begins to boil, reduce the heat to low, add salt and pepper to taste and heat until the mixture is warm throughout. The sauce should just moisten the mixture. If it is too wet, reduce it a little; if too dry, add a few tablespoons of water.

Trim the overhanging pastry from around the baked cases, then pour the macaroni mixture into each one and top with cheese. Scatter over half the chopped chives then place under a hot grill, on the lowest shelf, to melt the cheese until it starts to brown – this should only take a couple of minutes. Remove and scatter the remaining chives over the top. We serve this with Creole Tomato Chutney (see page 246) and a simple green salad.

White Chocolate Mash

In a cunning twist, the white chocolate replaces some of the usual butter with cocoa butter, elevating the humble spud to new heights of hedonism. This is the bestselling side dish in our restaurants. **See image overleaf, top right.**

Cocoa Factor: Medium | **Origin:** Any | At least 30%

Serves 4–6
500g potatoes, peeled
100g white chocolate,
  chopped into hazelnut-size pieces
100ml whole milk
100g butter
salt

Put the peeled potatoes in a pan of cold water and bring to a boil, then cook until soft enough to mash. Drain the potatoes and mash using a fork or potato masher.

Place the hot mashed potato in a large mixing bowl. Beat in the white chocolate, ensuring it all melts. Beat in the remaining ingredients until smooth. Add a pinch of salt to taste.

Roasted Parsnips with White Chocolate and Balsamic Dressing

You might not expect it, but white chocolate goes brilliantly with roasted parsnips, enhancing their natural sweetness. You can also add white chocolate to a parsnip purée, in the same way we add it to mashed potato (see White Chocolate Mash on page 149 and pictured opposite). The secret is balance – use the white chocolate sparingly to avoid over-sweetening. These parsnips go brilliantly with Roast Yard Bird (see page 80), Cocoa Brine Roast Turkey (see page 83) and Cocoa and Herb-Crusted Fillet of Pork (see page 77).

Cocoa Factor: Low | **Origin:** Any | At least 30%

Serves 4
500g parsnips, peeled and quartered lengthways
3 tablespoons sunflower oil
3 tablespoons White Chocolate Balsamic Dressing (see page 242)

Preheat the oven to 170°C/gas 3.

Place the parsnips in a pan and cover with cold water. Bring to a boil, then reduce the heat and simmer for 5 minutes. Drain immediately without running under water. Transfer the parsnips to a tray and allow to cool slightly.

Pour the oil into a roasting tin and heat on the hob until very hot but not burning. Carefully tip the parsnips into the hot oil. Using a tablespoon, coat each piece with hot oil to prevent them from sticking. Roast in the oven and cook for 20 minutes. Turn the parsnips over and roast for a further 15 minutes or until they are golden all over. Remove from the pan with a slotted spoon and drain on kitchen paper. Toss immediately with the White Chocolate Balsamic Dressing.

To Die For

Our greatest chocolate desserts

Rum and Raisin Semifreddo

Cocoa cream finds a perfect partner with rum-soaked raisins. A proper dessert for grown-ups. Make sure you use pure cocoa powder; non-Dutched (non-alkalised) cocoa powder is best as more of the antioxidants are retained during processing.

Cocoa Factor: Medium | **Origin:** Any | 100%

Serves 8

40g raisins
4 tablespoons dark rum
1 litre good quality vanilla ice cream, softened slightly

For the cocoa cream
100ml double cream
2 tablespoons cocoa powder
1 tablespoon caster sugar

Place the raisins in a bowl, then pour over the rum and leave to soften for 1 hour.

Transfer the rum and raisins to a small pan and heat for about 10 minutes until the rum has reduced slightly and the raisins are very soft. Alternatively, place in a small bowl, cover and heat in a microwave on high power for 1 minute. Leave to cool.

Spoon the softened ice cream into a large bowl and fold through the rum and raisins. Pour the mixture into a large, rectangular, freezer-proof mould (silicone is best) lined with cling film, leaving enough of an overhang to cover the top. Freeze until firm, preferably overnight.

To make the cocoa cream, combine all the ingredients in a bowl and whisk to the consistency of thick yoghurt.

Remove the semifreddo from the mould and peel away the cling film. Leave to soften slightly, then cut into slices and serve with the cocoa cream.

Chocolate Panna Cotta with Raspberry Sauce

The light texture of panna cotta is the perfect way to experience the flavour notes of good chocolate, so choose the best quality you can. The cocoa is mellowed by the cream, so don't settle for anything less than dark 70% chocolate. Chocolates with natural red fruit or red wine notes harmonise best with raspberries. Madagascan is the classic 'red fruit' chocolate, while Caribbean and Latin American chocolates often have red wine flavour notes.

Cocoa Factor: High | **Origin:** Madagascar, Caribbean, Latin America | 70–80%

Serves 4

sunflower oil, for greasing
3 gelatine leaves
250ml whole milk
250ml double cream
30g caster sugar
1 vanilla pod, split lengthways and seeds scraped out
50g dark chocolate
4 mint sprigs, to decorate

For the raspberry sauce

75g caster sugar
6 tablespoons water
splash of Chambord liqueur or raspberry vodka
175g fresh or frozen raspberries, plus extra to decorate
juice of 1 lemon

Lightly grease 4 ramekins with a little sunflower oil.

To make the panna cotta, soak the gelatine leaves in a little cold water until soft. Place the milk, cream, sugar, vanilla pod and seeds in a pan and heat gently until hot, but do not boil. Remove the vanilla pod and discard. Squeeze the water out of the gelatine leaves and add them to the pan, then take off the heat and stir until the gelatine dissolves. Place the dark chocolate in a mixing bowl and pour the hot cream mixture over the top. Stir until the chocolate melts and combines with the cream mixture. Pour the mixture into the ramekins and chill for at least 1 hour, until set.

To make the raspberry sauce, place the sugar, water, Chambord and raspberries in a pan and bring to a gentle boil. Reduce the heat and simmer, stirring, until the sugar dissolves. Take the pan off the heat and stir in the lemon juice. Using a hand blender, blitz the sauce until smooth, then pass through a sieve into a clean bowl to remove the raspberry seeds. To serve, run a knife around the edge of each ramekin and turn each panna cotta out on to a serving plate. Spoon the sauce over and around the base, then decorate with a sprig of mint and an extra raspberry.

Rhubarb and White Chocolate Custard

The richness of the white chocolate and vanilla custard balances the sharpness of rhubarb. Our white chocolate is made with 36% cocoa butter, and has a clean milky finish that elevates the custard into a truly unique version of a crème anglaise. If you use a sweeter type, cut the sugar in the recipe a little.

Cocoa Factor: Medium | **Origin:** Any | At least 30%

Serves 4–6

500g rhubarb, trimmed and cut into 7cm pieces
200g caster sugar
1 vanilla pod, split lengthways and seeds scraped out

For the white chocolate custard
200ml double cream
700ml whole milk
1 vanilla pod, split lengthways and seeds scraped out
4 large egg yolks
3 tablespoons cornflour
55g caster sugar
150g white chocolate, broken into small pieces

Preheat the oven to 200°C/gas 6.

Put the rhubarb in a roasting tin and spoon the sugar and vanilla seeds over the top. Cover the tin with foil, seal well, and roast for 10 minutes, until softened. Remove the tin from the oven and leave to stand, still covered with foil, for 10 minutes.

To make the custard, put the cream, milk and vanilla seeds in a large, heavy-based pan and gently bring to just below the boil.

Meanwhile, in a large bowl whisk together the egg yolks, cornflour and sugar. Gradually pour the hot milk on to the egg mixture, whisking continuously until the sugar dissolves.

Return the custard to the pan and heat until boiling. Turn the heat down and simmer for about 5 minutes, stirring continuously with a whisk to prevent the custard sticking and burning, until thickened.

Remove the pan from the heat and stir in the white chocolate until melted into the custard. Serve the rhubarb with the custard and decorate with a strip of vanilla pod, if you like.

The Rabot Mousse Collection

Why make just one mousse, when you can showcase the personalities of three varieties of fine single-origin cocoa for the same amount of work? This recipe uses a single smooth, creamy custard base to which you can add your preferred types of chocolate. Serve in small glasses for the perfect portion size – a shot glass or espresso cup is ideal.

We recommend using Saint Lucian 50% milk chocolate, Mekong Delta 80% chocolate from Vietnam, and Hacienda Iara 90% chocolate from Ecuador to experience a range of contrasting flavours. Each mousse is enhanced by carefully chosen toppings. Caribbean cocoa, with its complex flavour notes of red wine, leather and tobacco, responds well to a pinch of sea salt on top of the mousse. Vietnamese cocoa, with its red fruit notes, has a natural tartness and is perfectly matched with a kirsch-soaked cherry. And Ecuadorian cocoa's mellow, nutty flavours are ideal with a freshly roasted almond.

Cocoa Factor: High | **Origin:** Vietnam, Caribbean, Ecuador | Dark, up to 80%; Milk, 50%

Serves 6
2 egg yolks
25g caster sugar
225ml whipping cream
125ml whole milk
3 x 120g of your favourite milk or dark chocolates (see above), broken into small pieces
toppings of your choice (see above)

To make the basic mousse base, whisk the eggs and sugar in a bowl to combine. Bring 125ml of the cream and all of the milk to a boil in a small pan. Remove from the heat and pour one-third of the mixture over the egg yolks, and beat to combine. Pour back into the pan with the rest of the hot milk and cream mixture and heat gently over a low heat, stirring occasionally, until it coats the back of the spoon. (If you have a thermometer, the temperature should reach 74°C.) It is important not to let the mixture boil or it may split. As soon as the consistency is reached, pass through a fine sieve into a metal bowl and whisk for 3–4 minutes, which will help it cool slightly.

Divide the still warm custard evenly between 3 bowls. Beat a different chocolate into each portion of custard until completely melted to give you 3 different mousse bases. Chill in the fridge for 5–8 minutes to cool slightly.

Meanwhile, whip the remaining 100ml of cream to soft peak stage in a large bowl. Remove the chocolate custards from the fridge and beat each one for 10 seconds. Fold 1 tablespoon of the whipped cream into each one until completely combined. Gently fold one-third of remaining cream into each mix. Do not beat; you want to keep it lovely and airy to avoid a hard mousse. Pour into your desired serving vessels, cover with cling film and chill in the fridge for a couple of hours to set. Garnish with your chosen topping just before serving.

Chocolate Coffee Mousse with Cocoa Nib Shortbread

Dark chocolate and coffee are natural flavour partners, and the two beans have a lot in common: they grow in similar climates and are roasted in similar ways. We think this recipe represents the ideal balance of both. It's great to stick with the same origin for both your coffee and your chocolate – Java, Costa Rica or Brazil – but this recipe works with a wide range so go with your favourites. In keeping with the region they come from, this dessert is best accompanied with a glass of aged rum.

Cocoa Factor: High | **Origin:** Java, Costa Rica, Brazil | 65–85%

Serves 8

For the shortbread
2 egg yolks
65g caster sugar
100g plain flour
pinch of salt
1 teaspoon baking powder
75g unsalted butter, at room temperature
10g roasted cocoa nibs or 15g dark chocolate, finely chopped

For the mousse
125g dark chocolate, broken into small pieces
35g glucose syrup
35ml espresso/strong coffee
250ml whipping cream

You will need 8 x 125ml ramekins and 2 baking trays lined with baking parchment.

First make the shortbread. In a large bowl, whisk the egg yolks and sugar until light and fluffy. Sift the flour, salt and baking powder 3 times into a separate bowl to ensure even distribution. Using your fingertips, rub the butter and cocoa nibs or chocolate into the flour, then add to the egg and sugar mixture.

Gently bring the dough together, then wrap in cling film and chill in the fridge for at least 30 minutes. (NB – you can also freeze the shortbread dough if it is wrapped well. Defrost at room temperature until pliable but still firm before use.)

Preheat the oven to 150°C/gas 3. Roll out the dough on a floured surface to a thickness of 4mm. Use a cutter to cut out 8 discs the size of the ramekins (or use a sharp knife to cut round a ramekin as a template). Place the discs on one of the prepared baking trays and bake for 10–11 minutes, until a pale golden colour. Remove from the oven and allow to cool slightly before re-cutting to size. Allow to cool completely.

To make the mousse, gently melt the chocolate with the glucose syrup and espresso by microwaving it on medium power for 1 minute, then checking and stirring. Repeat for 30 seconds more and stir until completely liquid. Alternatively, melt together in a bowl set over a pan of simmering water for 1 minute or so. Make sure the bottom of the bowl doesn't actually touch the hot water and stir the chocolate occasionally. Whisk until smooth and shiny then leave it to cool to blood temperature.

Place the ramekins on the other prepared baking tray – it needs to fit in your fridge. Lightly whip the cream in a cold bowl, then fold one-third of it into the chocolate, mixing thoroughly but gently. Carefully fold in the remaining cream, taking care to keep the air in and create a light mousse. Pour into the ramekins and chill for at least 4 hours, until set.

To serve, place a piece of shortbread on a plate, then take a ramekin and place it upside down directly on the shortbread. Using the warmth of your hands, slowly work your way around the outside of the ramekin until the heat melts the mousse enough to allow the ramekin to slide off easily. Serve with vanilla ice cream or some rum-soaked dried fruits.

Gluten and Lactose-Free Chocolate Mousse

A creamy chocolate mousse that's easy to prepare and highly versatile. Choose a good quality dark chocolate for a naturally gluten- and lactose-free dessert. It can also be made with white, milk or single-origin chocolate if you can tolerate milk and want something lighter – caramel and high-cocoa milk (50% or higher) chocolate are highly recommended. Serve with fresh raspberries, peanut brittle, cocoa nibs or just on its own.

Cocoa Factor: High | **Origin:** Any | Dark, at least 70%; Milk, at least 50%

Serves 4

150g chocolate of your choice, roughly chopped
6 egg whites
pinch of salt
¼ teaspoon lemon juice
35g caster sugar

Place the chocolate pieces in a heatproof bowl set over a pan of barely simmering water, stirring until the chocolate has melted. Make sure the base of the bowl does not actually touch the hot water. Set aside and keep warm.

Whisk the egg whites, salt and lemon juice in a large bowl, then gradually add the sugar and continue whisking until soft peaks are formed. Quickly whisk one-third of the beaten egg whites into the chocolate mixture; this loosens and cools the melted chocolate for the next stage. (Whisking the mixture too slowly will cause the chocolate to solidify, which will result in a lumpy mousse.) Now fold in the remaining egg whites, using a metal spoon, until the mixture is streak-free. Be careful not to over mix and knock out the air bubbles.

Pour the mixture into a large serving dish or individual 200ml ramekins and chill in the fridge for at least 2–3 hours before serving.

The Nib of the Matter

How we make great chocolate

Step 1. Roasting the Beans

Roasting the bean develops its rich, chocolatey notes and roasted nutty flavours. We usually roast at between 125°C and 145°C for 20–40 minutes, depending on the type of bean and the desired flavour outcome. Roasting is the first opportunity for the couverturier (the maker of couverture, a technical term for any pure chocolate) to start influencing the flavour of the finished chocolate.

The finer the quality of the bean, the lower the temperature and time we want to roast it, to let the innate flavours of the bean take centre stage. The trick is to balance the nutty quality produced by roasting with the bean's natural flavour notes, which can be as diverse as red fruit, spices, yellow fruit, coffee, tobacco, leather and caramel, and can vary from region to region (see the Taste-o-Meter on pages 90–91).

A chocolatier working with low quality cocoa beans will compensate by giving them a higher and longer roast, sometimes imparting a slightly burnt flavour to the chocolate.

Step 2. Separating Shell from Nib

Roasting also cleans the bean and loosens the shell that covers the heart of the bean – the nib. To separate them, the beans are crunched and the light shells winnowed away. Unlike most chocolatiers, we keep our cocoa shells to use as an ingredient in everything from making Cocoa Beer to our Cocoa Infusion Teas (see page 208).

Step 3. Grinding and Conching

The roasted cocoa nibs are packed with flavour, and not all of them are used to make chocolate. We use a lot of nibs to prepare savoury dishes at our restaurants, and sell roasted cocoa nibs as well as whole beans in our stores. The rest are finely ground between granite rollers to make chocolate, in a process called conching. Cocoa nibs are 50% cocoa powder and 50% cocoa butter. Finely crushing the nibs releases the butter from the powder, making a paste (called cocoa mass or cocoa liquor) that looks like melted chocolate. In its early stages this is still quite bitter and rough.

After about 10 hours of grinding, sugar is added. The sugar is abrasive and helps to thicken the paste, balance the bitterness and release some of the cocoa's more delicate flavours. A mix of 30% sugar and 70% cocoa mass results in what we call a 70% dark chocolate. After at least two days of conching and continuous tasting, the couverturier will decide whether it is ready.

Milk, Dark or White?

During the conching process, the couverturier can add other ingredients to make a variety of chocolate grades. Dark chocolate is the simplest to make. Our minimum house grade of dark chocolate contains 70% cocoa, with the sugar added after 10 hours as usual. Depending on the recipe, we might add more cocoa butter and a natural emulsifier to balance and smooth it, making the chocolate easier to mould.

Milk makes a beautiful balance to the intensity of cocoa, smoothing, mellowing and taming it just like the milk in your cappuccino. Dried milk is added with the sugar, and at the end of the conching we add a little more cocoa butter to smooth the texture. Our house milk grades are 40%, 50% and 65% cocoa. And it's a simple step from milk chocolate to caramel chocolate: just add caramelised sugar.

Is white chocolate really chocolate? Purists say no, but it's still loved by many and is often an essential ingredient for light and fruity centres and our chocolate slabs. The ingredients are again very simple: cocoa butter (36% in our recipe, but most white chocolates have around 28%), milk powder and sugar. Conching isn't required as the flavours are already mellow and creamy.

Why no Vanilla?

Great chocolate doesn't really need vanilla. In fact, vanilla's strong influence can seriously obscure the flavour profile of a single-origin chocolate, and we rarely use it.

Despite its many excellent qualities, vanilla has something of a shady past in the chocolate world. Some chocolatiers use it as a way to mask 'off' flavours in poor quality beans and boost the flavour of low-cocoa chocolate. Sometimes they don't even use natural vanilla but artificial vanillin. Some chocolatiers also add an alkalising agent to darken the colour and smooth the flavour of chocolate, often to hide the use of poor quality ingredients.

We only use vanilla when a recipe really needs it – a custard-filled truffle wouldn't be the same without it, for example.

Step 4. Tempering

The chocolate is now ready to eat, but before we can mould it we have to temper it, heating and cooling the cocoa butter so that it sets in a strong crystal structure. Tempered chocolate is shiny, breaks with a satisfying snap and melts cleanly in your mouth. Untempered chocolate is weak, melts in your hands, looks dull and just tastes wrong.

We have sophisticated tempering machines to take care of this, but in our development kitchen we still temper chocolate by hand, first heating and then cooling molten chocolate using spatulas and a large marble slab. It's a tricky and occasionally messy process. But the rhythmic sound of metal on marble is quite musical and many chocolatiers say they find chocolate-tempering relaxing.

Step 5. Sculpting the Chocolate

We use a variety of moulds for shaping chocolate, which should be warm (around 25°C) to avoid giving the chocolate a temperature shock. The molten, tempered chocolate is poured into the moulds and any air bubbles tapped out. It's then put in a fridge and allowed to set. After setting, the moulded chocolate is removed and covered to avoid water damage through condensation. Finally, once it has risen to room temperature, the chocolate can be turned out and eaten.

Page 162: As the beans dry, they need to be turned for an even toasting
Opposite, top: Roasting beans in a small-batch hot air machine we had specially customised for cocoa
Opposite, below: Granite rollers do their work inside our conch

Make Your Own Dark Chocolate Bar from the Bean

Some hard work with a pestle and mortar is required here, but people are often surprised how simple it is to make chocolate from cocoa nibs. Nothing tastes better than a bar of 75% dark chocolate you've made yourself. This method produces un-tempered and un-conched chocolate (see page 163–164), which can be used as an ingredient in any dark chocolate recipe. Experiment with different origins to produce a range of flavour notes. Ecuadorian beans will give you a robust, woody, leathery flavour; red, fruity flavours come from Madagascar and Saint Lucian beans will give a more tannic flavour.

Cocoa Factor: High | **Origin:** Any

Makes 100g
100g roasted cocoa nibs (see opposite)
2 tablespoons unrefined caster sugar
4 tablespoons cocoa butter (see page 14)

You will need a stone pestle and mortar, and chocolate moulds or an ice-cube tray.

Preheat the oven to 120°C/gas ½.

Warm the nibs on a small tray in the oven for 30 minutes, stirring every 10 minutes, then take them out and leave to cool. Turn off the oven and place the mortar inside to heat up to body temperature, about 37°C.

Place the roasted nibs in the mortar and, using the pestle, grind them to a fine paste. This will take a good 15 minutes. When the nibs have turned to a thick liquid, add the sugar and grind again for 5 minutes or until smooth. Stir in the cocoa butter – it should melt; if not, put the mortar back in the oven to warm up to 45°C and stir again. The longer you can grind this mixture, the smoother the chocolate will be.

When you are satisfied that the chocolate is as smooth as possible, pour it into moulds or an ice-cube tray. Cover with baking parchment and chill for 40 minutes until set.

Roasting Cocoa Beans at Home

You can buy raw cocoa beans online and roasting them yourself in the oven is easy. Lay your raw beans out evenly on a metal tray. Roast them in the oven at 130°C/ gas ½ for 25 minutes, turning them halfway through.

Leave them to cool and then separate the cocoa shells from the beans with finger and thumb, one by one. Keep the light shells to make some delicious infusion drinks (see page 206). The heavy interior of the beans can be used whole or broken; it makes no difference to the taste or your chocolate.

Chocolate Soup with Floating Island

A beautifully soft and delicate meringue, surrounded by chocolate soup, with sliced bananas, flaked almonds and caramel drizzle: this is our homage to the Piton sea mountains that overlook our cocoa estate in Saint Lucia. It's also the most popular dessert at our Boucan restaurant. Straightforward chocolatey notes from the Caribbean or Latin America are best; avoid Madagascan, Vietnamese and other intensely fruity origins.

Cocoa Factor: Medium | **Origin:** Caribbean, Latin America | Dark, 70–80%; White, at least 30%

Serves 6

For the meringue
3 egg whites
100g caster sugar

To decorate
2 bananas, thinly sliced
4 tablespoons flaked almonds, toasted
1 quantity of Caramel Cocoa Sauce (see page 171)

For the chocolate soup
125ml whipping cream
150ml semi-skimmed milk
40g caster sugar
3 egg yolks
30g white chocolate, broken into small pieces
30g dark chocolate, broken into small pieces

Preheat the oven to 120°C/gas ½ and sparingly spray the insides of 6 x 135ml ramekins with a non-stick spray oil.

First make the meringue. In a large metal bowl, beat the egg whites and caster sugar just to combine – about 2 minutes. Place the bowl over a pan of simmering water but do not let the hot water touch the bottom of the bowl.

Whisk the egg and sugar mixture over a simmering heat until the sugar has dissolved and the egg whites are warm to the touch – this should take about 3 minutes. Now place the mixture in the bowl of a freestanding mixer and whisk to soft peaks. Alternatively you can continue whisking by hand.

Fill the prepared ramekins to three-quarters full with the meringue mixture then place them in a deep roasting tray. Add hot water to the tray so that it comes halfway up the outsides of the ramekins. Cover the cups and tray very loosely with foil and bake for 20 minutes until firm but not coloured. Carefully remove from the oven and use a tea towel to lift out the cups. Leave to cool.

Recipe continues

While the meringues are cooling, make the chocolate soup. Gently bring the cream and milk to a boil in a medium pan, then remove from the heat. In a large bowl, beat the sugar and egg yolks. Pour a quarter of the hot liquid into the eggs and beat well, then return this mixture back to the pan of milk and cream, whisking as you do. Stir over a low heat until the mixture thickens sufficiently to coat the back of a spoon – about 5–6 minutes.

Remove from the heat and beat in the broken chocolate until completely melted. Pass through a fine sieve into a bowl and leave to cool slightly. (The soup can be served warm or cold – you can cover with cling film and leave it until needed.)

Place a small ladleful of the soup in the bottom of 6 bowls. De-mould the meringues and sit them in the middle. Decorate with the thinly sliced bananas, toasted almonds and Caramel Cocoa Sauce before serving.

Caramel Cocoa Sauce

This sweet sauce is very versatile and great with all sorts of desserts. The cocoa nibs give it a lovely rich, dark colour. If you add half a teaspoon of salt along with the cream you will produce a wonderful salted caramel sauce.

Makes 250ml
75ml water
125g caster sugar
125ml double cream
1 tablespoon roasted cocoa nibs

Measure the water and sugar into a pan and stir briefly. Set the pan over a low heat and cover with a lid until all the sugar has dissolved, about 5 minutes. Remove the lid and turn up the heat to medium to high. Cook until you get a golden honey colour – this will take about 5–8 minutes. Keep watching the pan, as once the colour is reached you have to act quickly.

While the sugar is colouring, gently warm the cream and cocoa nibs in a separate pan. Do not boil.

When the caramel is the correct colour, immediately remove the pan from the heat. Take care because this caramel is very hot. Allow the caramel to settle for 10 seconds, then gently and slowly pour in the cream and nibs – be careful, as it may bubble and sputter up. Allow to cool for 1 minute, then whisk again to fully combine. Pour into a jug. Covered in cling film; the sauce will keep for up to 5 days in the fridge. Reheat gently before using.

Cheat's Chocolate Fondant

This is a simplified version of the classic chocolate dessert. By hiding your favourite filled chocolate in the centre of each pudding, where it will turn deliciously gooey like a fondant, you get to experiment with all sorts of flavours. From weighing out to eating, this recipe only takes 30 minutes, so it is perfect as a last-minute dessert. A purist approach would be to use a fabulous single-estate praline, but fruit, caramel or liqueur fillings all work well. Make sure you use pure cocoa powder. Non-Dutched (non-alkalised) cocoa powder is best as more of the antioxidants are retained during processing.

Cocoa Factor: High | **Origin:** Any

Serves 6
150g butter, melted, plus extra for greasing
45g cocoa powder, plus extra for dusting
150g unrefined caster sugar
150g self-raising flour
3 eggs
6 filled chocolates of your choice

Preheat the oven to 160°C/gas 3. Lightly butter 6 x 175ml ramekins and dust the insides with cocoa powder, shaking out any excess.

In a large bowl, mix together the sugar, flour and cocoa powder. Add the eggs and melted butter and mix to a smooth batter.

Half-fill each ramekin with the batter, then push in a filled chocolate. Cover the chocolate with more batter so that each ramekin is three-quarters full.

Place the ramekins on a baking tray and bake for 15–18 minutes, until the surface of the cake is fully cooked and springs back when touched. Serve immediately in the ramekins, or run a knife gently around the edge of each pudding and turn out on to a plate. Serve with a little cream.

The fondants can be made in advance and kept in the fridge for up to 4 hours. Just add 2 minutes to the cooking time above.

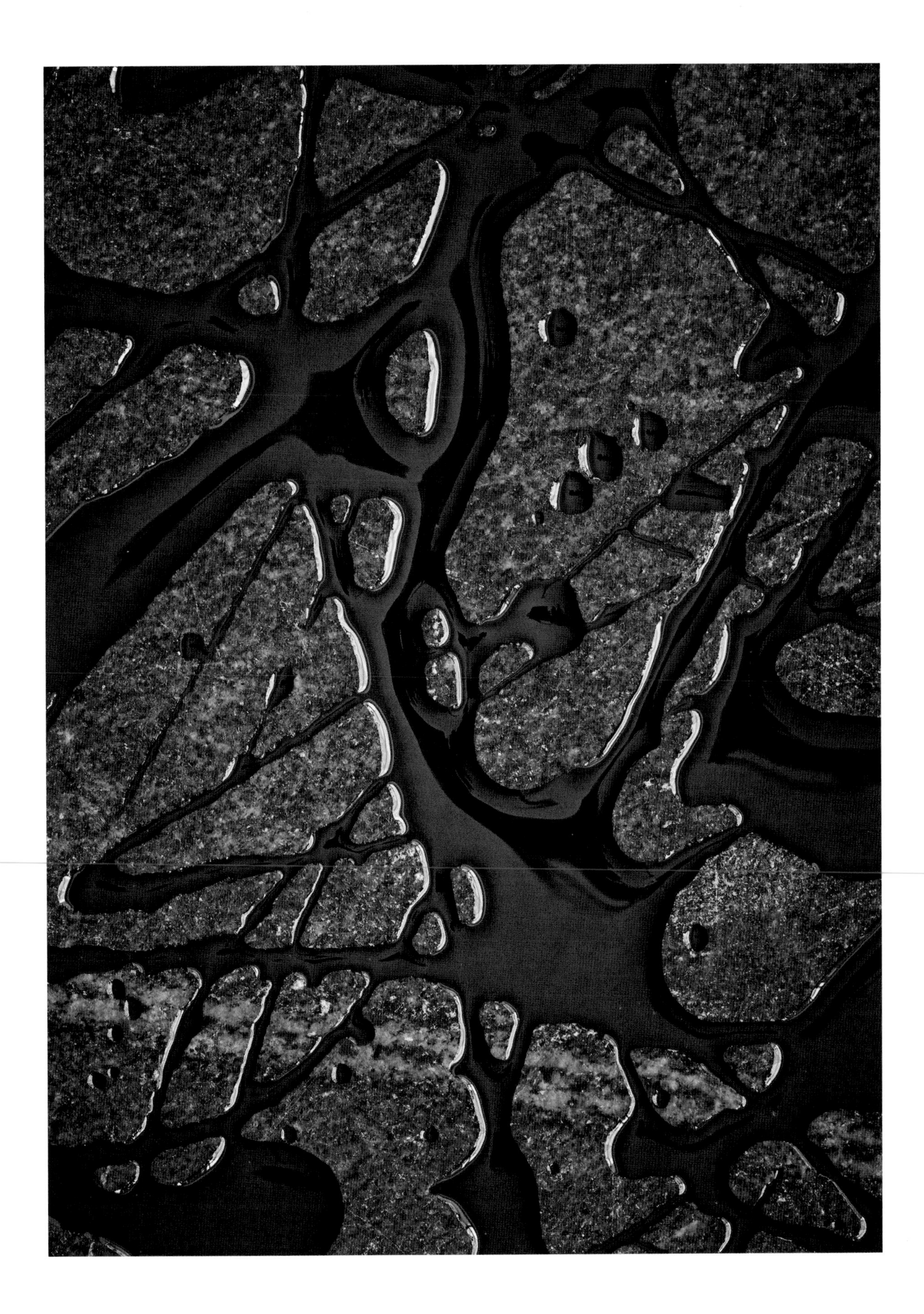

Chocolate Mousse Cake

This is a rich, fudgy bitter chocolate cake with a spectacularly contrasting milk chocolate mousse filling. It's definitely worth getting the very best chocolate you can for this recipe. Our original recipe uses Saint Lucian chocolate, but other Caribbean or Latin American chocolates will work well too. Bear in mind that the mousse will carry more chocolate flavour than the sponge.

Cocoa Factor: High | **Origin:** Caribbean, Latin America
Sponge, 70%; Mousse, 50%

Serves 6–8

140g butter, plus extra for greasing
85g dark chocolate
225g plain flour
100g cocoa powder
pinch of bicarbonate of soda
pinch of salt
450g caster sugar
3 eggs
300ml whole milk

For the chocolate mousse
350ml whipping cream
125ml whole milk
3 egg yolks
50g caster sugar
275g milk chocolate, broken into pieces

Preheat the oven to 160°C/gas 3, and butter and line 2 x 20cm round springform tins with baking parchment.

Melt the dark chocolate in 10-second bursts in the microwave, stirring frequently. Alternatively, melt the chocolate in a bowl set over a pan of simmering water for 2 minutes. Make sure the bottom of the bowl doesn't actually touch the hot water and stir the chocolate occasionally.

In a large bowl, mix together the flour, cocoa, bicarbonate of soda and salt. Using a freestanding or handheld electric mixer, beat together the butter and sugar until light and fluffy. Add the eggs one at a time, beating well between each addition.

Mix the flour and dry ingredients into the egg mixture. Combine the melted chocolate and milk and then whisk into the mix. Pour the mixture equally into the prepared tins and smooth the surface with the back of a spoon.

Bake the cakes for 50–55 minutes, or until a skewer inserted into the centre comes out clean. Cool the cakes in their tins on a wire rack for 15 minutes, then turn them out on to a rack to cool completely.

While the cakes are cooling, make the mousse. Measure 125ml of the cream into a pan along with the milk and bring to a boil. In a separate bowl, beat the egg yolks with the sugar, then pour the hot cream mixture over the eggs and mix well. Return the mixture to the pan and cook over a low heat until it coats the back of a spoon. Strain the custard through a fine sieve.

Melt the chocolate as before and then mix into the custard. Whip the remaining cream to soft peaks then fold a small amount into the chocolate custard. When the mixture is smooth, gently fold in the remaining cream.

De-mould the cooled cakes and slice each into 3 equal horizontal discs. Using a plate slightly smaller than the discs as a guide, cut around the plate to create neat discs of sponge. Place what was the top of the cake on the bottom of the springform tin, in the centre. Spread one-sixth of the chocolate mousse all over and around this layer of sponge, then place the tin in the freezer for 5 minutes to set slightly. Repeat with the other slices of sponge, ending with the bottom slice for the top, with the flat side up. Cover completely with the remaining chocolate mousse and level flat. Place in the fridge for 3 hours to set fully. De-mould the cake from the tin and slice to serve.

Sticky Ginger and Chocolate Pudding

We gave this classic winter dessert a praline twist with a generous dollop of hazelnut paste that works brilliantly with the ginger, pecan and walnut. Choose a chocolate with a robust flavour.

Cocoa Factor: Medium | **Origin:** Ecuador, West Africa | 70–85%

Serves 4

50g softened butter, cut into small pieces, plus extra for greasing
50g pecan or walnut halves, roughly chopped, plus extra to decorate
40g stem ginger in syrup, drained and roughly chopped
100g plain flour
90g light muscovado sugar
40g dark chocolate drops, roughly chopped
½ teaspoon ground ginger
½ teaspoon bicarbonate of soda
150ml soured cream
1 egg, lightly beaten
25g Chocolate Hazelnut Spread (see page 47)

Preheat the oven to 180°C/gas 4. Lightly grease 4 individual 125ml dariole moulds with butter. Spoon half the chopped pecans or walnuts and half the stem ginger into the bottom of each mould.

Mix together the flour and sugar in a large mixing bowl, then rub in the butter with your fingertips to make a crumbly mixture. Stir in the dark chocolate and ground ginger, then add the remaining nuts and the rest of the stem ginger. Divide 50g of this mixture equally between the moulds, spooning it over the nuts and stem ginger. Stir the bicarbonate of soda into the remaining mixture in the bowl. Mix together the soured cream and egg, then stir it into the crumb mixture to make a loose batter. Pour the batter over the crumbs in the dariole moulds almost to the rim.

Bake the puddings for 25–35 minutes or until risen – a skewer inserted into the centre should come out clean. Let the puddings sit for 10 minutes, then run a knife around the inside edge of the moulds and turn the puddings out on to serving dishes. Serve warm with a drizzle of the Chocolate Hazelnut Spread and a sprinkling of extra nuts.

White Chocolate Blueberry Cheesecake

The creaminess of white chocolate is perfectly balanced by sharp berries in this baked classic. Choose a white chocolate with the highest cocoa butter content you can find.

Cocoa Factor: Medium | **Origin:** Saint Lucia or any | At least 30%

Serves 10

75g butter, melted, plus extra for greasing
175g digestive biscuits
450g cream cheese
1 vanilla pod, split in half lengthways and seeds scraped out
4 eggs, separated
100g caster sugar
35g blueberry jam
handful of blueberries, to serve

For the white chocolate glaze
3 tablespoons whipping cream
100g white chocolate drops

Preheat the oven to 160°C/gas 3 and lightly grease a 23cm springform cake tin.

Place the biscuits in a food processor and pulse until they resemble coarse breadcrumbs. (Alternatively, place them in a plastic bag and crush with a rolling pin.) Mix the crushed biscuits with the melted butter and tip into the prepared tin, then press down into an even layer on the base and up around the side using the back of a spoon. Leave to chill and firm up in the fridge for at least 30 minutes while you make the filling.

Beat the cream cheese, vanilla seeds and egg yolks together in a large bowl until smooth and creamy. Whisk the egg whites to soft peaks then gradually add the sugar until the mixture is stiff and glossy. Fold the egg whites into the cream cheese mixture then transfer roughly one-sixth of the mixture into a separate bowl and stir in the blueberry jam until combined. Remove the cake tin from the fridge and pour the plain cheesecake mixture over the biscuit base. Spoon the blueberry mixture on top and use a skewer to swirl it into the plain cheesecake mixture, giving a marbled effect.

Bake the cheesecake for 35 minutes, until firm but slightly wobbly in the centre when shaken gently. Turn off the oven, open the door slightly and leave the cheesecake to cool completely.

To make the white chocolate glaze, pour the cream into a pan and heat until almost boiling. Place the white chocolate in a small bowl and pour the hot cream over, then beat until the chocolate melts. Pour the warm glaze over the cheesecake and spread it out until it covers the top in an even layer. Leave to cool, then place in the fridge for 3 hours to set.

When ready to serve, run a knife around the edge of the tin. Remove the cheesecake and transfer to a plate. Serve at room temperature with the blueberries scattered over the top.

Dizzy Praline Cake

This hazelnut chocolate cake is inspired by our Dizzy Praline chocolate, a firm favourite ever since the first Hotel Chocolat store opened ten years ago. This recipe uses ground hazelnuts combined with dark chocolate to recreate the smooth and seductive taste of praline. A straightforward type of chocolate is best for this recipe, so choose a house blend.

Cocoa Factor: High | **Origin:** House Blend | 70–75%

Serves 4

185g dark chocolate, broken into pieces
6 large eggs, separated
185g ground hazelnuts
115g caster sugar

To fill and decorate
150g Hotel Chocolat Chocolate Spread
  or a good quality chocolate spread
  or any of the ones on pages 47–53
100g dark chocolate, broken into pieces
100ml whipping cream, broken into pieces
50g white chocolate

Preheat the oven to 180°C/gas 4. Grease 2 x 18cm round cake tins and line with baking parchment.

Melt the dark chocolate for the cake in a bowl set over a pan of simmering water, stirring occasionally, for 2 minutes. Make sure the bottom of the bowl doesn't actually touch the hot water. Alternatively, melt the chocolate in a microwave, stirring every 10 seconds or so to ensure the chocolate does not burn.

Using an electric mixer, beat the egg whites until they form soft peaks. Carefully fold the ground hazelnuts into the egg whites. In a separate bowl, beat the egg yolks and sugar until thick and pale, then mix in the melted chocolate. Add the egg white mixture to the chocolate mixture and fold gently to combine.

Divide the batter equally between the prepared tins and bake in the centre of the oven for 20 minutes, or until the top is firm to the touch. Allow the cakes to cool completely in their tins before turning them out.

Sandwich the cakes together with the chocolate spread. To make it a showstopper, pipe on the spread for a beaded edge and smooth it over the middle. Melt the dark chocolate for the topping, as above, then quickly beat in the cream using a whisk, until smooth and glossy. Spread over the top of the cake. Melt the white chocolate in the same way as the dark chocolate, making sure it isn't hotter than 30°C, and then pipe a swirl of the melted white chocolate on the top of the cake. Leave to set before serving.

Bread and Chocolate Pudding

This ingenious recipe is not only a great way to use up leftover bread; it also makes fabulous use of those random pieces of dark and milk chocolate – any combination will work and taste delicious. We recommend using a dark chocolate with a high percentage of cocoa solids for a glamorous dessert, but you can even use white or caramel chocolate.

Cocoa Factor: High | **Origin:** Any | 30–90%

Serves 4

butter, for greasing
600ml milk
200g chocolate, dark or milk, or a combination
2 egg yolks
55g caster sugar (reduce this to 25g if using milk or white chocolate)
1 day-old baguette, cut into 1cm-thick slices

Preheat the oven to 160°C/gas 3 and butter an ovenproof dish.

Bring the milk to a boil in a pan, then remove from the heat and set aside. Put the chocolate, egg yolks and sugar into a food processor. Add the hot milk, leave to stand for a minute, then blend.

Arrange the slices of bread in the ovenproof dish, creating 2–3 layers. Pour the chocolate mixture over the bread and bake for 20–25 minutes. The top should look crisp and lightly browned. Leave to cool for 10 minutes, then serve the pudding on its own or with a scoop of vanilla ice cream.

Queen of Puddings

Raspberries and chocolate go well together in this traditional British dessert. A generous helping of milk chocolate makes for a richer and more indulgent custard, its usual egg flavour concealed by a darker edge.

Cocoa Factor: Medium | **Origin:** Any | 40–60%

Serves 6 or 8

225ml whole milk
225ml double cream
1 vanilla pod, split in half lengthways and seeds scraped out
100g caster sugar
5 egg yolks
100g breadcrumbs
finely grated zest of 1 lemon
200g raspberry jam

For the milk chocolate ganache
120ml whipping cream
200g milk chocolate, finely chopped

For the meringue topping
4 egg whites
110g caster sugar
1 tablespoon icing sugar, for dusting

Preheat the oven to 160°C/gas 3. You will need 6 x 150ml or 8 x 135ml ramekins.

To make the puddings, pour the milk and cream into a pan and stir in the vanilla seeds. Bring slowly to a boil over a medium to low heat. Meanwhile, put the caster sugar and egg yolks into a large bowl and whisk until the mixture is pale and fluffy. Remove the pan from the heat then slowly pour the egg mixture into the hot milk and cream, whisking continuously, then stir in the breadcrumbs and lemon zest.

Pour the pudding mixture into the ramekins and put them on a rack set in a roasting tin. Pour in enough just-boiled water to come halfway up the sides of the ramekins and carefully put the tin in the oven. Bake for 10–15 minutes or until the puddings are almost set but still slightly wobbly in the centre. Remove from the oven and allow to cool. Turn up the oven temperature to 190°C/gas 5.

To make the milk chocolate ganache, bring the cream to a boil then add the chocolate pieces. Remove from the heat and whisk until the chocolate melts, then set aside. Divide the raspberry jam between the cooled ramekins and spread it over the top of each pudding in an even layer. Gently pour the warm ganache over the jam.

To make the meringue topping, put the egg whites into a large clean bowl and whisk until stiff peaks form. Gradually whisk in the caster sugar, a tablespoon at a time. Spoon the meringue on top of the puddings, then sprinkle with icing sugar and bake for 8–10 minutes or until the meringue is crisp and lightly browned. Serve immediately.

Hot Chocolate Puddle Pudding

This luscious recipe loves a high-percentage chocolate, delivering a clean cocoa hit. Look for a chocolate that will give you a robust cocoa flavour. The beauty of this recipe is that you can enjoy it either as a 'self-saucing' pudding or cook it a little longer and create a soft, mousse-like dessert.

Cocoa Factor: High | **Origin:** Africa, House Blend | 70–85%

Serves 6–8

250g dark chocolate,
broken into small pieces
300ml semi-skimmed milk
50g butter, at room temperature
150g golden caster sugar
2 eggs, separated
25g self-raising flour
25g cocoa powder

You will need a shallow, 1.5 litre baking dish and a roasting tin large enough to hold the baking dish and act as a bain-marie. Preheat the oven to 190°C/gas 5.

Place the chocolate in a pan, pour in the milk and set over a low heat. Stir frequently to ensure the chocolate does not burn – you want the chocolate to melt into the warm milk.

In a separate bowl, cream the butter and sugar together until pale and fluffy. Gradually add the egg yolks, chocolate milk, flour and cocoa powder, stirring between each addition until fully combined.

In a separate clean bowl, whisk the egg whites until stiff peaks form. Using a metal spoon, fold one-third of the egg whites into the chocolate mixture, then fold in the remainder. Break up any larger clumps of egg white with the side of the spoon.

Place your baking dish in the roasting tin and pour the chocolate mixture into the baking dish. Pour hot water into the roasting tin so that it comes halfway up the side of the dish; this will act as a bain-marie and cook the pudding more gently. Carefully place on the middle shelf of the oven and cook for 25–35 minutes. The pudding should be dry on top but still have a slight wobble. Enjoy warm, served with either cream or ice cream.

Rabot Lava Cake

A favourite pudding cake with a bubbling interior of melted chocolate, making it a dramatic way to showcase the best chocolate you can lay your hands on. It is reminiscent of the dormant volcano in Soufrière near our cocoa estate in Saint Lucia and so we like to use a Saint Lucian chocolate, but you can use any you like. However, the quality of your cake depends entirely on the quality of your chocolate so choose wisely. We like to serve this with ice cream sprinkled with crushed roasted nibs.

Cocoa Factor: High | **Origin:** Saint Lucia or any | 65–80%

Serves 6

75g butter, plus extra for greasing
65g dark chocolate, broken into small pieces
2 large eggs
80g caster sugar
30g plain flour, plus extra for dredging

You will need 6 x 150ml dariole moulds. If you don't have dariole moulds then use ramekins of a similar size.

Melt the butter in a pan, add the broken chocolate and stir until melted. In a mixing bowl, whisk the eggs and sugar until combined. Mix the melted chocolate and butter into the beaten egg mixture. Sift the flour into the chocolate mixture and stir to combine. Put the mixture into an airtight container with a lid and leave in the fridge for 8 hours. This will allow the mixture to harden a little and develop its flavours.

When ready to cook, preheat the oven to 190°C/gas 5. Lightly butter the insides of the dariole moulds then dust them with flour. Shake out the excess flour. Place in the fridge for about 10 minutes so the butter sets.

Half-fill each mould with the chocolate mixture and place on a baking tray. Bake in the oven for about 8 minutes. The lava cakes should still be soft in the middle but the edges of the cake should have started to form a wall of cooked sponge about 5mm thick. Remove from the oven and leave to rest for a minute.

Gently loosen the edges of the lava cakes by running just the tip of a small knife around the inside rim of the mould. Carefully tip the mould upside down into the middle of a serving plate, then gently pull it up to reveal a fragile, light chocolate lava. Serve with whipped cream or your favourite ice cream.

White Chocolate, Lemon and Passion Fruit Tart

The sharpness of passion fruit, the creaminess of white chocolate: the two are just calling out for one another! The dramatic cocoa crust tastes and looks fabulous with a depth of flavour and touch of indulgence, while the white chocolate offsets the tang of the fruit. As always with white chocolate, try to source a less sweet one, ideally with at least 30% cocoa butter.

Cocoa Factor: Medium | **Origin:** Any | At least 30%

Serves 8

270g plain flour,
plus extra for dredging
4 tablespoons cocoa powder
125g butter, at room temperature,
plus extra for greasing
2 tablespoons caster sugar
1 egg, beaten
1–3 tablespoons milk

For the white chocolate and passion fruit filling
2 passion fruits, halved
3 eggs
1 egg yolk
finely grated zest of 1 lemon
juice of 3 lemons
juice of 1 orange
150ml double cream
75g caster sugar
75g white chocolate,
broken into small pieces

To serve
100g white chocolate,
broken into small pieces
3 passion fruits, halved,
seeds and juice scooped out

First make the pastry. Put the flour, cocoa powder, butter, sugar and egg in a food processor and pulse-chop briefly to combine. If the mixture looks too dry, add a little milk. Turn the mixture out on to a floured surface and gently bring it together into a dough. Wrap well in cling film and chill in the fridge for 30 minutes.

Remove the dough from the fridge and roll it out on a floured surface to the thickness of a pound coin. Butter and flour a 26cm flan tin/pie tin and set it on a baking tray. Line the tin with the pastry, pressing it right into the corners of the tin and bringing it up over the sides, leaving an overhang. Rest the pastry in the fridge for another 30 minutes. Preheat the oven to 180°C/gas 4.

Recipe continues

Line the pastry with baking parchment so that it comes up over the edges and fill the lined pastry case with baking beans or uncooked rice. Place in the oven and bake for 18 minutes. Remove the tray from the oven, remove the paper and beans/rice, then return to the oven and bake a further 5 minutes until the pastry is cooked and golden. Take the pastry out and leave to cool. Trim the edges with a sharp knife to give a neat finish. Turn the oven down to 160°C/gas 3.

While the pastry is cooling, make the filling. Scoop out the seeds from the passion fruit and press them through a fine sieve, keeping the juice and discarding the seeds. Whisk the eggs, egg yolk and lemon zest in a bowl. Add the lemon juice, orange juice and the strained passion fruit juice. Mix well then set aside. Pour the cream into a pan and bring slowly to a boil. Whisk in the sugar and stir until dissolved. Remove from the heat and add in the white chocolate. Whisk until fully melted and combined, then leave to one side to cool slightly before mixing it into the egg and juice mixture.

Pour the filling into the pastry base and bake in the oven for 25 minutes, until the filling has just set in the middle – it should wobble slightly when removed from the oven. Leave to cool completely before removing from the tin.

To serve, gently heat the white chocolate in a microwave, stirring every 10 seconds or so to ensure the chocolate does not burn. Alternatively, you can melt the chocolate in a bowl set over a pan of simmering water, stirring occasionally, until completely melted. Make sure the bottom of the bowl doesn't actually touch the hot water. Spoon the passion fruit over the tart and drizzle with the melted white chocolate.

Super Quick Microwave Chocolate Sauce

The quickest way to make a proper chocolate sauce, this recipe breaks all the rules, with no bain-maries and no fuss. Be careful not to burn the chocolate – lots of short bursts of heating and stirring is the secret. Pour over sliced banana and ice cream or put it into a cup and dip away with biscuits, fruit and nuts. Go wild with your choice, amplifying the personality of your chocolate in this warm sauce. We prefer a dark 70–85% chocolate, but high-cocoa milk chocolate works well too, and you can even use this method for white or caramel chocolate.

Cocoa Factor: High | **Origin:** Any | Dark, 70–85%; Milk, 50–70%

Makes 175g
100g chocolate of choice
75ml milk (skimmed, whole, almond or soya)

Break the chocolate into small pieces and place in a small ceramic jug or mug. Microwave for 30 seconds on full power then remove and stir. Microwave for further 10-second bursts, stirring thoroughly after each one until melted (do not let the chocolate burn). Pour in the milk in 3 equal additions, stirring vigorously each time to make a glossy emulsion. If the sauce isn't liquid enough, add a small amount of extra milk.

Simple Chocolate Cream

Cocoa Factor: High | **Origin:** Any | 70–90%

Makes 200g
100g homemade chocolate (see page 166)
100ml whipping cream

In separate bowls, gently warm the cream and melt the chocolate to about 35°C. You can do this either in bowls set over pans of simmering water, making sure the bowls do not actually touch the hot water, or in a microwave.

Using a metal spoon, quickly and firmly stir the cream into the chocolate; it will go lumpy at first but keep going until it becomes smooth. Use the ganache as it is, dipping fresh fruit, biscuits or bread into it while warm. Alternatively, pour into a bowl, cover with cling film and chill to set into a truffle mousse.

On the Verandah

Cookies, cakes and snacks for afternoon tea

Plantation Scones

There's something deeply comforting about the gentle spice mix of cinnamon, nutmeg and allspice – the classic flavour of most West Indian home-baked goodies. These go beautifully with a steaming mug of hot chocolate (see pages 212–215). Instead of spices and cocoa nibs, try it with orange zest and dark chocolate chips. We like to use Madagascan nibs and dark chocolate but the recipe works with a wide variety of fruity dark chocolates.

Cocoa Factor: Low | **Origin:** Madagascar, Caribbean, Venezuela | 65–80%

Makes 6–8

Basic scone recipe
250g plain flour
pinch of salt
40g caster sugar
1 tablespoon baking powder
40g butter
130g buttermilk
1 egg, beaten and mixed with an equal quantity of milk, to glaze

Spiced
½ teaspoon ground ginger
½ teaspoon ground nutmeg
2 pinches of ground cloves
15g roasted cocoa nibs

Citrusy (pictured)
1 teaspoon grated orange zest
50g dark chocolate chips

Preheat the oven to 180°C/gas 4 and line a baking tray with baking parchment.

Mix the flour, salt, sugar and baking powder in a bowl, adding the spices and nibs or orange zest and chocolate chips, depending on the recipe you choose.

Rub in the butter using your fingertips to create a fine, sandy crumb. Gently fold in the buttermilk until just combined. It is fine to leave a little flour unmixed to avoid overworking.

Turn on to a floured work surface and gently roll to a thickness of 2.5cm. Use a cutter to stamp out the scones – don't twist, or your scones will rise unevenly. Dip the cutter in flour in between each stamp. Gently re-roll the remainder and cut out in the same way.

Brush each scone with a little egg wash, then place on the baking tray and bake for 10–12 minutes. Remove from the oven when golden. Cool on a wire rack and cover with a clean cloth to keep moist until ready to eat.

Illegal Parkin

Parkin is a Yorkshire classic, so when we opened our restaurant in Leeds we wanted to pay homage to it but add a twist. We were a little concerned that we were being a bit naughty with a local icon; however we think the dark chocolate adds a fantastic warming depth and is a natural partner with ginger and spices. With so much going on, choose a chocolate with a straightforward cocoa hit.

Cocoa Factor: Medium | **Origin:** Africa | 70–85%

Serves 12

200g butter, plus extra for greasing
200g self-raising flour, plus extra for dredging
55g treacle
200g golden syrup
200g soft brown sugar
35g dark chocolate, finely chopped
pinch of salt
4 teaspoons ground cinnamon
1 teaspoon ground ginger
1 teaspoon ground allspice or finely grated zest of 1 orange
60g dark chocolate chips
150g medium oatmeal
2 eggs, beaten
4 tablespoons milk

Preheat the oven to 140°C/gas 2 and butter and flour a 20cm square cake tin. In a pan over a low heat, melt the treacle, syrup, sugar and butter, then stir in the chopped chocolate to melt. Remove from the heat and allow to cool for 5 minutes.

In a large bowl, sift and thoroughly mix the flour, salt, cinnamon, ginger, allspice or orange zest, chocolate chips and oatmeal. Now mix this spiced flour into the cooling syrup mix. Beat in the eggs and milk. Pour the batter into the prepared tin and bake for 1 hour and 10 minutes, until firm to the touch. Remove from the oven and cover loosely with foil, then leave to cool in the tin.

Once cold, the cake should be kept in an airtight container in a cool place. It will keep for up to 4 days and is best eaten after a day or two, once the flavours have matured.

Flourless Chocolate Mousse Cake with Chocolate Rum Fruit

This is a rich, moist, dark chocolate cake, whose bitterness works well with the acidity and sweetness of its fruit accompaniment. It also happens to be naturally gluten-free, so even more of us can enjoy it. It is a great way to showcase the flavours of top-quality dark chocolate, with only a few other ingredients added. Choose something fruity, like Madagascan chocolate, and use the same chocolate for the rum fruit sauce.

Cocoa Factor: Medium | **Origin:** Madagascar | 70–85%

Serves 6–8

150g butter, plus extra for greasing
50 g caster sugar, plus extra for dusting
300g dark chocolate, broken into pieces
6 eggs, separated
1½ teaspoons ground cinnamon

For the fruit
1 tablespoon water
50g caster sugar
30g Cocoa Nib Butter (see page 232), cold and diced
20g dark chocolate, broken into small pieces
100g strawberries, washed, hulled and halved
100g raspberries
2 teaspoons light rum

Preheat the oven to 180°C/gas 4 and butter the inside of a 13cm-wide, 7.5cm-deep springform tin, then dust with caster sugar.

First, make the cake. In the microwave, melt the chocolate and butter at 10-second intervals until they are liquid and smooth. Alternatively, you can melt the chocolate in a bowl set over a pan of simmering water, stirring occasionally, for 2 minutes. Make sure the bottom of the bowl doesn't actually touch the hot water. Beat together well.

Using a mixer or a hand whisk, beat the egg yolks, cinnamon and 2 tablespoons of the sugar for 30 seconds on high speed. Beat the egg yolk mixture into the melted chocolate and butter.

In a separate, clean bowl, beat the egg whites with the remaining sugar to form stiff peaks. Beat a quarter of the whites into the chocolate mixture, then gently fold in the remaining egg whites.

Pour the cake mixture into the prepared tin and bake for 20 minutes. It will have risen a little and be slightly soft in the middle. Remove from the oven and cover tightly with foil, then allow to cool to room temperature.

While the cake is cooling, prepare the fruit. Put the water in a medium frying pan and sprinkle over the sugar, then leave it to stand for 3–4 minutes. Cook the syrup over a medium to high heat until it turns a very pale golden colour. Stir in the diced Cocoa Nib Butter and chopped chocolate, add the strawberries, raspberries and rum, then cook for 30 seconds. Remove from the heat and leave to cool a little.

To serve, cut wedges from the mousse cake – bear in mind this is rich, so a little goes a long way – spoon over some of the fruit and drizzle some of the syrup over the cake. For absolute indulgence, serve with whipped cream.

Chocolate Fudge

A rich and indulgent treat, best made with dark chocolate to give the fudge a strong cocoa depth and to balance out the cream, butter and sugar. Experiment with single-origin high-cocoa chocolates to experience the subtle difference in flavours. You will need a sugar thermometer for this recipe.

Cocoa Factor: High | **Origin:** Any | 70–100%

Makes about 24 pieces
60g butter, plus extra for greasing
210ml double cream
340g caster sugar
170ml liquid glucose
200g dark chocolate,
 broken into small pieces

Butter a lipped 20 x 20cm baking tray and line it with baking parchment.

Put the cream, sugar and glucose in a heavy-based pan over a medium to high heat. Bring to a gentle boil and cook until the mixture reaches 120°C on the sugar thermometer – try not to shake or stir the pan too much during this time.

Add the butter and stir until the temperature of the mixture reaches 120°C again.

Remove from the heat and stir in the chocolate until it is melted, then work quickly to pour the fudge into the baking tray. Leave at room temperature to set for about 30 minutes before cutting into 3cm squares and serving. If it doesn't get eaten immediately, it will last for a few days in an airtight container.

Truffle Doughnuts

Delightfully gooey, these are almost like chocolate lava cakes in doughnut form. They are best eaten warm, almost straight out of the fryer, just dusted with a little cinnamon sugar. Your choice of truffle will determine the flavour of the doughnut, so choose your favourite – pure chocolate truffles and rum truffles work especially well.

Cocoa Factor: Medium | **Origin:** Any | Any

Makes 8

250g strong white flour,
  plus extra for dusting
pinch of salt
½ teaspoon ground cinnamon
40g caster sugar
150ml lukewarm water
1 teaspoon butter, softened
1½ teaspoons instant dried yeast
vegetable oil, for deep-frying
8 chocolate truffles

For the cinnamon sugar
1 teaspoon ground cinnamon
75g caster sugar

Sift the flour, salt, cinnamon and sugar into a large mixing bowl. Add the water, butter and yeast and bring the dough together. Knead the dough for 5 minutes, then cover with cling film and prove in a warm place until doubled in size – about 45 minutes.

Tip the risen dough on to a floured surface. Using the palm of one hand, stretch out the dough away from you then bring the edges in and roll it into a tight ball. Repeat a couple of times then leave to rest on the work surface while you heat the oil.

Half-fill a pan with the vegetable oil and heat to 150°C. If you don't have a kitchen thermometer, tear off a piece of dough about the size of a cherry and drop it into the hot oil. It should gently turn golden brown in about 2 minutes. If it's too hot, turn off the oil and leave to cool for 10 minutes, before reheating gently. While the oil is heating, mix the cinnamon and sugar in a bowl and set aside.

Take a small handful of the dough and shape into a disc about 5cm in diameter. Place a truffle in the centre and wrap the dough around. Seal the dough completely, making sure there are no gaps, otherwise the dough will burst and the truffle will melt into the oil. Repeat with the rest of the dough.

Using a slotted spoon, slip each doughnut into the oil and fry for about 5 minutes, turning halfway through cooking. You will probably need to do this in batches of 2 or 4 – do not overcrowd the pan as it will cause the temperature of the oil to drop. When they are cooked, they should be a golden sandy colour. Drain well and roll each doughnut in the cinnamon sugar while still warm.

Double Nut Brownies

The ideal brownie is just on the right side of gooey. The secret to achieving that perfect bite is to use a relatively small amount of plain flour. Another tip is to tap the side of the tray on the worktop when you pull it out of the oven. This releases air from under the crust and will help the surface drop, creating that desired fudgy texture. Use your favourite chocolate to provide little bursts of flavour in these brownies – both high-percentage milk and dark chocolates work well. Leave them for a day and the taste and texture will get even better.

Cocoa Factor: Medium | **Origin:** Any | Dark, 70–85%; Milk, 40–70%

Makes 16

100g butter, at room temperature
200g caster sugar
½ vanilla pod, split lengthways and seeds scraped out
2 eggs, beaten
55g plain flour
35g cocoa powder
½ teaspoon baking powder
35g hazelnuts, roughly chopped
35g pecans, roughly chopped
75g chocolate chips

Preheat the oven to 180°C/gas 4 and line an 18cm square cake tin with baking parchment.

Cream together the butter, sugar and vanilla seeds using an electric whisk, or mix by hand. Add in the eggs, flour, cocoa powder and baking powder and combine thoroughly, then fold in the hazelnuts, pecans and chocolate chips. Pour into the prepared tin.

Bake for 30 minutes until dry on top and firm to the touch, but be careful not to overcook. Leave to cool before cutting into pieces.

Chocolate Chip Cookie-in-a-Cup

Perhaps the simplest cookie recipe ever invented, and a lot of fun for kids in the kitchen. It takes only 45 seconds to cook in the microwave, leaving you with a soft cookie full of perfectly gooey chocolate chips that you can eat straight from the cup. Dress this recipe up or down as you like – it works with the full spectrum of chocolate, from a good white to single-estate dark. You can also make this recipe with a tablespoon each of oats and raisins instead of chocolate chips, or with a tablespoon each of cocoa powder and ground coffee if you want a bit of a caffeine kick.

This cookie is just as tasty made with gluten-free flour, and you can also use dairy-free butter or coconut oil and two teaspoons of dairy-free milk instead of an egg yolk.

Cocoa Factor: Medium | **Origin:** Any | Any

Makes 1 cookie-in-a-cup

1 tablespoon butter
2 tablespoons caster sugar
½ teaspoon vanilla extract
pinch of salt
1 egg yolk
2 teaspoons milk
3 tablespoons flour
2 tablespoons chocolate chips
(milk or dark, whichever is your favourite)

Put the butter in your cup and microwave for 10 seconds, then add the sugar and mix until fully combined. Add the vanilla extract, salt, egg yolk and milk, and mix until fully combined. Fold in the flour and then the chocolate chips. Smooth out the top of the mixture with the back of a spoon to create a tidy finish and wipe away any unwanted mixture around the sides of the cup.

Microwave for 40–50 seconds on full power. (The cookie might look pale but it will continue to cook as it cools.) Serve warm, maybe with a dollop of whipped cream or ice cream, and eat with a spoon.

The Crownie

It's not quite a cookie and not quite a brownie, it's the Crownie: a densely chocolatey, soft yet crunchy biscuit packed with whole hazelnuts. The added sugar has a mellowing effect, so try making these with a high-percentage dark chocolate for a more intense experience. Choose a chocolate with a roasted nut flavour such as those from Venezuela or Ecuador. Enjoy warm while the chocolate within is just molten.

Cocoa Factor: High | **Origin:** Venezuelan Chuao, Ecuador, House Blend | 70–85%

Makes 16

200g butter, at room temperature
50g golden caster sugar
100g soft light brown sugar
1 egg, beaten
275g plain flour
25g cocoa powder
1 teaspoon baking powder
200g dark chocolate, chopped into small pieces
200g whole roasted hazelnuts

Preheat the oven to 160°C/gas 3 and line 2 baking trays with baking parchment.

In a mixing bowl, cream the butter and sugars together until pale and fluffy, then beat in the egg. Add the flour, cocoa powder and baking powder, and stir until combined. Add the chocolate and hazelnuts, then use your hands to bring everything together into a dough.

Using your hands, form 16 balls and place them evenly on the prepared baking trays before pressing them down to a thickness of 1.5cm. Bake for 10–12 minutes on the middle shelf of the oven. They should be cooked but still slightly squidgy in the middle, and will smell amazing. Serve warm, perhaps with ice cream.

Mixers & Shakers

Cocoa teas, hot chocolates and cocoa cocktails

Cocoa Infusion Tea

An undiscovered pick-me-up that's better than coffee, this brilliant beverage was somehow lost in the steam of history's teapot.

The shells covering cocoa nibs are usually discarded after the beans are roasted or, at best, used as mulch for the garden. What a shame. A simple infusion of cocoa shells in hot water is so refreshing, and rich in antioxidants and gentle stimulants. It has the taste of chocolate with zero calories. You can buy cocoa shells online or from Hotel Chocolat in the form of ready-to-infuse cocoa shells blends. You can even roast your own beans and keep the shells to make your own (see page 167). See pages 26–27 for more information on cocoa's health-giving qualities.

You can blend cocoa with ordinary teas, using a traditional tea strainer. Feel free to experiment with a mix of loose leaf and shells. You can enjoy your brew hot or chilled, black or white, and even enhance with a touch of nutmeg and cinnamon. Do note, though, that the freshness of the shells is important.

Cocoa Factor: High | **Origin:** Any

Serves 1

Basic cocoa shell tea
2 heaped teaspoons cocoa shells

For Assam tea with cocoa shells
1 heaped teaspoon Assam tea leaves
1 heaped teaspoon cocoa shells

For peppermint tea with cocoa shells
1½ teaspoons peppermint tea leaves
½ teaspoon cocoa shells

For Earl Grey tea with cocoa shells
½ teaspoon Earl Grey tea leaves
1½ teaspoons cocoa shells

Simply pour hot, but not boiling, water over your desired blend and brew according to the tea you've used. Pure cocoa shells should be left for at least 5 minutes.

White Chocolate Jasmine Tea

A superb new take on traditional hot chocolate. The delicate floral flavours of jasmine sit perfectly alongside the gentle creaminess of white chocolate. Choose a white chocolate with a low sugar content and the highest cocoa butter content you can find – at least 30%.

Cocoa Factor: Medium | **Origin:** Any | At least 30%

Serves 1
200ml milk
2 teaspoons loose-leaf jasmine tea
30g white chocolate, finely chopped

Gently warm the milk and tea in a small pan. Remove from the heat, cover with the lid and leave to steep for 5 minutes. Reheat the milk and then gently whisk until slightly frothy. Measure the chocolate into a cup and strain a little of the milk over the top. Stir to melt the chocolate and make a paste then pour over the rest of the jasmine milk. Stir and drink.

White Chocolate Chai Tea

A twist on a classic hot chocolate, made with a blend of spices and Assam tea. The white chocolate adds extra creaminess and takes the place of the sugar usually added to chai. Choose a high-percentage white chocolate so it's not too sweet. This can be also be enjoyed cold in summer, served over ice. As an alternative, replace the white chocolate with dark chocolate and sweeten with a tablespoon of honey.

Cocoa Factor: Medium | **Origin:** Any | At least 30%

Serves 4–6
400ml water
1 teaspoon ground nutmeg
1 teaspoon ground ginger
1 teaspoon ground cinnamon
1 teaspoon ground peppercorns
6 cloves
6 green cardamom pods, slightly crushed
400ml whole milk
2 Assam tea bags
80g white chocolate, finely chopped

Place the water and spices in a small pan and bring to a boil. Remove from the heat, cover with a lid and allow to steep for 10 minutes.

Add the milk, bring back up to a simmer and stir gently to ensure the milk doesn't boil up. Add the tea bags, remove from the heat, cover and allow to steep for 5 minutes. After 5 minutes, stir through the white chocolate – there will be enough heat left in the tea to melt it fully. Strain the tea into glasses to enjoy!

Coconut Milk Hot Chocolate

A classic combination of dark chocolate and coconut in a smooth hot chocolate. Go for real indulgence by topping with coconut whipped cream. The coconut milk dilutes the dark chocolate, effectively turning it into milk chocolate, so use a high-percentage chocolate for a strong cocoa presence. Any good quality chocolate works well here, but our favourite is an Ecuadorian variety, which has a nutty flavour profile. The image opposite also shows Salted Caramel Hot Chocolate (see page 214).

Cocoa Factor: High | **Origin:** Ecuador or any | 70–90%

Serves 1
200ml coconut milk
40g dark chocolate shavings

For the coconut whipped cream
70g coconut cream, chilled
2 teaspoons icing sugar

To make the coconut whipped cream, empty the coconut cream into a bowl, discarding any liquid. Add the icing sugar and whisk together to a firm cream.

To make the hot chocolate, gently heat the coconut milk in a pan over a low to medium heat. Measure the chocolate into a serving cup. When the milk is hot, pour a small amount over the chocolate and mix to form a smooth paste. Add in the remaining milk and stir well. Serve topped with the coconut whipped cream.

Salted Caramel Hot Chocolate

This is one of the most popular drinks in our cafés. It's essentially a salted caramel sauce that gets diluted into hot milk – or you can pour it over chopped bananas. A good robust flavour is required here so don't choose anything too fruity. Avoid Madagascan or Vietnamese; house blends are fine. **See image on page 213, back.**

Cocoa Factor: Medium | **Origin:** Caribbean, Latin America | 70–80%

Serves 1

For the chocolate salted caramel sauce
(this makes enough for 8 drinks)
200ml double cream
½ teaspoon salt
150g sugar
40g butter
50g dark chocolate, finely chopped

For the drink
150ml skimmed milk
2 tablespoons chocolate salted caramel sauce

First make the sauce. Gently warm the cream with the salt in a small pan over a low heat. Set aside.

Take a deep, heavy-based pan and set it over a medium to high heat. When warm, add about a quarter of the sugar. As it starts to melt at the edges, add a third of the remaining sugar. Add the sugar in 2 more batches as soon as the previous batch melts at the edges. Stir the caramel as little as possible during this time. If it starts to darken and bubble too rapidly, take it off the heat and gently stir; it should bubble and warm slowly and evenly. When all sugar has melted and you have a golden caramel, take the pan off the heat and stir in the butter. The caramel will bubble, but continue to stir until mixed through. If the mixture gets too thick, place it back over the heat.

Place the caramel over the heat again and add in the warm cream. You will need to do this in stages as the caramel will bubble up. When all the cream is added, cook over a medium heat for 2 minutes. Take off the heat and allow to cool slightly, then stir through the chopped chocolate.

To make the drink, gently warm the milk in a small pan, whisking continuously to create a good foam. When warm, take the pan off the heat and stir through the chocolate salted caramel sauce. Pour into a cup and enjoy!

Hazelnut Hot Chocolate

Here we've turned the classic praline partnership of hazelnut and chocolate into an exceptionally tasty hot chocolate. You can also experiment with different milk and nut paste combinations – almond milk with smooth salted peanut butter is particularly good. The hazelnut milk dilutes the dark chocolate and has a natural sweetness, so use a high-percentage chocolate. Something with a roasted nut profile, like a good Ecuadorian, or a balanced house blend are good options. You can buy hazelnut paste in most supermarkets and health food shops.

Cocoa Factor: High | **Origin:** Ecuador, House Blend | 70–85%

Serves 1
200ml hazelnut milk
1 heaped teaspoon hazelnut paste
40g dark chocolate shavings
(or use good quality chocolate
and make your own shavings)

Gently heat the hazelnut milk and paste together in a pan, stirring continuously. Measure the chocolate into a serving cup. When the milk is hot, pour a small amount into the cup and mix with the chocolate to form a smooth paste. Add in the remaining milk, stir and drink while hot.

Almond Milk Peanut Chocolate Shake

In a blender-blitz of genius, almond milk and banana come together with naturally dairy-free dark chocolate and peanut butter to create a delicious shake. By adding almond milk you're turning the dark chocolate into a milk chocolate drink, so it's best to use a high-cocoa chocolate. For a dairy version, try cow's milk and a scoop of vanilla ice cream; hazelnut paste works well too.

Cocoa Factor: High | **Origin:** Any | 70–90%

Makes 1 large glass
50g dark chocolate
20ml boiling water
150ml almond milk
1 small banana
30g smooth peanut butter

Mix together the chocolate and hot water so that the chocolate melts and becomes a thick paste. Put this paste into a blender along with the remaining ingredients and blitz until smooth. Serve over ice.

This can be made in advance and stored in the fridge for 24 hours.

Rabot 1745 Rum Sour

The bestselling cocktail at our Rabot 1745 restaurant in London's Borough Market, with a dash of cocoa bitters for a piquant tang that pairs beautifully with mellow rum. We like Chairman's Reserve rum because it's made in Saint Lucia, not far from our plantation.

Cocoa Factor: Low
Origin: Caribbean

Serves 1
50ml Chairman's Reserve
 or another light amber rum
2 tablespoons lime juice,
 plus lime wedges to serve
2 teaspoons clear honey
6 dashes chocolate bitters
 (or Angostura bitters)
pinch of freshly grated nutmeg
pinch of roasted cocoa nibs,
 ground for 30 seconds
 in a pestle and mortar (optional)

In a cocktail shaker combine all the ingredients except the cocoa nibs, if using, and lime wedges. Strain through a fine strainer into a tumbler. Sprinkle over the ground nibs, garnish with lime wedges and serve.

Praline Soother

Apply all the secrets of making great pralines to a gentle after-dinner cocktail. The chocolate needs to be mellow to match the mood of the cocktail so avoid a fruity cocoa from Madagascar or Vietnam. Choose a good house blend or a chocolate from the Caribbean or Latin America.

Cocoa Factor: Medium
Origin: House Blend, Caribbean, Latin America | At least 40%

Serves 1
25g dark chocolate, broken into pieces
50ml coconut milk
50ml Frangelico liqueur
50ml coconut cream
25ml vodka
3 ice cubes

Melt the chocolate in the microwave on medium power for 30 seconds. Take out and stir until just melted. Alternatively, melt it in a bowl set over a pan of simmering water, making sure the bottom of the bowl doesn't actually touch the hot water and stirring occasionally. Mix the coconut milk into the melted chocolate to form a liquid. Now add this and all the other ingredients to a cocktail shaker. Add 3 ice cubes and shake until thoroughly mixed.

Pretty Pink

Our bar in London's Borough Market overlooks Bridget Jones' flat from the movie, so we mixed up a suitable cocktail we thought she would like. Opposite, centre.

Serves 1

25ml gin (we use our own Cocoa Gin)
juice of ¼ lemon
3 fresh raspberries
1½ teaspoons rose water
1 teaspoon sugar cane syrup
50ml dry Prosecco
rose petal, to garnish

Shake all the ingredients except the Prosecco together in a cocktail shaker – hard enough to encourage the raspberries to start releasing their juice. Pour and double strain into a chilled coupe glass, then top up with Prosecco. Float a rose petal on the top for maximum schmaltz.

Aged Rum Fizz

We started making this in our bar at Boucan, Saint Lucia – around us we had fabulous aged rum, made by our friends down the road, our own direct-bottled Prosecco and loads of fresh mint from the chefs' herb garden. Opposite, left.

Cocoa Factor: Low
Origin: Caribbean

Serves 1

50ml aged golden rum of choice (we use Chairman's Reserve Forgotten Casks)
3 drops of Angostura or cocoa bitters
4 mint leaves
juice of 1 lime
4 teaspoons honey water (1 teaspoon honey mixed with 3 teaspoons hot water)
25ml dry Prosecco

Combine all other ingredients apart from the Prosecco in a cocktail shaker. Strain into a short tumbler filled with crushed ice. Top with Prosecco.

Ginger Fizz

An old recipe that we've revived in our bar in Borough Market. We like to think of it as a London version of a Moscow Mule. See image on page 221, right.

Serves 1
2 thick slices of fresh ginger
50ml gin
juice of 1 small lemon
4 teaspoons honey water
(1 teaspoon honey mixed with
3 teaspoons hot water)
25ml ginger ale
2 thin slices of fresh ginger, to garnish

Muddle the thick slices of fresh ginger in the bottom of a Boston glass, then add the gin, lemon juice and honey water. Pour into a cocktail shaker, shake and pour over crushed ice in a short tumbler. Top up with ginger ale and garnish with 2 thin slices of fresh ginger.

Mulled Wine Bellini

Jazzing up this winter classic with cocoa powder gives it a smooth, rounded flavour that blends exquisitely with citrus and spices. Make sure you use pure cocoa powder. See image on page 221, back.

Cocoa Factor: Low
Origin: Any

Makes about 500ml
750ml red wine
400g caster sugar
2 cinnamon sticks
5 star anise
8 cloves
35g cocoa powder
juice of 1 orange and 3 strips of peel
juice of ½ lime and 2 strips of peel
1 tablespoon Grand Marnier
Prosecco, to top

Place 500ml of the wine in a large pan along with the sugar and spices and bring to the boil. Simmer just until the sugar has dissolved. Turn up the heat and cook for about 10 minutes, or until reduced by half (it should have the consistency of single cream). Remove from the heat. Whisk in the cocoa powder. Add the orange juice and peel, and the lime juice and peel. Whisk well. Add the Grand Marnier and the remaining wine. Allow to cool.

Strain the liquid through a fine sieve. At this point it can be stored in the fridge for a few days. To serve, pour 2 teaspoons of the mulled wine into the bottom of a flute and top up with Prosecco.

Fortified Coconut Water

Our secret plantation soother – pure coconut water and Saint Lucian rum. Rehydrates with every sip, perfect as a Sunday morning pick-me-up.

Serves 1
50ml golden rum
(we use Chairman's Reserve)
ice
coconut water

Pour the rum into a short tumbler, add ice and top up with coconut water until you reach your preferred flavour balance. Remember that the ice will melt and further dilute the drink.

Intense Chocolate Shot

This drink is a revelation: you can quickly and simply turn just about any top quality dark chocolate into a light chocolate drink. Replacing the milk with water creates a drink that is sharper, cleaner and more in tune with the flavour of the bean. Try it with different grades of chocolate for a range of intensities, but it really needs to be at least 70%–85%; 90% and even 100% cocoa work well. If you like it a bit sweeter, add some sugar or honey, to taste.

Cocoa Factor: High
Origin: Any | 70%–100%

Serves 1
2–3 tablespoons finely chopped dark chocolate, to taste
100ml boiling water

Measure the chocolate into a small espresso-sized cup. Pour over a small amount of hot water, just enough to melt the chocolate into a thick paste. Top up with the rest of the warm water, stir and drink.

The Pantry

Condiments, glazes, spreads and gravies with a cocoa flourish

Cocoa Nib Crispbread

Cocoa nibs add a subtle, earthy depth and satisfying extra crunch to this bread, ideal for scooping up dips. Pairing perfectly with the Spiced Aubergine Salad (see page 128) or used to scoop up the Hummus (see page 129) or Smoked Mackerel Ganache (see page 228), they are always best eaten while still a little warm.

Cocoa Factor: Medium | **Origin:** Any

Serves 4
375g plain flour
1½ teaspoons bicarbonate of soda
1 teaspoon salt
200ml skimmed milk
1 egg
1½ tablespoons sugar
1½ tablespoons sunflower oil
1½ tablespoons roasted cocoa nibs, finely crushed

Preheat the oven to 170°C/gas 3 and line 3 baking trays with baking parchment.

Place all the ingredients in the bowl of mixer and mix well for 2 minutes. Remove the bowl and cover loosely with cling film to stop the mixture drying out as you work with it. Lightly flour your work surface and use a rolling pin to roll out one-sixth of the dough (about the size of a tennis ball) as thinly as possible. Scatter over some more flour if it is too sticky. Keep dusting the dough with flour, turning it over and rolling each side until it is 2–3mm thick.

Cut the rolled-out dough into 5 x 15cm rectangles. Lay in a single layer on a lined baking tray and cover with another layer of baking parchment. Repeat with another tennis ball-sized amount of the dough, layering the next batch of dough rectangles on top of the baking parchment. Bake in the oven for 12–15 minutes until golden – they should be crisp and snap nicely. Roll out the rest of the dough while the first batch is cooking and repeat using the remaining trays.

Remove from the oven, cool and store in an airtight container for up to 3 days.

Smoked Mackerel Ganache

A superb ganache that can be spread on bread or toast, or served at breakfast with poached eggs (see page 36). Horseradish cuts through the richness of the mackerel, while the opulence of cocoa butter in the white chocolate replaces cream and provides a sweetness to offset the tangy edge. Choose a white chocolate with the highest cocoa butter content you can find – at least 30%.

Cocoa Factor: Low | **Origin:** Any | At least 30%

Serves 6
125g peppered smoked mackerel
100g cream cheese
zest and juice of ½ lemon
2 tablespoons White Chocolate Horseradish (see page 231)
salt and freshly ground pepper

Skin the mackerel and make sure there are no bones in it. Break into smallish pieces. Place in a bowl along with all the other ingredients and use your hands to mix everything until completely combined. Taste for seasoning and adjust if necessary. Store in an airtight container in the fridge for up to 3 days.

White Chocolate Horseradish

Sharp, fiery, grated horseradish is tempered by the soft and subtle sweetness of white chocolate. Choose a chocolate with the highest cocoa butter content you can find. This is the best-selling cocoa condiment in our range.

Cocoa Factor: Low | **Origin:** Any | At least 30%

Makes 160g
50g white chocolate
110g creamed horseradish

Gently melt the chocolate in a bowl set over a pan of simmering water, making sure the bottom of the bowl doesn't actually touch the hot water.

While the bowl is still sitting over the pan, add the creamed horseradish and mix until fully combined with the chocolate. Remove the bowl from the pan and beat for 1 minute further. Allow to cool and store in an airtight container in the fridge until needed – it will keep for up to 2 weeks.

Chocolate Aioli

This aioli has the texture of an exquisite emulsion, just like a ganache, with the bitterness of dark chocolate cutting through the rich mayonnaise and the sweetness of slowly roasted garlic. Best eaten at room temperature, it is great with fish and boiled or steamed vegetables. You need a chocolate with a robust flavour here to stand up to the garlic. To make plain aioli, simply leave out the chocolate.

Cocoa Factor: Medium | **Origin:** Ghana, Côte d'Ivoire | 70–100%

Makes 200g
8 garlic cloves, unpeeled
1 tablespoon olive oil
20g dark chocolate,
 broken into small pieces
170g mayonnaise
½ teaspoon lime juice
1½ teaspoons roasted cocoa nibs

Preheat the oven to 180°C/gas 4 and line a baking tray with baking parchment.

Toss the garlic in the olive oil and place on the prepared tray. Roast for 15 minutes or until tender. Leave to stand for 10 minutes or until cool enough to handle, then squeeze the garlic from its skin. Discard the skins and set aside to cool completely. Mash the cloves to a purée using a fork.

Gently heat the chocolate in a microwave for 10 seconds, then give it a stir; it needs to be just liquid. If still slightly lumpy, microwave again for 5 seconds until liquid. Alternatively, you can melt the chocolate in a bowl set over a pan of simmering water, stirring occasionally, until the chocolate becomes liquid. Make sure the bottom of the bowl doesn't actually touch the hot water.

Mix the garlic and mayonnaise into the chocolate in 4 stages, incorporating each part thoroughly before adding the next. Finally, stir in the lime juice and cocoa nibs. Store in the fridge in an airtight container until needed (it will keep for up to 2 weeks).

Chocolate Bacon Spread

The rich balance of flavours in this deviously delicious recipe works on the same principle as bacon with maple syrup or cranberry. The resulting smoky and salty ganache makes an amazingly indulgent dip, and it's particularly superb spread on bread in a roast chicken club sandwich. Adding cream effectively makes the dark chocolate more like a strong chocolate milk, so stick with a high percentage of cocoa solids.

Cocoa Factor: High | **Origin:** Any | 70–90%

Makes 200g
65ml whipping cream
65g dark chocolate,
broken into small pieces
20g crispy bacon (supermarkets
sell this in packets), crushed or chopped finely
45ml whole milk

Pour the whipping cream into a medium pan and bring to a gentle simmer over a low heat. Remove the pan from the heat and whisk in the chocolate until melted. Add the bacon and milk and blitz in a blender until smooth.

Place in an airtight container and store in the fridge for up to 1 week.

Cocoa Nib Butter

This is a great alternative to chocolate spread on your toast in the morning. We also use it in sauces, to coat cooked vegetables, sauté meats and fish, flavour our delicious Roast Yard Bird (page 80) – the list goes on! It has a savoury chocolate flavour that is very versatile and very addictive. Since cocoa nibs are made up of 50% cocoa butter, they melt readily in the mouth after a few chews, joining with the butter and chocolate for a savoury-chocolatey experience.

Cocoa Factor: Medium | **Origin:** Any | 70–90%

Makes 250g
225g butter, at room temperature
1 tablespoon roasted cocoa nibs, slightly crushed
10g dark chocolate, finely grated
pinch of table salt
twist of freshly ground black pepper

In a large bowl, mix all the ingredients together quickly using a wooden spoon. Unroll about 40cm of cling film and place the butter on top. Mould into a 5cm round cylinder before rolling up tightly and twisting the ends like a Christmas cracker to seal. Store in the fridge for up to 5 days, or you can freeze it for 2 months – just slice off rounds whenever you want to use some.

Cocoa Nib Pesto

Not the usual pesto as we know it, but by now you may realise we do things a bit differently here. The ingredients in this pesto are very much Caribbean, and the recipe was developed on the Rabot Estate with local products in abundance.

Cocoa Factor: Medium | **Origin:** Any

Makes 140g
20g cashew nuts
1 tablespoon pine nuts
1 tablespoon desiccated coconut
large bunch of basil, leaves picked
1½ tablespoons roasted cocoa nibs
1 teaspoon salt
4 tablespoons olive oil

Place all the ingredients in a blender and pulse until combined but with a slightly chunky texture. Place in an airtight container and store in the fridge – it will keep for up to 1 week.

Cocoa Mint Sauce

Mint sauce is much more versatile than traditionalists would have you believe; try it with poached fish, chicken and pork, as well as the classic lamb, and use it in dressings. Cocoa nibs add earthier notes, providing a contrast to the vinegar and fresh mint.

Cocoa Factor: Low | **Origin:** Any

Serves 4
bunch of mint, leaves only
2 tablespoons caster sugar
30ml white wine vinegar
1½ tablespoons roasted cocoa nibs

Place everything in a blender and blitz until combined but still slightly chunky. This sauce will keep in the fridge for up to 2 days.

Cocoa Chilli Oil

Chilli and cocoa was originally a Mayan flavour combination and has stood the test of time for good reason. This is a special recipe used by the chefs in our Boucan restaurant in Saint Lucia: extra-virgin olive oil rounded by rich notes of cocoa nibs and beans, with a kick of red chilli. Shake to wake the chilli flakes, then drizzle lightly over chicken, fish, pasta, pizza or roasted vegetables. Try crushing the cocoa nibs for some fabulous bread-dipping.

Cocoa Factor: Medium | **Origin:** Any

Makes 450ml
20g roasted cocoa nibs
450ml olive oil
1 teaspoon dried red chilli flakes
2 whole dried red chillies

Preheat the oven to 140°C/gas 1.

Place the nibs on a tray and cook for 15 minutes. Gently warm the olive oil in a saucepan. Add the cocoa nibs, chilli flakes and whole chillies to the oil. Remove from the heat and leave the oil to cool slightly.

When the oil has cooled, carefully pour it into a sealable glass bottle or airtight container using a funnel. Add the cocoa nibs, chilli flakes and dried chillies from the pan. Seal the bottle.

Keep the bottle in a cool, dark place, shaking it once a week. As time goes by the oil will become redder and hotter. If it gets too hot, just top it up with more olive oil. It will keep for up to 1 month.

Chocolate Balsamic Dipping Sauce

Dark cocoa and sharp balsamic vinegar are in perfect yin-and-yang balance in this sauce, which is great with bread, vegetables or cooked meats. If you prefer your sauce to be less sharp, whisk in a little honey. Caribbean and Latin American chocolates have notes of leather, wine, tobacco and spice, which partner well with balsamic vinegar. Serve with White Chocolate Balsamic Dressing (see page 242).

Cocoa Factor: High | **Origin:** Caribbean, Latin America | 70–90%

Makes 190ml
70g dark chocolate, broken into pieces
80ml olive oil
1½ tablespoons sunflower oil
1 tablespoon balsamic vinegar
salt

Gently melt the chocolate for 15 seconds in the microwave, remove and stir. Continue to heat in 10-second bursts until the chocolate has just melted, taking care not to burn the chocolate. Alternatively, melt the chocolate in a bowl set over a pan of simmering water for 2 minutes. Make sure the bottom of the bowl doesn't actually touch the hot water and stir the chocolate occasionally.

Combine the oils in a measuring jug, using a whisk, then slowly pour and beat them into the melted chocolate. Whisk until thoroughly blended and smooth. Finally whisk in the balsamic vinegar until smooth and combined, and add a little salt to taste. Store in an airtight container. If the sauce is not being used right away it may be stored in the fridge for up to 1 week, but let it come up to room temperature before using.

White Chocolate Balsamic Dressing

A simple dressing that is great with sharp salads or brushed over roasted vegetables or sautéed green beans at the last minute to add unusual extra flavour. The soothing properties of cocoa butter bring delicious balance to the soy and vinegar. Try it with the Cocoa Gin-Cured Salmon (see page 123). Use a white chocolate with the highest cocoa butter content you can find – at least 30%. See image on page 241.

Cocoa Factor: Low | **Origin:** Any | At least 30%

Makes 190ml

70g vanilla white chocolate or regular white chocolate, broken into pieces
100ml sunflower oil
1½ tablespoons white balsamic vinegar
1 teaspoon light soy sauce

Gently melt the chocolate in the microwave for 15 seconds. Remove and stir. Repeat for another 15 seconds until the chocolate has melted completely. Be careful as white chocolate can burn easily. Alternatively, melt the chocolate in a bowl set over a pan of simmering water until melted. Make sure the bottom of the bowl doesn't actually touch the hot water and stir the chocolate occasionally.

Whisking all the time, slowly pour the oil into the melted chocolate until thoroughly blended and smooth. Finally, whisk in the balsamic vinegar, followed by the soy sauce. Store in an airtight container in the fridge for up to 1 week.

Chocolate Grain Mustard

It sounds like the ravings of a madman, but once you have tried this you'll be putting it on everything. The hot, fiery mustard pairs magnificently with the depth and mild sweetness of dark chocolate, producing a taste reminiscent of black olives. Try using this as a tapenade or dressing, or spread it on ham and cheese sandwiches for a unique twist.

Cocoa Factor: Medium | **Origin:** Any | 70–90%

Makes 200g
75ml whipping cream
60g dark chocolate,
broken into small pieces
2 teaspoons grain mustard
1 teaspoon English mustard
50ml cold water

Pour the whipping cream into a medium pan and bring to a gentle simmer over a low heat. Remove the pan from the heat and whisk in the chocolate until melted.

Beat in the mustards and finally the cold water, mixing everything thoroughly. The mixture will appear watery, but place it in an airtight container and leave to cool and firm up in the fridge for 2 hours. It will keep in the fridge for up to 1 week.

Cocoa Nib Breadcrumbs

Excellent as a crust when frying fish or chicken, grilling meats or roasting vegetables such as pumpkin, these breadcrumbs work best of all with deep-fried foods. The cocoa nibs introduce a delightful crunch and a slightly bitter, nutty taste to the crumbs, bringing as much in texture as they do in flavour.

Cocoa Factor: High | **Origin:** Any

Makes 300g
250g dry breadcrumbs
(panko are great as they give a crisper texture to fried foods)
40g roasted cocoa nibs, crushed
2 pinches of salt
6 twists of the peppermill

Mix everything together well and store in a dry place in a sealed container. They will keep for 2–3 weeks.

You can also add spices to these breadcrumbs: try creole spices, curry powder, or whatever takes your fancy.

Spiced Chilli Chocolate Glaze

This is our favourite glaze for burgers – it's rich, spicy and moreish – but it works equally well with pork, chicken or fish. Just brush it on at the last minute and let the heat of the cooked meat gently melt it. Don't put it back under the grill, as the chocolate will burn and taste bitter.

Cocoa Factor: High | Origin: Any | 70–100%

Makes 150g
100g dark chocolate, broken into pieces
pinch of jerk spices (store-bought, or see below to make your own)
50ml sunflower oil

Melt the chocolate in the microwave on medium power for 10 seconds. Give the chocolate a stir then repeat at 10-second intervals until the chocolate is liquid, but not hot. Alternatively, melt the chocolate in a bowl set over a pan of simmering water for 2 minutes. Make sure the bottom of the bowl doesn't actually touch the hot water and stir the chocolate occasionally.

Whisk in the spices and then slowly add the sunflower oil in 3 parts. Ensure each addition of oil is fully incorporated before adding more, and you'll end up with a smooth emulsion.

Leave to cool until needed. If you're not using it all immediately, store in a sealed plastic container in the fridge for up to 1 week.

Jerk Seasoning

This makes more than you need for the glaze but it will keep well in a lidded container in a cupboard for up to 3 months.

2 tablespoons black peppercorns
2 tablespoons ground cinnamon
1 tablespoon dried thyme
1 teaspoon ground pimento
1½ teaspoons cayenne pepper
½ nutmeg, finely grated

Dry-fry the black peppercorns in a small pan over a medium heat for about 2 minutes, until they are aromatic. Tip into a blender, spice grinder or mortar. Add the remaining ingredients and grind to a fine powder.

Creole Tomato Chutney

A tangy, fruity chutney which has a cocoa-Caribbean twist. Cocoa is in the back of the orchestra of flavours but its subtle role adds depth and texture. Cherry tomatoes are the best for this, otherwise use plum tomatoes. It is a fantastic last-minute glaze for grilled meats or fish, works well in dressings for salads, and is a wonderful addition to sauces and marinades. It also loves cheese and cold-cut meats, and makes a great salsa-style dip. This is one of the most popular cocoa condiments in our range.

Cocoa Factor: Low | **Origin:** Any

Makes 300g

250g red onions, peeled and finely sliced
500g tomatoes, roughly chopped
3 garlic cloves, peeled and grated
½ red chilli, finely chopped (optional)
2cm piece of fresh ginger, peeled and finely chopped
125g brown sugar
75ml red wine vinegar
2 cardamom seeds
1 teaspoon creole seasoning
1 tablespoon roasted cocoa nibs

Tip all the ingredients into a large heavy-based pan and bring to a gentle simmer, stirring frequently. Simmer for 1 hour, then bring to a gentle boil so that the mixture turns dark, jam-thick and shiny. Pour into sterilised jars (see below) using a funnel and allow to cool before covering. The chutney will keep unopened for 6 weeks. Once opened, store in the fridge and use within 1 week.

To sterilise the jars, wash the jars, lids and bands/seals in hot soapy water and rinse well. Place the jars upright in a large pan and cover with cold water. Bring to a boil and leave for 15 minutes, adding the lids and seals. Turn off the heat and leave for 10 minutes. Using tongs, lift out the jars and place upside down on a clean towel. Turn over and fill the jars almost to the top while both the chutney and jars are still warm. Add the seals and lids and screw down fully.

Cocoa Onion Gravy

Slowly cooking the onions releases their sugars and they caramelise, giving a rich, dark colour and a slightly bittersweet taste that works well with the bitterness of cocoa beer.

Cocoa Factor: Low | **Origin:** Any

Serves 4

1 quantity of Cocoa Beer-Braised Onions (see page 76)
500ml good chicken stock
1 tablespoon plain flour
4 thyme sprigs
salt and freshly ground pepper

Heat the onions in a heavy-based pan over a gentle heat, then drain in a sieve to remove any excess fat. Bring the stock to a boil in a separate pan then set aside while you prepare the onion base.

Return the onions to the pan and add the flour. Stir over a medium heat for 1 minute. Add half the chicken stock and the thyme. Stir until a smooth, loose paste has formed. Add the remaining stock and bring to a boil, stirring as you go. Simmer gently for 4 minutes. Taste for salt and pepper and adjust as needed.

Any Roast Gravy

This recipe is a good base for all gravies. Depending on which roast you are making, add the appropriate stock.

Serves 4–6

500ml chicken or beef stock, or use any quality stock cubes
all juices left in the roasting tin once meat has been removed
1 teaspoon cornflour
1 tablespoon cold water

Bring the stock to a boil in a pan over a low to medium heat. Meanwhile, tilt the roasting tin slightly, to gather all the residue and juices into one corner. Gently skim off any excess fat using a spoon. Set the roasting tin flat again and add the warmed stock. Using a wooden spoon, scrape up all the bits off the bottom of the tray and mix them into the stock.

Return the stock and roasting juices to the pan and bring to a boil, then simmer for 5 minutes. Mix together the cornflour and cold water to make a paste. In a steady stream, pour and stir this into the pan, then bring to a boil once more and reduce until the gravy just coats the back of a spoon. Pour the gravy through a fine sieve into a clean pan, then keep and reheat to serve if necessary.

Yorkshire Nib Puddings

Cocoa nibs give these puddings a nutty texture and a warming, unusually light chocolate taste. They add depth to any dishes they are served with, complementing and enhancing the textures and flavours.

Cocoa Factor: Low | **Origin:** Any

Makes 6
2 eggs
150ml whole milk
110ml water
150g plain flour
20g roasted cocoa nibs,
broken to the size of a rice grain
beef dripping or sunflower oil
2 pinches of salt

Break the eggs into a large mixing bowl and whisk for 5 minutes, then beat in the milk and water. Add the flour to the egg mixture. Starting in the centre of the bowl, slowly whisk the flour to make a batter. Add the cocoa nibs. When all the ingredients are fully incorporated, cover with cling film and chill for 30 minutes. Preheat the oven to 220°C/gas 7.

Put a tablespoon of sunflower oil or beef dripping into 6 Yorkshire pudding moulds and set on a baking tray. Place this in the oven for 5 minutes to allow the oil or fat to get hot. During this time take out the batter, add the salt and whisk again for 30 seconds.

Carefully remove the baking tray with the Yorkshire pudding moulds from the oven. Add the batter until the moulds are two-thirds full. Return to the oven and bake until golden and risen. This should take around 12–15 minutes. Remove the puddings from the moulds.

They can now be left to cool and reheated in the oven when needed at a temperature of 190°C/gas 5 for 3 minutes.

Index

Picture Credits

Hotel Chocolat: Pages 6, 7, 8, 11, 64–5, 66 (top), 162

Tom Mannion: Pages 12, 28, 66 (middle), 67, 78, 104–5, 106, 107, 112, 143 (top, 2nd, 3rd), 165 (top), 255

Roland Pupupin: Page 57

Fredrik Ahlin: Page 66 (bottom)

Stephen Bond: Pages 117, 143 (4th), 165 (bottom)

Kathrin Koschitzki: Page 122 (styled by Elodie Rambaud)

Acknowledgements

This book would not have been possible without the imagination, courage, graft and support of the following people, who made cocoa cuisine a reality:

Libby Thirlwell for acting as a human guinea pig for my cocoa experiments at home over the last eight years and for her supremely intelligent insights.

Phil and Judy Buckley, who have built every stage of our project at Rabot Estate in Saint Lucia and continue to be an inspiration.

Jon Bentham, not only the mastermind behind our imaginative menus, but the man responsible for our quality, day in day out.

The dedicated teams at our restaurants in Saint Lucia, London and Leeds who have truly embraced the cocoa lifestyle.

And, of course, Peter Harris, my long-time business partner, who has taken the project to his heart and shares the vision of what we are trying to do, making it happen every day.

A special thanks, also, to the government and people of Saint Lucia, who welcomed our idea to make local cocoa-growing truly sustainable and connected to a new luxury food experience. We feel very at home now. There's still lots left to do.

Angus Thirlwell, CEO & Co-Founder, Hotel Chocolat

A New Way of Cooking with Chocolate is the result of the collective ingenuity, dedication and hard work of the following contributors: Jon Bentham, Angus Thirlwell, Megan Roberts, Adam Geileskey, Angela Summers, Terry Waters, Iain Ball, Alexandra Hare, Claire Haddad, Kiri Kalenko, Louise Cox, Emma Cope, Rhona MacFadyen, Rachel Smith, Jessica Howe, Paul Matthews, Andy Simpson and Lauren Tann-Trankle.

From the start, Headline understood our vision for this book and shared our incredible passion to create a unique and innovative cookbook that was like nothing else out there. We have worked with a fantastic and truly dedicated group of people to deliver the book you now hold in your hands.

Recipes on pages 70, 132 and 135 were created and developed by Megan Roberts.

Executive Chef Jon Bentham

Jon Bentham is an unsung hero of London's gastronomic revival in the 1990s. He worked for chefs like John Burton-Race, Stephen Bull and Gary Rhodes in key roles in Britain's finest Michelin-starred kitchens.

In 2000, Jon moved to Saint Lucia, falling in love with the culture and creole cuisine, before joining Hotel Chocolat in 2010 to help create a unique cocoa cuisine menu for the Boucan restaurant on our plantation.

Chef Tom Kerridge, who opened The Hand and Flowers, the world's first-ever two Michelin-starred pub, has called Jon 'The most influential chef in my career. I learnt so much from Jon... His understanding of food was phenomenal – and not just British, but world food.'

First published in 2015
by HEADLINE PUBLISHING GROUP

1

Cataloguing in Publication Data is available from the British Library

Hardback ISBN 9781472224545

Food photography by Nassima Rothacker
(for location photography credits, see page 254)
Project Editor Laura Herring
Copy editor Emily Sweet
Food stylists Rich Harris and Katy Ross
Props stylist Jenny Iggleden

Colour reproduction by Born Group

Printed and bound by Mohn Media

Headline's policy is to use papers that are natural, renewable and recyclable products and made from wood grown in sustainable forests. The logging and manufacturing processes are expected to conform to the environmental regulations of the country of origin.

HEADLINE PUBLISHING GROUP
An Hachette UK Company
338 Euston Road
London NW1 3BH

www.headline.co.uk
www.hachette.co.uk

PAUL HOLLYWOOD

A BAKER'S LIFE

1KG

PAUL HOLLYWOOD

A BAKER'S LIFE

from childhood bakes to five-star excellence

B L O O M S B U R Y
LONDON • OXFORD • NEW YORK • NEW DELHI • SYDNEY

Bloomsbury Publishing
An imprint of Bloomsbury Publishing Plc

50 Bedford Square, London WC1B 3DP, UK
1385 Broadway, New York, NY 10018, USA

www.bloomsbury.com

BLOOMSBURY and the Diana logo are trademarks of Bloomsbury Publishing Plc

First published in Great Britain 2017

Family photographs on pages 5, 6, 12, 61,110, 160 and 250 courtesy of Paul Hollywood. Photograph of the Breadwinner bakery on pages 6 and 61 courtesy of The Press, York. Photograph on page 207 © Love Productions 2012. Archive photograph of Paul on page 110 courtesy of Eaton Estate, part of the Grosvenor Estate.

British Library Cataloguing-in-Publication Data
A catalogue record for this book is available from the British Library.

Library of Congress Cataloguing-in-Publication data has been applied for.

ISBN: HB: 978-1-4088-4650-6
ePub: 978-1-4088-4651-3

10 9 8 7 6 5 4 3 2 1

Project editing: Janet Illsley
Design and art direction: Smith & Gilmour
Photography: Martin Poole
Recipe development and food styling: Claire Bassano
Props styling: Rachel Jukes
Proof reading: Sally Summers
Index: Hilary Bird

Printed and bound in Germany by Mohn Media

TO MY NAN AMY AND MY MUM GILL, YOU'VE BEEN THERE FROM THE START OF THE JOURNEY, BIG LOVE TO YOU

BREADWINNER
for fresh bread
BREADWINNER
CYPRUS

FIVE DECADES OF BAKING

All my life, I have been surrounded by great baking. I've been in the industry for more than thirty years, and yet every day I learn something new.

My childhood was in Merseyside and I grew up eating my mum's bakes at home – her ginger biscuits are legendary – and I was always in and out of my dad's bakeries. Following in his footsteps, I did an apprenticeship in high-street bakeries, then began working in five-star hotels. I moved to Cyprus in my late twenties, living and baking there for six years, as well as travelling around the Mediterranean and Middle East, learning about many different styles of bread and pastry.

Coming back to Britain, I set up my own bakeries and I also started to teach baking on television shows. Then one day I got a call asking me to audition as a presenter for a new programme: *The Great British Bake Off*. So started a whole new chapter in my life. Through television, books and other forms of teaching, I'm proud to have been part of a revival of baking in Britain, and the celebration of one of our great national traditions.

You don't have to go to college to make a career in baking. I learnt on the job; from reading and by watching other people, but most of all from doing. I've taught perhaps forty people how to bake professionally over the years, some of them from scratch. What matters most, whether amateur or professional, is hands-on experience and the ability and willingness to pick things up.

What other qualities help? If you're making puff pastry, croissants, crème pât, bread or any number of other things, you need patience. And to be patient, you need passion. Because even if you fail, you'll do it again and again until you get it right; once you've got it right, you'll never forget.

The other key lesson is the importance of touch. If I go into a bakery, I can put my finger in a dough and tell you how that bread will come out of the oven – how it'll bake, how it'll look, what the crust is going to be like. That's purely the result of experience, which anyone can build up day by day. Get the knowledge in your fingertips.

My dad always encouraged me to use my hands, and I've passed that on to everyone who's ever worked with me. Do something by hand, however much it seems like hard work, and you'll get to know the texture of what you're making. This goes for fillings and decoration too. A lot of people over-whip cream. If you use an electric whisk, you should always under-whip and then take it to the right consistency by hand, lifting the whisk up to see when it's ready.

Cooks go by their own tastebuds, altering recipes to suit their preferences – putting a little bit more in, tasting as they go. Baking is a different sort of skill. Bakers are scientific. You can play with the flavours in a bake but there's an underlying strategy and science. You have to do things precisely, weighing up the ingredients and getting the timing right. It's all about the chemistry, such as the rising agent's reaction to liquid, and how the salt and fat work with the flour and yeast. Fermentation is key – the way that a dough's flavour develops over time and how this is affected by the temperature of the air and water.

Ingredients make a real difference too – the type of butter and the eggs used in a mixture and the way they emulsify. And then there's the importance of using your oven properly, taking care over any decoration and knowing the simple tricks that make a bake look great.

There are two aspects to any bake: one is the base recipe; the other is flavour. Follow the base recipe to the letter initially – whether it's a Victoria sponge, Genoise, bread or croissant, don't change the recipe. When it comes to flavours, though, you can play around. You might think you need some more raspberries, or cut them back, or change onions to mushrooms. But only do that after you've mastered the base recipe first and made it two or three times, so you have confidence in what you're doing.

Ingredients do differ and you have to notice and respond to that as you bake. Different brands of flour may absorb up to five per cent more or less liquid. A good flour will absorb more liquid, which will give your bake more volume. Try the same recipe with different flours and you'll see the difference, and discover your own preferences.

There's a plethora of equipment around these days to make baking easier. But in the end I prefer to use as little kit as possible. All you really need is a bread scraper, a good serrated knife and digital scales.

A set of digital scales is the item of equipment that has really changed home baking, and is essential. I started with balance scales at work and they were fine for 20kg quantities, but when you're dealing in hundreds of grams digital precision makes a real difference.

Bread scrapers are great for cutting dough and scraping it off surfaces, or smoothing icing on the top or sides of a cake. When you get one for the first time, you realise what you've been missing. I've used a Scotch scraper for forty years and I'll never be without one.

A serrated knife is the most effective tool for cutting bakes. You can use it for cutting a sponge into discs, just as you do for slicing bread.

Bakeware is much better than it used to be. It's worth buying good-quality trays and tins, as they'll last longer and won't warp. If you buy decent kit, the only thing you'll ever have to change is the battery in your digital scales.

Baking teaches you patience and creativity, but more than that it teaches you what goes into your food. It helps you learn about ingredients and what they do in pastries, cakes and pies. It's also a family thing. Once a recipe is good, you can pass it on to the rest of your family so they continue to make it. That's why it's very nostalgic – when people watch *Bake Off* and see a particular kind of cake, they think, 'My grandma used to make a cake like that and it was delicious,' then they want to make it themselves.

Home baking and passing down these recipes has long been a tradition in Britain. We have always been good bakers in this country, but people sometimes forget that fact. I think people here are bakers before they are cooks. One reason is that cooking can be about sourcing special ingredients, whereas baking starts with the basics. Flour, sugar, salt and yeast are what we use – all raw ingredients that you have already in the cupboard.

Anyone can bake, and you can start at any age. If you can get a few core bakes right – a Victoria sandwich, a favourite bread, a beautiful brioche, a buttery croissant – you will enter a whole new world of enjoyment, and save yourself money in the shops at the same time.

Over the years, I've not only perfected my techniques and recipes, but also come to understand what it means to be a baker. The things I've learnt from decades as a professional are just as useful for the home baker who wants to make a weekend loaf, a batch of biscuits, a pie, a pud, a tart or a celebration cake. So this is what I'm sharing with you now – the recipes, lessons and experiences from my baker's life.

A NOTE ON OVEN TEMPERATURE

The baking times in my recipes are for conventional ovens. If you are using a fan-assisted oven, you will need to lower the oven setting by around 10–15°C. Ovens vary, so use an oven thermometer to verify the temperature and check your bakes towards the end of the suggested cooking time.

My Favorite Recipe for
By
Serves
Philadelphia Cream Cheese
Pie Crust
PIGEON PIE
BONED CAPON
PIPED HAM

NOSTALGIC BAKES
MY EARLY YEARS

YOU ASSOCIATE YOUR childhood with food because it makes such an impact at the time. Sweet foods and other bakes are treats. They mean you've been good, or are having a good time. These are the moments that you find yourself remembering decades later.

Baking is in my genes. My dad was a baker and when I was born in 1966 we lived in a flat above his shop. He would start work at 4am and the flat was permanently full of the smell of bread. When my mum came down to gel the doughnuts she would hang me on a baby bouncer at the bottom of the stairs by the shop. I'd bounce away for hours, watching people bake.

We moved to a semi-detached house in Wallasey, in the Wirral, when I was very young and that's where I grew up. We were a very tight community where everyone knew each other and the kids all played outside in the street. My mum still lives in the same house, and she was born and raised in the next road.

My mum hates cooking but she's creative – she worked as a graphic artist – and her pastry work and her biscuits were great. We were much involved in the church and that's where I saw a lot of cakes, bread and, predominantly, tray bakes. If someone had a birthday, we'd have a big bash or we'd go on an outing, perhaps to the seaside, and everyone would bring food to the table – my nan and mum included. Nowadays people are baking at home much more again but there was a gap of around twenty years when people just bought pre-made food. What I am part of now is a return to that ethos of baking yourself.

On a Saturday, my mum used to make a fruit pie for Sunday lunch, all from scratch. The fruit – rhubarb, apples or pears – was always home-grown. I would climb the apple tree in our garden with my two younger brothers, Jason and Lee, partly to pick apples and partly to get onto the shed roof to be naughty and throw stones.

Saturday was a fun day; there was no school and my dad was off work so I'd get to see him. In the afternoon, he'd bake bread rolls, making dough in a bowl, shaping the buns and putting them on a tray to rise in front of a gas fire with a damp cloth over the top. I remember lifting the cloth to have a quick look. They were growing. Then he baked them off, and they were absolutely delicious. I would recognise that flavour anywhere; it's the taste of something home-made. My dad was a baker who knew his stuff, and he understood that the longer you rise a bread before you knock it back and let the shaped loaf prove (grow again), the greater the flavour. It's down to fermentation – one of the most important lessons for any baker.

While the rolls were proving, I remember Dad sitting down and watching the wrestling on a Saturday – invariably Big Daddy was up against Giant Haystacks – and we'd be there, me and my two brothers. Then we would watch a bit of the *Generation Game*, a TV game show where novices tried to copy a skill demonstrated by a professional. At the age of six, I remember seeing a guy plaiting bread and being fascinated. Thirty-odd years later, I went on the *Generation Game* myself and plaited bread, just like that baker.

My nans – Olive and Amy – lived in flats above shops in big Victorian houses and they each had a minute kitchen and a pantry. The smell of baking always struck me in my dad's mum's house. She ran a launderette until she was eighty. Tough as old boots. She used to say to me, 'Your dad's the best baker in the country. He works all the hours God sends.' So I grew up with this sense of good baking.

Both sides of the family were grafters. My great-great-great grandfather on Mum's side used to run across Scotland and back in a week, delivering and collecting the post for his community on the west coast. It was the equivalent of about twenty-one marathons a month. I didn't know that when I was growing up,

but I had a lot of energy as a child – in double-games I would opt to run round and round a field without stopping – and later on, I regularly did thirteen- or fourteen-hour shifts as a baker.

My dad built up a chain of bakeries in the Northeast and as a child and teenager I'd go along with him to help out or watch the lads work. There was a very old stainless steel machine that was used to pierce each doughnut, then you'd pull two levers to inject the perfect amount of jam. Sometimes I'd do it with my brother and we'd go ge-dung, ge-dung, ge-dung, putting more and more jam in until the doughnuts became like jam bombs.

My dad's bakeries were all open plan. In the front, there was the shop area displaying all the cakes and cream cakes, the steak and kidney pies, the sausage rolls and the bread on racks. Then you would swing round to a pâtisserie area with rum truffles and little brownies. I used to disappear off and talk to the people in the shop, to ask if I could take a cream doughnut. It would seem almost as big as my head but I'd eat the lot. My dad would go mad, saying, 'Why's he doing that – he won't eat his dinner!'

I had no idea that I wanted to be a baker back then. At the time I was just fascinated by baking and everything that went with it – the white aprons hanging on washing lines with Dad's checks, white t-shirts and long white coats. If I hugged my dad when he came back from work, he always had that smell of bread. Years later, I remember coming home from my bakery and my lad Joshua saying to me: 'Dad, you smell like a loaf!'

MY MUM'S GINGER BISCUITS

MAKES 25–30

Mum used to make these easy biscuits several times a week. Not only are they a doddle to make but they've got the right balance of being crispy and chewy. You can use butter instead of margarine if you like; they taste great either way.

110g margarine
110g caster sugar
110g golden syrup
225g self-raising flour, plus extra for dusting
2 tsp ground ginger

Heat your oven to 180°C/Gas 4. Line two large baking trays with baking parchment.

Melt the margarine, caster sugar and golden syrup together gently in a saucepan over a medium heat. Once melted, remove from the heat and let cool slightly. Add all of the dry ingredients to the pan and stir to combine and make a smooth dough.

Once the dough is cool enough to handle, use lightly floured hands to roll into balls, each the size of a 50p piece. Place them on the baking trays, leaving enough room in between to allow them to spread during cooking. Mark the top of each ball with a fork.

Put the baking trays into the oven and bake for about 10–12 minutes, or until the biscuits are golden brown. Remove from the oven and leave to cool and firm up slightly on the tray, then transfer to a wire rack to cool completely.

MILLIONAIRE'S SHORTBREAD WITH SALTED CARAMEL

MAKES ABOUT 12 BARS

What is there not to like about a caramel chocolate biscuit? I've tried some good shop-bought millionaire's shortbread but it's even better if you make it yourself, as you can choose the chocolate and cut it into the size of pieces you want. I've updated this childhood favourite by adding salt to the caramel and a topping of macadamia nuts. This version is a great favourite of my son Josh.

For the base
150g unsalted butter, softened
75g caster sugar
175g plain flour
A pinch of fine salt
25g fine semolina or ground rice

For the salted caramel filling
120g condensed milk
60g golden syrup
150g unsalted butter
150g soft light brown sugar
1 tsp sea salt flakes

For the topping
200g dark chocolate (I use chocolate with 40% cocoa solids, like Bourneville), cut into small pieces
50g macadamia nuts, roughly chopped

Heat your oven to 150°C/Gas 2. Line a shallow 27 x 18cm baking tin with baking parchment.

To make the base, in a bowl, cream the butter and sugar together until light and fluffy. Add the flour, salt and semolina or ground rice and mix with a spoon and then your hands to form a smooth dough; try not to overwork it.

Press the mixture into the prepared tin and prick the surface all over with a fork. Bake for 35–40 minutes until pale but cooked through.

For the salted caramel filling, weigh all the ingredients except the salt into a pan. Melt over a medium heat, stirring occasionally, and then bring to the boil. As it boils, keep stirring – the caramel bubbles will become larger and the mixture will thicken and turn a rich, glossy caramel colour.

Pour the caramel evenly over the shortbread, sprinkle on the sea salt flakes and leave to cool and set.

For the topping, melt the chocolate in a heatproof bowl suspended over a pan of simmering water, making sure the bottom of the bowl doesn't touch the water.

Pour the melted chocolate over the caramel layer so it is completely covered, spread to level and smooth the surface with a palette knife. Scatter over the macadamia nuts. Leave to set completely, then cut into bars.

MADE IN ENGLAND

JAM TARTS

MAKES 15–20

My mum used to make these for us when we were little, often using leftover pastry from a pie. She'd dollop brightly coloured Robinson's strawberry or raspberry jam into the pastry cases. Her tip is to not fill them too much or the jam can gurgle over and make a mess. Jam tarts are simple to make but we love them and they're worth rediscovering for family teas or children's parties. They are very basic, very cheap – and a treat.

170g self-raising flour, plus extra for dusting
85g cold unsalted butter or margarine, cut into small dice
1–3 tbsp cold water
About 15 tsp jam (any flavour)

Heat your oven to 200°C/Gas 6 and have ready two shallow 12-hole bun trays.

Put the flour into a bowl, add the butter or margarine and rub in with your fingers until the mixture resembles breadcrumbs. Stir in just enough water to bring it together to form a dough.

Roll out the pastry dough on a lightly floured work surface to a 4mm thickness. Using a 6.5–7cm fluted pastry cutter, cut out 15–20 circles.

Use the pastry rounds to line the bun trays (you'll probably have some spare hollows). Add a scant teaspoonful of jam to each pastry case – not too much or it will ooze everywhere. Re-roll the leftover pastry to make more tarts or use a star cutter to cut lids and position on top of the jam filling.

Bake in the oven for about 25–30 minutes, until the pastry is pale brown, checking after 20 minutes.

Leave the tarts to cool in the trays for 5 minutes, then carefully remove and place on a wire rack. Leave to cool completely.

STICKY GINGER TRAY BAKE

MAKES 15 SLICES

The beauty of a tray bake is that it's easy to transport in the tin you bake it in and then cut into portions to share out. Ginger is a simple way of flavouring a sponge and stem ginger adds a little texture, as well as a fresh and fragrant kick. The ginger syrup soaks into the sponge and makes it shine on top.

220g unsalted butter, softened
220g soft dark brown sugar
3 large eggs, beaten
220g self-raising flour
1 tbsp ground ginger
4 knobs of stem ginger, chopped into small pieces
2 tbsp stem ginger syrup

For the ginger syrup
60g soft dark brown sugar
100ml water
½ tsp ground ginger

Heat your oven to 180°C/Gas 4. Line a 30 x 20cm baking tin with baking parchment.

In a large bowl, cream the butter and sugar together until light and fluffy. Add the beaten eggs a little at a time, beating well to incorporate each addition. Sift the flour and ground ginger together over the mixture and gently fold in. Finally, fold in the chopped stem ginger and syrup.

Pour the mixture into the prepared tin and gently level the surface. Bake for 25–30 minutes, until risen and springy to the touch. Leave to cool slightly.

For the syrup, gently heat the sugar, water and ground ginger together in a small pan until the sugar is dissolved. Bring to the boil and let the syrup bubble away until it thickens a little.

While the tray bake is still warm, make small holes all over the surface with a skewer then pour on the syrup, so it seeps into the holes. Leave to cool completely. Cut into pieces to serve.

ORANGE & WALNUT TRAY BAKE

MAKES 15 SLICES

Here's a tray bake based on an afternoon cake I love, walnut with orange instead of the more usual coffee and walnut. The softness of the sponge, the walnuts and the intense flavour from the citrus fruit make it delicious with a cup of tea.

220g unsalted butter, softened
220g caster sugar
3 large eggs, beaten
Finely grated zest of ½ orange plus 2 tbsp juice
1 tsp orange extract
220g self-raising flour
100g chopped walnuts

For the topping
60g unsalted butter, softened
250g full-fat cream cheese
200g icing sugar, plus extra for dusting
Finely grated zest of 1 orange
1 tsp orange extract
60g walnut halves

Heat your oven to 180°C/Gas 4. Line a 30 x 20cm baking tin with baking parchment.

In a large bowl, cream together the butter and sugar, until light and fluffy. Gradually add the beaten eggs, beating well after each addition. Add the orange zest, juice and extract and stir to incorporate. Gently fold in the flour and chopped walnuts.

Tip the mixture into the prepared tin and gently level the surface. Bake for 25–30 minutes, until risen and springy to the touch. Leave to cool slightly in the tin before removing and transferring to a wire rack. Leave to cool completely.

For the topping, beat the butter, cream cheese and icing sugar together until smooth, then beat in the orange zest and extract.

Spread the icing over the top of the tray bake with a palette knife or the back of a large spoon and decorate with the walnut halves. Cut into pieces to serve.

COCONUT TRAY BAKE

MAKES 12–15 SLICES

There's something very British about a tray bake. This one has pretty pink icing dusted with desiccated coconut and was considered a favourite back in the seventies. Coconut is a tropical ingredient but it's a long-standing part of British baking, both as a flavouring and as a decoration – think of the Snowball and coconut macaroons. You can even serve this tray bake as a dessert, with plenty of custard – a popular school-dinner pud.

200g unsalted butter, softened
200g caster sugar
3 large eggs, beaten
1 tsp vanilla extract
200g self-raising flour
100g desiccated coconut
2–3 tbsp milk

For the topping
150g icing sugar
1–2 tbsp cold water
A few drops of pink food colouring
40g desiccated coconut

Heat your oven to 180°C/Gas 4. Line a 30 x 20cm baking tin with baking parchment.

In a large bowl, cream the butter and sugar together until light and fluffy. Gradually add the beaten eggs, beating well after each addition, then stir in the vanilla extract. Add the flour and desiccated coconut and gently fold in. Finally add enough milk to achieve a loose enough consistency for the mixture to drop easily off a spoon.

Pour the mixture into the prepared tin and gently level the surface. Bake for 25–30 minutes, or until risen and springy to the touch. Allow to cool slightly in the tin, then remove and place on a wire rack. Leave to cool completely.

To make the topping, sift the icing sugar into a bowl and add 2 tsp water with a few drops of pink colouring. Mix until smooth, then add more water, 1 tsp at a time, until you have a smooth, spreadable icing.

Pour the icing onto the centre of the coconut cake and use a palette knife to spread it out to the edges. While the icing is still wet, sprinkle over the desiccated coconut. Leave to set before cutting into pieces.

CHOCOLATE TEA CAKES

MAKES 12

As a kid I loved Tunnock's Tea Cakes and I'm still partial to them now. There's that great moment when you bite through the crispy shell, hit that marshmallow and then the biscuit underneath. These are fun to make, too.

For the biscuit bases
200g plain flour, plus extra for dusting
½ tsp baking powder
A pinch of fine salt
50g cold unsalted butter, cut into small dice
50g caster sugar
2–3 tbsp milk

For the filling
3 large egg whites
150g caster sugar
2 tbsp glucose syrup

For the topping
300g dark chocolate (I use chocolate with 40% cocoa solids, like Bourneville), cut into small pieces

For the biscuit bases, line two baking trays with baking parchment. Sift the flour, baking powder and salt together into a bowl. Add the butter and rub in using your fingertips until the mixture resembles fine breadcrumbs. Stir in the sugar. Incorporate enough milk to bring the mixture together to form a ball.

On a lightly floured surface roll out the dough to a 5mm thickness and stamp out 12 discs using a 7cm plain cutter. Place on the prepared trays. Chill for at least 30 minutes. Heat your oven to 170°C/Gas 3½.

Bake the chilled dough discs for 12–15 minutes until lightly browned. Transfer the biscuits to a wire rack to cool and firm up.

For the filling, put all the ingredients into a large heatproof bowl set over a pan of hot (but not boiling) water, making sure the bottom of the bowl doesn't touch the water. Using a hand-held electric whisk, beat for about 8 minutes until you have a stiff, smooth and silky meringue mixture (the aim is to gently melt the sugar as you whisk).

Spoon the mixture into a piping bag fitted with a medium plain nozzle and pipe a mound on each cooled biscuit base, leaving a small margin around the edge. Place the biscuits on a wire rack over a sheet of baking parchment.

For the topping, melt 200g chocolate in a bowl over a pan of hot water, making sure the bowl is not touching the water. Remove from the heat and add the rest of the chocolate so that it melts. Leave to cool slightly; it must not be too hot or it will melt the meringue.

Spoon the chocolate onto the tea cakes to coat completely, allowing the excess to fall onto the parchment below, and smooth with a palette knife. If the chocolate gets too cool, put the bowl back over the pan of hot water briefly. You can also re-melt the chocolate that has fallen onto the parchment. Allow the chocolate to set before serving.

Photographs overleaf

CHOCOLATE CORNFLAKE CAKES

MAKES 12

A staple at kids' parties, these are just as popular now as they were in the sixties and seventies when I was growing up. A great first recipe to introduce children to baking , there are only three ingredients and it gets them into stirring well to ensure all the cornflakes are coated. Of course, the best bit is licking the bowl when you've finished.

40g unsalted butter
125g dark chocolate (I use chocolate with 40% cocoa solids, like Bourneville), cut into small pieces
75g cornflakes

Line a 12-hole bun tray with paper cupcake cases.

Put the butter and chocolate into a large pan and gently melt together over a low-medium heat, stirring until combined and smooth.

Remove the pan from the heat and add half the cornflakes. Stir until these are coated in chocolate, then add the remaining cornflakes and stir until they are all coated in chocolate.

Divide the mixture between the paper cases and leave to cool and set before eating.

MARSHMALLOW CRISPY RICE BARS

MAKES 9 LARGE OR 12 MEDIUM BARS

When my mum used to make these, we'd never leave the mixture to set. By the time she'd tipped it into the tin, we'd be spooning it up. Leave it be until firm... if you can. You can cut it into as many pieces as you like. The mixture is very sweet so some will prefer just a small nugget, others a large bar.

50g unsalted butter
2 tbsp golden syrup
200g marshmallows
125g crispy rice cereal
20g mini marshmallows, to finish

Line the base and sides of a 20cm square tin with baking parchment.

Put the butter, golden syrup and the 200g marshmallows into a large saucepan and heat gently until melted, stirring constantly to combine and prevent the mixture sticking.

Remove the pan from the heat, add the rice cereal and mix until well coated in the marshmallow mix.

Transfer the mixture to the prepared tin. As it is very sticky, cover the surface with a sheet of baking parchment and then press down well to level the surface. Remove the parchment and gently but firmly press down onto the mixture with the back of a large metal spoon.

Scatter mini marshmallows over the surface and leave to cool, then cut into squares and remove from the tin.

TEA LOAF

MAKES 1 LARGE TEA LOAF

When I started baking, ingredients and kitchen kit used imperial measurements. Nowadays, everything is metric but many bakers and recipes still refer to loaf tins in pounds. This tea loaf is always baked in a 2lb tin (that's 900g in metric), with dimensions of roughly 23 x 13 x 7cm.

150g sultanas
150g raisins
150g currants
150ml strong hot black tea
225g self-raising flour
175g demerara sugar
1 large egg, beaten
3–4 tbsp milk

Put the dried fruit into a bowl, pour over the hot tea and stir well, then cover with cling film and leave to soak overnight.

The next day, heat your oven to 160°C/Gas 3. Line a 900g (2lb) loaf tin with baking parchment.

Drain the soaked fruit and place in a large bowl. Add the flour, sugar, beaten egg and enough milk to give a dropping consistency, mixing well to combine.

Spoon the mixture into the prepared loaf tin and level the surface with the back of a spoon. Bake for about 1 hour, or until a skewer inserted into the centre comes out clean.

Leave the loaf to cool in the tin for 5 minutes, then remove and place on a wire rack to finish cooling.

Slice, spread with butter and enjoy.

SALLY LUNN

MAKES 1 LOAF

The bakeries in the Northwest have a certain style. In other parts of the country, a Sally Lunn refers to a round tea bread or smaller buns. For us, it is a large, oval-shaped fruited bun, covered in icing, but made with the same enriched buttery dough, studded with dried fruit. It's best eaten freshly made.

450g strong white bread flour, plus extra for dusting
3 tbsp caster sugar
7g instant dried yeast
7g fine salt
40g unsalted butter, cut into small pieces, softened, plus extra for greasing
125ml whole milk
About 125ml cold water
75g mixed dried fruit
Finely grated zest of 1 orange
Finely grated zest of 1 lemon
1 tsp ground cinnamon
50g glacé cherries, chopped

For the icing
200g icing sugar
20–30ml water

Put the flour and sugar into a large bowl. Add the yeast to one side of the bowl and the salt to the other. Add the butter, milk and three-quarters of the water. Using the fingers of one hand, mix everything together. Add the remaining water, a little at a time, until all the flour is incorporated – you want a soft but not soggy dough. (You may not need all the water or you may need a bit more; it depends on the flour.)

Tip onto a lightly floured surface and knead for 5–10 minutes until you have a soft, smooth dough. Place in a lightly greased bowl, cover with a tea towel and leave to rise for 1–3 hours, until doubled in size.

Meanwhile, mix the dried fruit with the citrus zests, cinnamon and glacé cherries. Line a large baking tray with baking parchment.

Tip the risen dough out onto a lightly floured surface and knock back by folding it inwards repeatedly until all the air is knocked out. Shape into a large rectangle and scatter the fruit mix over the surface. Fold the dough over to encase the fruit, then knead to distribute it evenly.

Dust the work surface with more flour and roll out the dough to a large rectangle, with a long side facing you. Fold each end into the middle, then roll up and turn over so the join is underneath. Roll the dough lightly, applying more pressure at the ends to create a long oval shape.

Lift the loaf onto the prepared baking tray and place in a large, clean plastic bag. Leave to prove for about an hour, until doubled in size.

Heat your oven to 190°C/Gas 5. Take the baking tray out of the plastic bag and place in the oven. Bake for 30–35 minutes until the loaf is risen and golden brown. Transfer to a wire rack to cool.

For the icing, sift the icing sugar into a bowl and mix in enough water to make a thick but spreadable icing that coats the back of a spoon. Spread the icing evenly over the top of the cooled loaf and leave to set. Slice and serve with butter for spreading.

CUSTARD TART

SERVES 8

As a lad, I found custard tarts from the bakery irresistible: a hand-held treat in a foil cup. Here is my recipe for a family-sized version, which makes a lovely pud. Don't stint on the nutmeg – this fragrant spice gives the tart its character.

For the pastry
200g plain flour, plus extra for dusting
2 tbsp icing sugar
100g cold unsalted butter, cut into small dice
1 medium egg, beaten
½ tsp lemon juice
2–3 tsp very cold water

For the custard filling
250ml whole milk
350ml double cream
8 medium egg yolks
80g caster sugar
¼–½ whole nutmeg

For the pastry, mix the flour and icing sugar together in a bowl. Add the butter and rub in until the mixture resembles fine breadcrumbs. Make a well in the centre. In a jug, lightly whisk the egg with the lemon juice and 2 tsp cold water, then pour into the well. Mix into the flour, using one hand to bring the pastry together and adding a splash more water if needed. As the dough comes together, gently knead into a ball. Wrap in cling film and rest in the fridge for at least 30 minutes.

Transfer the dough to a lightly floured work surface and roll out to a circle, about 3mm thick and large enough to line a 20cm loose-based tart tin. Lift the pastry into the tin and press into the edges, leaving the excess hanging over the top. Prick the base all over with a fork, then chill in the fridge for 15 minutes. Heat your oven to 200°C/Gas 6.

Line the pastry case with a sheet of baking parchment and fill with baking beans. Bake 'blind' for 12–15 minutes, or until the pastry is dry to the touch and golden around the edge. Remove the beans and parchment and bake for a further 5–8 minutes, until the pastry case is crisp and light golden brown all over. Let cool, then use a small, sharp knife to trim away the excess pastry from the edge. Turn the oven down to 150°C/Gas 2.

For the filling, pour the milk and cream into a pan and slowly bring to the boil. Meanwhile, whisk the egg yolks and sugar together in a bowl, then pour on the hot, creamy milk, stirring as you do so. Strain through a sieve into a jug and allow to settle for a few minutes.

Pour the custard into the tart case, then finely grate the nutmeg over the surface until it is completely covered. Bake for 30–35 minutes, or until the custard is just set.

Place the tart in its tin on a wire rack to cool; the custard will firm up as it cools down. You can keep this tart, covered, in the fridge, for a day or two but bring it back to room temperature before serving.

TRIFLE

SERVES 6

To this day, no one makes trifle as good as my mum. She doesn't include any sherry in her recipe and that's how I like it – with no booze, just simple home-made sponge, fruit jelly, custard and cream.

For the trifle sponge
4 medium eggs, separated
125g caster sugar
125g plain flour
½ tsp baking powder
1 tbsp granulated sugar, for sprinkling

For the custard
300ml whole milk
300ml double cream
1 vanilla pod, split lengthways
4 large egg yolks
3 tbsp cornflour
2 tbsp caster sugar

For the fruit jelly
2 x 135g packets strawberry jelly, broken into cubes
300ml boiling water
500ml cold water
400g strawberries, hulled and halved

For the topping
600ml whipping cream
1 chocolate Flake bar

For the trifle sponge, heat your oven to 190°C/Gas 5 and line a baking tin, about 20 x 27cm, with baking parchment.

In a large bowl, whisk the egg yolks with 50g of the caster sugar until the mixture is smooth, thickened and paler in colour. In another, clean bowl, whisk the egg whites until stiff, then gradually add the remaining caster sugar, whisking well between each addition, to make a smooth, glossy meringue. Gently fold the meringue into the egg yolk mixture, a spoonful at a time, until it is all incorporated.

Sift the flour and baking powder together over the mixture then fold in carefully, using a spatula, until evenly combined. Pour into the prepared tin and sprinkle the granulated sugar over the surface. Bake for 20 minutes, then lower the oven setting to 150°C/Gas 2 and bake for another 20 minutes. Transfer to a wire rack to cool.

To make the custard, pour the milk and cream into a pan. Scrape in the seeds from the vanilla pod and add the empty pod. Heat gently until the milk is almost boiling. Meanwhile, beat the egg yolks, cornflour and sugar together in a bowl. Discard the vanilla pod, then slowly pour the hot creamy milk onto the beaten mixture, whisking as you do so. Pour back into the pan and stir over a low heat until the custard thickens. Take off the heat and cover the surface with cling film to prevent a skin forming.

Put the jelly cubes into a heatproof bowl, pour on the boiling water and stir until the cubes melt. Add the 500ml cold water and stir.

Cut the sponge into squares and layer in the base of a serving bowl (about 25cm diameter and 10cm deep). Scatter over the strawberry halves, then cover with the jelly and refrigerate until set. Pour the custard over the jelly and chill to set again.

When ready to serve, whip the cream until thick and spread over the custard layer. Crumble the chocolate Flake over the surface to finish.

NO-BAKE CHEESECAKE

SERVES 6

There are different kinds of cheesecake and the no-bake version is the one from my childhood. The key is to have the right amount of gelatine to make it firm enough to slice but still gently creamy. Decorate the top as you like.

For the base

100g unsalted butter, melted, plus extra for greasing

150g digestive biscuits

For the filling

6.5g leaf gelatine (about 4 sheets Costa brand)

325g full-fat cream cheese

2 tbsp caster sugar

1 tsp vanilla extract

175ml double cream

60ml just-boiled water

For the topping

4g leaf gelatine (about 2½ sheets Costa brand)

150ml red berry juice (any flavour – it's the colour that matters)

150g fresh or defrosted frozen summer berries

Grease a 20cm loose-based cake tin with butter.

For the base, put the digestive biscuits into a strong plastic bag and bash with a rolling pin to a crumb-like texture. Tip into a bowl, add the melted butter and stir until all the crumbs are coated. Spoon into the prepared tin, press down firmly onto the base and chill until set firm.

For the filling, put the gelatine leaves into a heatproof bowl, cover with cold water and set aside to soften. Meanwhile, in a large bowl, mix the cream cheese with the caster sugar and vanilla extract, beating until smooth. In another bowl, whip the cream to soft peaks and then fold into the cream cheese mixture.

Lift the gelatine leaves out of their bowl and squeeze to remove any excess water. Pour away the water then put the gelatine back into the bowl. Immediately pour on the 60ml just-boiled water and stir until the gelatine has dissolved, then fold into the cream cheese mixture until well combined.

Pour the filling mixture onto the chilled biscuit base. Smooth and level the surface, using a small, angled palette knife or the back of a large spoon. Place in the fridge to set.

For the topping, put the gelatine leaves into a small heatproof bowl, cover with cold water and leave to soften. Heat the berry juice in a pan but do not let it boil. Squeeze the gelatine to remove any excess water and discard the water in the bowl. Put the gelatine back into the bowl, pour over the hot berry juice and stir to dissolve. Leave the liquid to cool until slightly thickened but still pourable.

Pour the thickened berry juice over the top of the set cheesecake and arrange the berries on top. Place in the fridge until set.

Carefully remove the cheesecake from the tin and transfer to a flat serving plate shortly before serving.

APPLE PIE

SERVES 6

My mum's fruit pies were really good. She'd put sugar on the top before baking and add a little bit more after, to create the sugar crumb coating – delicious. The Bramleys came from our garden. She liked to serve the pie warm with Bird's custard, never cream. My tip is to sprinkle custard powder onto the base of the pastry case: this avoids a soggy bottom by soaking up some of the juices; it also gives a hint of subtle custard flavour to the filling.

For the pastry
275g plain flour, plus extra for dusting
2 tbsp icing sugar
140g cold butter, cut into small dice
3–4 tbsp cold water

For the filling
3 large Bramleys or other cooking apples
4 tbsp caster sugar
3 tbsp water
2 tbsp custard powder

For the glaze
1 medium egg, beaten
3 tsp caster sugar, for dusting

For the pastry, mix the flour and icing sugar together in a bowl. Add the butter and rub in until the mixture resembles fine breadcrumbs. Using one hand, mix in just enough water to bring the pastry together and gently knead into a ball. Wrap in cling film and place in the fridge to rest while you make the filling.

Peel and core the apples, then cut into slices, about 4cm long and 5mm thick. Tip into a saucepan and add the caster sugar and water. Cook over a medium heat, stirring occasionally, until the apples soften but still hold their shape. Leave to cool.

Heat your oven to 200°C/Gas 6 and have a 24cm pie plate ready.

Divide the pastry into 2 pieces, roughly two-thirds and one-third. Lightly flour your work surface and roll out the larger piece of pastry to a 2–3mm thickness. Use this to line the base of the pie plate. Roll out the remaining pastry to form the lid for the pie and set aside.

Sprinkle the custard powder over the pastry base and spoon the cooled apple filling on top. Brush the pastry edges with some of the beaten egg, then lift the pastry lid on top. Press the pastry edges together and crimp with a fork or pinch between your thumb and finger, then trim away any excess. Use the pastry trimmings to make leaves or other decorations, sticking them on top of the pie with a little beaten egg.

Brush the top of the pie with beaten egg then sprinkle with 2 tsp of the caster sugar to glaze. Make 2 or 3 small slits in the top to let the steam out. Bake for 30–35 minutes, until the pastry is golden brown. Sprinkle an extra 1 tsp sugar over the surface.

Leave the pie to rest for 15 minutes before serving. Enjoy with ice cream, cream or custard.

CREAMY MUSHROOM VOL-AU-VENTS

MAKES 8

Vol-au-vents of various types often appeared at family gatherings when I was growing up. I liked a mushroom filling and remember using tinned mushroom soup as the base for a slightly dubious batch when I was at art school. This is a more refined version, with tasty dried porcini mushrooms and tarragon adding another layer of flavour to the button mushrooms.

500g block of ready-made all-butter puff pastry
Plain flour, for dusting
1 medium egg, beaten, to glaze

For the filling
10g dried porcini mushrooms, finely chopped
150ml just-boiled water
40g unsalted butter
100g baby button mushrooms, wiped and halved or quartered
20g plain flour
75ml double cream
1 tbsp finely chopped tarragon
Salt and black pepper

Line a large baking tray with baking parchment. Cut the puff pastry block in half. Roll out one half on a lightly floured surface to a 5mm thickness and use a 6.5cm fluted cutter to stamp out 8 rounds. Use a 3.5cm plain cutter to cut out the middles from these. The little rounds will form the vol-au-vent tops, while the rings will become the sides.

Roll out the other portion of puff pastry to a 3mm thickness and cut out 8 bases using the 6.5cm fluted cutter. Place the vol-au-vent bases and little tops on the prepared baking tray. Prick the bases with a fork, then brush the edge of each base with beaten egg and stick a pastry ring on top. Brush the surface of the rings and the little tops with beaten egg. Place in the fridge for 30 minutes. Meanwhile, heat your oven to 200°C/Gas 6.

Bake the vol-au-vent cases for 15–20 minutes until risen, crisp and golden. Transfer to a wire rack to cool.

To make the filling, put the dried porcini in a small heatproof bowl, add the boiled water and leave to soak for at least 30 minutes. Heat 20g of the butter in a frying pan until melted and foaming then add the button mushrooms. Cook on a high heat until starting to turn golden. Season with salt and pepper then remove from the pan and set aside.

Melt the remaining 20g butter in the pan, then stir in the flour. Add a little of the soaked porcini with some of the liquor, stirring as it comes to the boil. Continue to slowly add the porcini and liquor until you have a smooth, thick sauce. Stir in the button mushrooms and cream. Taste to check the seasoning and add the chopped tarragon.

Fill the cooked vol-au-vent cases with the mushroom mixture, top with the pastry lids and serve.

NAN'S MINCE & ONION PLATE PIE

SERVES 4–6

As a kid I loved my nan's mince, onion and potatoes. That's all it was – minced beef, onion and potato, but boy did it taste good. This is the original recipe, which has been turned into a simple plate pie that nan would approve of. I love the crispness, flavour and gloss you get from the lard in the pastry. (I've used the same filling to create the posh puff pastry pithivier on page 55.)

For the pastry
300g plain flour, plus extra for dusting
A pinch of fine salt
80g cold unsalted butter, cut into small dice
70g cold lard, cut into small dice
4–6 tbsp cold water
1 medium egg, beaten, to glaze

For the mince and onion filling
1 tbsp sunflower or vegetable oil
400g beef mince
1 onion, chopped
1 tbsp plain flour
1 large potato, peeled and cut into bite-sized dice
300ml water
1 beef stock cube
Salt and white pepper

First make the filling. Heat the oil in a wide pan over a high heat. When hot, add the mince and onion and cook until the meat begins to brown, stirring from time to time to separate any lumps of meat. Lower the heat, add the flour and cook, stirring, for 2–3 minutes.

Add the potato and water, then crumble in the stock cube. Season with salt (allowing for the saltiness of the stock cube) and pepper. Bring to the boil, then cover, lower the heat and simmer for 20–25 minutes until the gravy thickens and the potatoes are cooked through. Taste and add more salt and/or pepper if needed. Allow to cool, then chill.

To make the pastry, put the flour and salt into a bowl. Add the butter and lard and rub in using your fingertips until the mixture resembles breadcrumbs. Add just enough cold water to bring the dough together. Form into a ball, wrap in cling film and rest in the fridge for 30 minutes.

Heat your oven to 200°C/Gas 6. Have ready a 23cm metal pie plate. Divide the pastry into two pieces, roughly two-thirds and one-third. Lightly dust your work surface with flour and roll out the smaller piece into a circle, about 3mm thick and slightly larger than your pie plate. Line the pie plate with this piece of pastry. Roll out the remaining pastry to a larger circle, about 26cm, ready to use as a lid.

Spoon the chilled filling into the pastry-lined dish. Brush the pastry edges with beaten egg, then lift the pastry lid over the filling. Crimp the pastry edges firmly together with a fork, or pinch together using your thumb and forefinger, then trim away any excess pastry. Brush the top with beaten egg and make a small slit to let out the steam.

Bake the pie for 30–35 minutes until golden brown. Leave to rest for 10–15 minutes before serving.

BEEF & POTATO PITHIVIER

SERVES 4–6

This appealing French pie takes my nan's mince and onion filling (see page 52) to another level. In this recipe, it's important to use good puff pastry, made with butter – I prefer to roll out a block but you can use pre-rolled – and to mark it carefully with the tip of a knife in the traditional way.

- 500g block of ready-made all-butter puff pastry
- 1 quantity mince and onion filling (see page 52), cooked and chilled
- 1 medium egg, beaten, to glaze

Cut the puff pastry block into two pieces, roughly two-thirds and one-third. Roll the smaller piece of pastry to a 4mm thickness and cut out a 25cm diameter circle for the pie base. Lift this onto a baking tray. Roll out the remaining pastry and cut out a larger circle, about 28cm, for the pie lid.

Spoon the chilled mince and onion filling onto the pastry base, leaving a 2cm clear margin around the edge. Brush the pastry edge with beaten egg. Lift the pie lid into position over the filling and press the pastry edges together to seal.

Use the tip of a sharp knife to score two horizontal lines around the side of the pie (this helps it to rise better). Brush the top of the pie with beaten egg. Now lightly score parallel curved lines, radiating from the centre to the edge of the pastry; this is to create a decorative effect – don't cut through the pastry. Make a small hole in the centre of the pie to let out the steam.

Place the pie in the fridge for at least 30 minutes to rest. Meanwhile, heat your oven to 200°C/Gas 6.

Bake the pie for 35–40 minutes, until the pastry is risen and golden. Leave to stand for at least 5 minutes before cutting.

FINGER ROLLS
FOR HOT DOGS OR FISH FINGERS

MAKES 12

These long rolls, with their soft, slightly sweet centre, are the perfect casing for hot dogs or fish fingers, so I've also included a great recipe for home-made fish fingers opposite. Before cooking them, I coat the fish in salt and sugar, then wash it off. This draws out some of the moisture and means you get a firmer texture and better flavour.

- 500g strong white bread flour, plus extra for dusting
- 10g instant dried yeast
- 10g fine salt
- 40g caster sugar
- 50g unsalted butter, cut into small dice, softened
- 170ml whole milk
- About 150ml cold water
- Oil, for oiling

Put the flour into a large bowl and add the yeast to one side and the salt and sugar to the other. Add the butter, milk and three-quarters of the water. Stir the mixture together with the fingers of one hand. Gradually add the remaining water a little at a time until all the flour is incorporated and you have a rough dough. The dough should be soft but not soggy. (You may not need all the water or you may need a little more; it depends on the flour.)

Tip the dough out onto a lightly floured surface and knead it for 5–10 minutes. At first it will be wet but as you knead it will become smooth and silky.

Place the dough in a lightly oiled bowl, cover and leave to rise until doubled in size. This will take at least an hour and can take up to 3 hours, depending on the temperature. Line two baking trays with baking parchment.

Divide the dough into 12 equal pieces. Roll each into a ball between the palms of your hands, then roll into fingers, about 12cm long, on a lightly floured surface. Place 6 fingers on each of the prepared trays, leaving a 1cm gap between to allow a little room for them to expand – but not too much as you want them to be touching once risen.

Place each tray in a large, clean plastic bag and leave to prove for 45–60 minutes, until doubled in size. Meanwhile, heat your oven to 220°C/Gas 7.

Remove the trays from the plastic bags. Dust the finger rolls with flour and bake for 10–15 minutes, until golden brown. Leave on the trays for 5 minutes, then transfer to a wire rack to cool. They are perfect filled with sausages and ketchup, or the fish fingers on the opposite page.

HOME-MADE FISH FINGERS

Cut 400g skinned and boned haddock or cod loin fish into 12 fingers, each about 8cm long and 1.5cm wide. Mix 70g fine salt and 70g caster sugar together in a bowl. Coat each fish finger in the salt and sugar mix then place on a baking tray. Leave for 30 minutes or so, to draw out any liquid from the fish and firm up the flesh. Take 3 shallow bowls: put 50g plain flour in one, lightly beat 2 large eggs in another, and tip 150g golden breadcrumbs into the third.

Carefully rinse all the salt and sugar from the fish and pat dry with kitchen paper. Dip each fish finger in flour, dusting off any excess, then dip in the egg and finally coat in the breadcrumbs. Dip each fish finger again in the egg and crumbs to give a second coating. In a large frying pan, heat enough sunflower oil to shallow-fry the fish fingers. Fry them in batches until golden brown and crispy, turning once.

SESAME-TOPPED BUNS
FOR BURGERS

MAKES 8

The first burger I ever ate was at a Wimpy, when that restaurant chain was the coolest thing on the planet. Here's my recipe for home-made buns with sesame seeds on top, to make your burger special. I've also given a recipe for the burgers, as making your own means you can use good-quality mince and add extra tasty seasoning.

500g strong white bread flour, plus extra for dusting
7g fine salt
7g instant dried yeast
40g unsalted butter, cut into small dice, softened
2 tsp caster sugar
About 225ml whole milk
About 100ml cold water
50g sesame seeds, for sprinkling
Oil, for oiling

Put the flour into a large bowl and add the salt to one side and the yeast to the other. Tip in the butter pieces and sugar. Combine the milk and water in a jug, then pour three-quarters into the flour mixture and turn the mixture around with the fingers of one hand to mix. Continue to add the remaining liquid, a little at a time, until all the flour is incorporated. The dough needs to be soft, but not soggy. (You may not need all the liquid or you may need a little more; it depends on the flour.)

Tip the dough out onto a lightly floured surface and knead it for 5–10 minutes until smooth and elastic. Place in a lightly oiled bowl, cover and leave to rise for about an hour. Line two baking trays with baking parchment.

Tip the dough onto a lightly floured surface and knead to knock out any air. Divide the dough into 8 equal pieces and shape each into a smooth ball by placing it in a cage formed by your cupped hand on the work surface and moving your hand around in a circular motion, rotating the ball rapidly. Place on the trays, allowing room to spread.

Place each baking tray in a large, clean plastic bag and leave the rolls to prove until doubled in size. This will take about an hour or longer, depending on the temperature. Heat your oven to 200°C/Gas 6.

Just before baking, remove the trays from the plastic bags. Brush the tops of the rolls with water and sprinkle with sesame seeds. Bake for 15 minutes then lower the oven setting to 160°C/Gas 3 and bake for a further 5–10 minutes, until risen and golden brown. Transfer to a wire rack to cool.

MY HOME-MADE BURGERS

Heat 2 tsp oil in a frying pan and cook 1 diced, small onion gently until softened; leave to cool. Put 100g fresh breadcrumbs into a large bowl, pour on 100ml milk and leave to soak for 5 minutes or until all the milk is absorbed. Add 600g good-quality minced beef, the cooled onion, 1 crushed garlic clove, 1 tsp mustard powder, ½ tsp celery salt and ½ tsp fine salt. Work with your hands, squeezing the mixture together so it is thoroughly combined.

Divide the mixture into 8 equal pieces, roll into balls and flatten to shape into burgers. Cover loosely with cling film and refrigerate for at least 30 minutes to firm up slightly until ready to cook.

Heat your grill to high. Place the burgers on a baking tray and grill, about 6–7cm from the heat, for 6 minutes. Turn over and cook the other side for 6 minutes or until the meat is cooked through. Serve each burger in a sesame-topped bun with lettuce, sliced tomato, gherkins, sliced red onion and mayonnaise.

BEGINNER'S BREAD

APPRENTICE BAKER

I DEFY ANYONE TO MAKE one loaf and never make another. All it takes is that little bit of ambition to have a go in the first place – and it's easier than you think.

Bread-making machines can be a good way to start, as all you have to do is weigh up ingredients and then leave the machine to it. The next step is to make a loaf that you knead yourself; you'll have more control this way because when you touch a dough, you can feel that it's lively and good, and you can smell it as well.

How did I learn? In my mid-teens, I'd followed my mum's path and went to Wallasey Art School, where I got particularly into sculpture. My dad now lived in York and had a chain of about eighteen bakeries. When Dad asked me if I wanted to become a baker, I initially said no. Then he offered to pay me £500 – a lot of money in those days – if I'd cut my long hair and join the industry. That put things in a different light for a seventeen-year-old! I set out to become a baker.

My dad put me to work with the best guys he had at each of the bakeries, to train me in their particular skills; they were mostly old school bakers and all great at their jobs. I also picked up the basic know-how of working in a bakery, such as not to just grab a tray but always tap it first to avoid getting burnt.

Being the son of the boss means you always get the toughest jobs. I had a lot to prove, so I had to work twice as hard as anyone else. The shift started at one o'clock in the morning and we finished about ten hours later.

I used to like working through the night, when it was quiet, finishing midway through the day with a huge sense of relief. But this was six days a week and it was gruelling work. I was only young when I started, and I was working alongside big stocky lads from Bootle. These lads were much bigger than me and they were lugging flour bags I could barely lift – a minimum of 16kg and you'd sometimes carry a couple on each shoulder when the flour delivery for the week came on a Thursday. You build up your body quickly carrying sacks like that, as well as big hot trays on your fingertips. Within six months, I was as quick and strong as they were.

When you begin as an apprentice baker, you're a mixing lad or a table hand. Mixing starts with measuring. This is as important for the home baker as for the professional. If you don't weigh up the ingredients properly at the beginning – a half ounce out, either way – you've screwed up the whole process. And, just as for the home baker, the quality of the ingredients has got to be right: put rubbish in, you'll get rubbish out.

The next job I learnt was to 'scale off' 1lb or 2lb pieces of dough on an old-fashioned scale with weights on one side and a pan on the other. You had to do it quick: bang, bang, bang, bang. There might be six or seven guys waiting to mould the dough into cobs, cottage loaves or tin loaves.

After that, you moved on to the table. Moulding is a manual skill. Once you've got it, it never leaves you. Some are faster than others; I tended to be fairly quick. I am rubbish at academic stuff, but manual? You show me something once and I won't stop until I've mastered it.

Finally comes the most important job – and this person really runs the bakery – feeding the oven. My first was an eight-foot oven with five decks and three trays on each one. It was huge and made your back strain from lifting trays and filling it from top to bottom. You cannot, *cannot* have an empty space in the oven from the moment you start to the end of the day. Electric or gas, that oven's costing you money and you have to keep it baking at all times.

You spend the whole shift juggling and figuring out where the heat is in your oven and the best position to bake things in. Every deck has its own character. You have to know where the

hot spots are, the best place for the Genoise or the barm cakes. Learn to love your oven and it can be your best friend – or else it can be your worst enemy.

In a bakery shift, you start with the breads. Because they need the greatest heat, they go in when the oven has been fired up. You pop the meringues in last thing, when the oven is cooling down, leave the oven door open and take the trays out the next day, first thing. Early on, I made the classic mistake of coming in, closing the oven door, firing up the oven and burning all the meringues.

My dad's chain of bakeries was what we called 'hot bread shops', designed so you could see and talk to the baker working at the back. Old dears would come in and say, 'Put that loaf back in and burn it for me.' They like bread darker in the North, with more of a caramel colour and a crust; down South they prefer it lighter. Looking back, working in this type of shop meant I saw that bakers didn't have to be stuck away but could be out and about, talking about what we do.

One day when I was working in the Lincoln shop, the head baker didn't turn up. As assistant baker, I took over. It all turned out beautifully. I was really proud of the cakes, scones, pies, breads, baps, barms, sticks, tin breads. Everything was great. I thought: I understand now. All it took was someone to be off for me to take responsibility and to do it myself.

The lessons I learnt translate to home baking. First of all, get stuck in. Making bread is so satisfying and every time you learn more about each stage. Get a decent set of digital scales and weigh your ingredients accurately. Get your oven clean so you haven't got hot spots in there. Try not to open the oven door too often. Ideally, have an oven with a glass front and clean the front window, then either turn the light on inside or use a torch if you need to look inside without opening the door. Make the same recipe several times and, best of all, take notes of what the difference is between bakes.

The initial mixing of the dry ingredients takes place in a large bowl. The flour goes in first, followed by the salt and yeast. It's important to keep these two ingredients separate – adding them to opposite sides of the bowl – as the salt will slow down (or even kill) the yeast in its concentrated form.

Different flours absorb different amounts of water. Add about three-quarters of the water quantity given in a recipe and mix it into the flour with your hands, adding as much as you need of the rest, or some more. You learn how to feel how much water is needed through experience. For continental breads or sourdough loaves with a more open structure, wetter is better. It is easier to mix very wet doughs, such as baguette dough, in a food mixer.

You then tip the whole dough out onto a work surface. If it's a dough with butter in it, I'd use a little dusting of flour. For other doughs, I began to advise oiling the work surface because so many people were coming up to me and saying that their bread was tight, with small holes and a poor rise. This can partly be down to putting too much flour on the work surface as you knead. By oiling the surface instead, you keep the dough soft, it doesn't stick so much and, crucially, you don't get any more flour going in.

There is no hard-and-fast rule for kneading bread. Some people slap a wet dough on the work surface, some people stretch it. I tend to constantly roll, roll, stretch, stretch. Each of these techniques builds up the gluten that makes the bread rise and hold its shape. Everyone has a way that works for them.

You then need to let the dough rise. Slower is better as it means more flavour. That's why I recommend using cold rather than warm water and leaving the dough in a cool place – even the fridge sometimes – so that the yeast works less quickly. Some of the doughs in this chapter use relatively little yeast, which also promotes a slow rise.

After the initial rise, you need to knock back and shape the dough. Knocking back gets rid of the air pockets and creates a uniform texture so the dough rises evenly. To do this and to shape the dough, for most breads you just fold and fold. It's a bit like folding paper: the dough becomes stronger, and the finished loaf is more able to hold its shape. This is especially important for breads you make without a tin. For baguettes, I let the dough rise in a square or rectangular tub that's not too deep – an old ice-cream tub works well – so you can tip the dough onto the work surface without losing too much air. You then knock it back less, and shape the loaf more carefully.

Next comes the final rise, or proving. Give dough plenty of time to prove. Again, you learn by touch when a loaf is ready to go in the oven: it should spring back when gently pressed with a finger. You want to catch the dough when it is at the top of its rise, before the yeast is exhausted and the dough stops rising and starts to slacken.

For novices, I'd recommend starting with soda bread, without a shadow of a doubt. It's simple and doesn't need proving at all. Kids won't be bored and it'll take 45 minutes from the time you start to the time you bring it out of the oven. The next stage is making bread in a tin. There's only one way that a tin bread can rise, and that's up. Then make rolls and build up to bigger cobs. Finally you can get on to sourdough, which is more complex and harder to handle but worth the effort; for some it's really the ultimate bread.

Once you've finished your loaf and it's come out of the oven, the killer is leaving it to cool when all you want to do is eat it. Leave it on your wire rack, admire it, photograph it, Instagram it, Tweet it, tell all your friends. *Then* you slice it.

The time you really want your own loaf is in the morning when you wake up and remember that you've got that bread downstairs that you made yesterday. Stick a slice in the toaster. Butter, jam or marmalade, mug of tea, first bite: that's when you realise your life has changed forever.

FLOURY BAPS

MAKES 12

These are my version of the rolls that my dad made at the weekend and left to prove in front of our gas fire. This was the first recipe that really showed me the magic of bread; how ingredients put together from the cupboard would mysteriously rise and then make a bake with a beautiful home-made taste.

500g strong white bread flour, plus extra for dusting
7g instant dried yeast
7g fine salt
40g caster sugar
40g unsalted butter, cut into small pieces, softened
About 320ml cold water
Oil, for oiling

Put the flour into a large bowl and add the yeast to one side and the salt and sugar to the other. Add the butter and about three-quarters of the water. Turn the mixture around with the fingers of one hand to mix, gradually adding more of the water, until you have picked up all the flour. The dough needs to be soft but not soggy. (You may not need all of the water or you may need a little more; it depends on the flour.)

Tip the dough out onto a lightly floured surface and knead it for 5–10 minutes. At first the dough will be wet but as you knead it will become smooth and silky.

Place the dough in a lightly oiled bowl, cover with a clean tea towel and leave to rise until doubled in size. This will take at least an hour and can take 2–3 hours or longer.

Tip the dough out onto a lightly floured surface and fold it inwards repeatedly until all the air is knocked out. At this stage, you're starting to form the structure of the dough so it rises upwards rather than spreading outwards.

Divide the dough into 12 equal pieces. (Until you can instinctively determine the correct size of each roll, it's a good idea to weigh the whole dough and divide the figure by 12, then check you have the correct weight for each piece.)

Lightly dust your work surface with flour. Shape each piece of dough into a smooth ball by placing it in a cage formed by your cupped hand on the work surface and moving your hand around in a circular motion, rotating the ball rapidly. Sit the rolls on a floured surface and cover with a clean tea towel. Leave to rest for 30 minutes. Line two baking trays with baking parchment.

Remove the tea towel and use a rolling pin to flatten each ball of dough so it doubles in width. Place on the prepared trays, leaving enough space in between for them to expand.

Place each tray in a large, clean plastic bag and leave to prove for 45–60 minutes, or until doubled in size. Meanwhile, heat your oven to 220°C/Gas 7.

Remove the trays from the bags and lightly dust the surface of the rolls with flour. Bake for 10–15 minutes or until risen and golden brown. Leave to cool on the tray for 5 minutes and then transfer to a wire rack to finish cooling.

TV ROLLS

MAKES 6

These are known as 'TV rolls' because of the square mould used to cut them out in bakeries, including my dad's. You'll discover that they go slightly odd shapes when they bake, but that doesn't matter.

- 500g strong white bread flour, plus extra for dusting
- 10g instant dried yeast
- 10g fine salt
- 20g unsalted butter, cut into small pieces, softened
- About 320ml cold water
- Oil, for oiling

Put the flour into a large bowl and add the yeast to one side and the salt to the other. Add the butter and pour in three-quarters of the water. Turn the mixture around with the fingers of one hand to mix then continue to add more of the water, a little at a time, until all the flour is incorporated and you have a rough dough. The dough needs to be soft but not soggy. (You may not need all the water or you may need a little more; it depends on the flour.)

Turn the dough out onto a lightly floured surface and knead it for 5–10 minutes, working through the wet stage until it becomes soft and smooth.

Put the dough into a lightly oiled bowl, cover with a clean tea towel and leave to rise until doubled in size. This will take at least an hour and can take 2–3 hours or longer, depending on the room temperature. Line a roasting tin (not a shallow baking tray) with baking parchment.

Tip the dough onto a lightly floured work surface and fold it inwards repeatedly to knock out the air.

Shape the dough into a chunky rectangle, 4–5cm high. Cut this into 6 equal squares, using a sharp knife or pizza wheel. Place the rolls in the prepared tin, leaving enough space in between for them to double in size.

Place the roasting tin in a large, clean plastic bag and leave to prove for about an hour until the rolls have doubled in size. The dough is ready when it springs back when lightly prodded. Meanwhile, heat your oven to 200°C/Gas 6.

Remove the tin from the bag and dust the rolls with flour. Bake for 15 minutes, or until the rolls are risen and golden brown. Transfer to a wire rack to cool.

SPLIT TIN LOAF

MAKES 1 LARGE LOAF

This is the staple white bread that my dad used to make in his bakeries. It uses a small amount of yeast and a lengthy eight-hour fermentation, because allowing the dough to rise slowly gives the best flavour.

- 500g strong white bread flour, plus extra for dusting
- 2g instant dried yeast (½ tsp)
- 10g fine salt
- 40g unsalted butter, cut into small pieces, softened
- About 320ml cold water
- Oil, for oiling

Put the flour into a large bowl and add the yeast to one side and the salt to the other. Don't put the salt onto the yeast, as it can kill the yeast, or at the very least slow it down.

Add the butter and three-quarters of the water. Turn the mixture around with the fingers of one hand to mix and continue to add the remaining water, a little at a time, until all the flour is incorporated. The dough needs to be soft but not soggy. (You may not need all of the water or you may need a little more; it depends on the flour.)

Tip the dough out onto a lightly floured surface and knead it for 5–10 minutes. Work it well, going through the initial wet stage until the dough becomes smooth and elastic.

Put the dough into a lightly oiled bowl, cover with a clean tea towel and leave to rise in a cool place (but not the fridge) for at least 8 hours or overnight. Taking time over this stage helps the dough to develop more flavour.

Lightly oil a 900g (2lb) loaf tin. Tip the dough onto a lightly floured surface and fold it inwards repeatedly until all the air is knocked out. At this stage, you are starting to form the structure of the dough to encourage it to rise upwards rather than spreading outwards (the tin also helps with this).

Shape the dough into an oblong by flattening it and folding the sides into the middle. Roll up the dough so the top is smooth and you have a join in the middle on the underside. Place the dough in the prepared tin with the join underneath.

Put the loaf tin inside a large, clean plastic bag and leave the loaf to prove until it has doubled in size. This will take at least an hour and can take 2–3 hours. The dough is ready when it springs back quickly when gently prodded with a finger. Meanwhile, heat your oven to 220°C/Gas 7 and place a roasting tin in the bottom.

Remove the proved loaf from the bag. Dust the surface of the loaf with flour and then use a sharp knife to make a 2cm deep slash along the top, nearly to the ends. Carefully pour enough hot water into the tin in the oven to almost fill it – this will create steam.

Bake the loaf for 15 minutes then lower the oven setting to 190°C/ Gas 5 and bake for a further 25–30 minutes. Remove the loaf from the tin and tap the base: it should sound hollow. If not, put the loaf back in the tin and return to the oven for another 5 minutes. Remove the loaf from the tin and transfer to a wire rack. Leave to cool completely.

WHOLEMEAL TIN LOAF

MAKES 1 LARGE LOAF

Wholemeal flour keeps the best bits of the wheat kernel and more of the fibre than white flour, resulting in a loaf with more nutrients and flavour – you can really taste the earthiness, especially if you use stoneground flour. It's one of my favourite ingredients and makes a loaf that I love. Like the split tin loaf on the previous page, it has a small amount of yeast and a long, slow fermentation, to allow the dough to rise slowly for optimum flavour.

350g strong stoneground wholemeal bread flour, plus extra for dusting the loaf
150g strong white bread flour, plus extra for dusting the work surface
2g instant dried yeast (½ tsp)
10g fine salt
40g unsalted butter, cut into small pieces, softened
20g malt extract
About 340ml cold water
Oil, for oiling

Put both flours into a large bowl and add the yeast to one side and the salt to the other. Add the butter, malt extract and about three-quarters of the water. Turn the mixture around with the fingers of one hand to mix (or use a round-bladed knife first and then your fingers) and continue to add more of the water, a little at a time, until all of the flour is incorporated. The dough needs to be soft but not soggy. (You may not need all of the water or you may need a little more; it depends on the flour.)

Tip the dough out onto a lightly floured work surface and knead for 5–10 minutes, working the dough through the initial wet stage until it is smooth and silky.

Place the dough in a lightly oiled bowl. Cover with a clean tea towel and leave to rise in a cool place (but not the fridge) for at least 8 hours or overnight. This long, slow rise allows plenty of time for the flavour to develop.

Lightly oil a 900g (2lb) loaf tin. Tip the dough onto a lightly floured surface and fold it inwards repeatedly until all the air is knocked out.

Shape the dough into an oblong by flattening it and folding the sides into the middle. Roll up the dough so the top is smooth and you have a join in the middle on the underside. Place in the prepared loaf tin with the join underneath.

Put the tin inside a large, clean plastic bag and leave until doubled in size. This will take at least an hour and can take 2–3 hours, depending on the room temperature. When you prod it lightly with your finger, the dough should spring back quickly. Meanwhile, heat your oven to 220°C/Gas 7 and put a roasting tin in the bottom.

Remove the tin from the plastic bag and dust the surface of the loaf with wholemeal flour. Use a sharp knife to make a 2cm deep slash along the top, almost to the ends. Carefully pour enough hot water into the roasting tin in the oven to almost fill it – this will create steam.

Bake the loaf for 15 minutes then lower the oven setting to 190°C/ Gas 5 and bake for a further 25–30 minutes.

Remove the loaf from the tin and tap the base: it should sound hollow. If not, put back in the tin and bake for another 5 minutes. Remove the loaf from the tin and transfer to a wire rack. Leave to cool completely.

COTTAGE LOAF

MAKES 1 LARGE LOAF

Traditionally, bakers used to bake what were called 'oven bottom breads' on the floor of the oven in order to get a heavier, tastier crust. At home, we bake such loaves on a tray and the recipe can be formed into any shape you like – cob, bloomer or, as here, into a classic cottage loaf. Make sure you shape the loaf well so it rises and holds without the help of a loaf tin.

- 500g strong white bread flour, plus extra for dusting
- 5g instant dried yeast
- 7g fine salt
- 50g lard, cut into small pieces, softened
- About 350ml cold water
- Oil, for oiling

Put the flour into a large bowl and add the yeast to one side and the salt to the other. Add the lard and pour in about three-quarters of the water. Turn the mixture around with the fingers of one hand to mix then continue to add more of the water, a little at a time, until all the flour is incorporated. The dough needs to be soft but not soggy. (You may not need all the water or you may need a little more; it depends on the flour.)

Tip the dough onto a lightly oiled surface and knead for 5–10 minutes, working through the initial wet stage until it is smooth and silky.

Place the dough in a lightly oiled bowl, cover with a clean tea towel and leave to rise until doubled in size. This will take at least an hour and can take 2–3 hours or longer, depending on the room temperature. Line a baking tray with baking parchment.

Tip the dough out onto a lightly floured surface and fold it inwards repeatedly until all the air is knocked out. At this stage, you're starting to form the structure of the dough so it rises upwards rather than spreading outwards. This is especially important in a free-standing loaf without a tin to support the bread's rise.

Tear off a third of the dough and set aside. Shape the larger piece into a ball. To do this, first flatten the dough into a rough rectangle then roll it up into a thick oblong. Repeat this several times, getting the dough nice and tight. Now fold the two ends in towards the centre and press them down, so you end up with a chunky, squarish shape. Turn the dough over, so that the join is underneath.

Continued overleaf

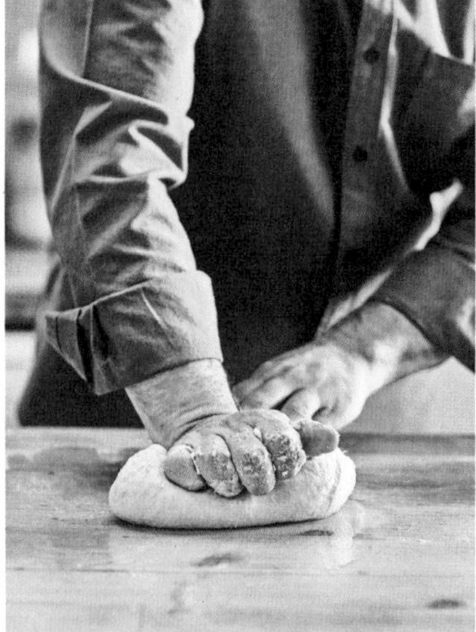

With your palms turned upwards, put your hands on each side, slightly under the dough. Move the cob around, slightly pushing the dough neatly under itself as it turns. You are gently forcing the sides of the dough down and underneath, to create a smooth, taut top. Try to avoid using too much extra flour during shaping if you can. Slightly flatten the ball of dough and place on the prepared baking tray.

Shape the other piece of dough into a smaller ball, using the same technique, and flatten slightly. Place the smaller ball on top of the larger ball. Dust your middle finger and forefinger with flour and push them through the centre of the loaf all the way to the bottom. This helps to join the two pieces firmly together.

Use a sharp knife to make vertical slashes at even intervals around the top and lower parts of the loaf.

Place the tray inside a large, clean plastic bag and leave the dough to prove for at least an hour, or until well risen. When prodded lightly with your finger, the dough should spring back quickly. Don't rush this stage; if the shaped loaf is under-proved it can spring up in the oven and tip over. Meanwhile, heat your oven to 220°C/Gas 7.

Remove the proved loaf from the bag and dust with flour. Bake for 15 minutes, then lower the oven setting to 190°C/Gas 5 and bake for a further 20–25 minutes, until crusty and golden brown.

When tapped on the bottom, the loaf should sound hollow. If not, put it back into the oven for another 5 minutes. Transfer the cooked loaf to a wire rack to cool.

GRANARY STICKS

MAKES 6

Granary (or malted) flour changed the way people thought of bread when it became popular in the seventies and eighties. It is essentially white flour with added flakes of malted wheat, and a nutty flavour. We called these 'sticks' in the bakeries where I worked because they are long, thin rolls, like mini-baguettes. You'll need to make the dough a day ahead, as it has a long, slow rise.

Olive oil, for oiling
150g strong white bread flour, plus extra for dusting
225g granary (malted) flour
5g instant dried yeast
7g fine salt
350ml cold water

Lightly oil a 2–3 litre rectangular or square plastic container, such as an ice-cream tub. (It's important to use this type of container as it helps shape the dough and improve its structure.)

Put the flours into a food mixer fitted with the dough hook. (As this dough is wet and tricky to handle, and needs a long knead, it's far easier to use a mixer.) Add the yeast to one side and the salt to the other. Start mixing on a slow speed, then slowly add the water.

As the dough starts to come together, continue to mix on a slow speed for 5 minutes and then increase the speed to medium and mix for a further 10–15 minutes or until you have a glossy, elastic dough. The dough should be very elastic and when pulled it should stretch so it's almost transparent without breaking. If it breaks, continue to mix for another 5 minutes.

Tip the dough into the prepared tub, cover with a clean tea towel and leave it to rise in the fridge for 24 hours. Line two baking trays with baking parchment, or use a bread stick tray.

Coat the work surface with a little olive oil then carefully tip the dough onto it. Rather than knocking it back, handle the dough gently so you keep as much air in as possible. This helps to create the irregular, airy texture of a really good baguette. The dough will be wet to the touch but still lively.

Divide the dough into 6 pieces. Shape each piece into an oblong by flattening the dough out slightly and folding the sides up into the middle. Then roll up each piece into a sausage – the top should be smooth with a join running along the length of the base.

Beginning in the middle, roll out each sausage with your hands to lengthen it. Don't force the dough to elongate by pressing heavily.

Concentrate on the backwards and forwards movement and gently use the weight of your arms to roll out the dough to about 15cm in length; the sticks should be about 5cm in diameter.

Lay the bread sticks on the prepared trays and place each tray inside a large, clean plastic bag. Leave to prove in the fridge for 24 hours. The long proving time helps the dough to develop more flavour.

Heat your oven to 220°C/Gas 7 and put a roasting tin in the bottom of the oven to heat up. Remove the trays from the bags and dust the bread sticks lightly with more white flour .

Carefully pour enough hot water into the roasting tin in the oven to almost fill it – this will create steam. Bake the granary sticks for 20 minutes or until they are golden brown and sound hollow when tapped on the bottom. Transfer to a wire rack to cool.

MILK LOAF

MAKES 1 LARGE LOAF

With its soft crumb and rich taste, this loaf is popular in the North and has always been a firm favourite in my family. Traditionally, it's made in a cylindrical tin marked with round circles, which helps prevent a thick crust forming and gives a soft, springy loaf.

- 500g strong white bread flour, plus extra for dusting
- 7g instant dried yeast
- 7g fine salt
- 60g unsalted butter, cut into small pieces, softened
- About 340ml whole milk
- Oil, for oiling

Put the flour in a large bowl and add the yeast to one side and the salt to the other. Add the butter and pour in about three-quarters of the milk. Turn the mixture around with the fingers of one hand to mix. Continue to add more of the milk until all the flour is incorporated. The dough needs to be soft but not soggy. (You may not need all the milk or you may need a little more; it depends on the flour.)

Tip the dough out onto a lightly floured surface and knead it for 5–10 minutes until you have a smooth dough.

Place the dough in a lightly oiled bowl, cover and leave to rise until doubled in size. This will take at least an hour and can take 2–3 hours or longer, depending on the room temperature.

Lightly grease a cylinder milk loaf tin or a 900g (2lb) loaf tin.

Tip the dough onto a lightly floured surface and fold it inwards repeatedly until all the air is knocked out.

Shape the dough into an oblong by flattening it and folding the sides into the middle. Roll up so the top is smooth and you have a join in the middle on the underside. Place the dough in the prepared tin with the join underneath.

Put the tin inside a large, clean plastic bag and leave to prove until the dough has doubled in size and springs back quickly when lightly prodded with a finger. Meanwhile, heat your oven to 200°C/Gas 6.

Remove the proved loaf from the bag. If using a milk loaf tin, place the other half of the tin on top and close. Bake the loaf for 30–35 minutes, until golden brown. Remove the loaf from the tin and place on a wire rack. Leave to cool completely.

FOUR-SEEDED MALTED BREAD

MAKES 1 LARGE LOAF

This is a loaf that I created for Mary Berry, packed with seeds. She likes it toasted with marmalade for breakfast and I would recommend you eat it that way too, or for lunch with a bowl of soup.

500g granary (malted) flour
5g instant dried yeast
10g fine salt
40g lard, cut into small pieces, softened
About 350ml cold water
Olive oil, for oiling
50g poppy seeds
50g linseeds (also known as flaxseed)
70g sunflower seeds
70g pumpkin seeds

For the topping
50g sesame seeds
50g linseeds (flaxseed)

Put the flour into a large bowl and add the yeast to one side and the salt to the other. Add the lard and pour in about three-quarters of the water. Turn the mixture around with the fingers of one hand to mix, adding more of the water until all the flour is incorporated. The dough needs to be soft but not soggy. (You may not need all the water or you may need a little more; it depends on the flour.)

Lightly oil your work surface then tip the dough onto it and knead for 5–10 minutes, working through the initial wet stage until it is smooth and silky.

Place the dough in a lightly oiled bowl, cover with a clean tea towel and leave to rise until doubled in size. This will take at least an hour and can take 2–3 hours or longer.

Meanwhile, mix the seeds for the loaf in a bowl and set aside. Put the seeds for the topping into a small bowl, cover with boiling water and leave to soak and swell while the dough is rising.

Tip the dough onto a lightly floured surface and knock out the air by folding it inwards repeatedly. Flatten into a rectangle and scatter the dry seed mix over the surface. Fold the dough repeatedly until the seeds are evenly incorporated.

Flatten the dough into a rectangle again and fold the sides up into the middle. Now roll up so you have a lozenge-shaped bloomer, with a smooth top and a join along the underside. Line a baking tray with baking parchment.

Spread out the soaked seeds on a tray. Roll the loaf in the seeds to form a seeded topping; make sure they cover the top and sides of the loaf. Place the loaf on the prepared baking tray with the join underneath.

Put the tray inside a large, clean plastic bag and leave the loaf to prove until it has risen and doubled in size. This will take at least an hour and may well take longer. The dough is ready when it springs back quickly when lightly prodded with a finger.

Heat your oven to 200°C/Gas 6 and place a roasting tin in the bottom of the oven.

Remove the tray from the bag. Using a sharp knife, make 3 diagonal cuts, about 2cm deep, in the top of the loaf.

Carefully pour enough hot water into the roasting tin in the oven to almost fill it – this will create steam. Slide the bread tray into the oven and bake for 15 minutes then lower the oven setting to 190°C/Gas 5. Bake the loaf for a further 25–30 minutes.

Remove the loaf from the tin and tap the base: it should sound hollow. If not, put the loaf back in the oven for 5 minutes or so. Once cooked, place the loaf on a wire rack to cool.

GARLIC BAGUETTES

MAKES 2 MINI BAGUETTES

Garlic bread was incredibly popular when I was growing up. This one has roasted garlic within the dough as well as plenty of garlic butter. You can make the dough by hand but it is wet and difficult to handle, plus it requires a long knead, so I'd recommend using a food mixer if you can. You'll need to prepare the dough a day ahead as it needs a long, slow rise.

100ml olive oil, plus extra for oiling
6 garlic cloves, peeled
250g strong white bread flour, plus extra for dusting
5g instant dried yeast
5g fine salt
160ml cold water

For the garlic butter
175g unsalted butter, softened
4 garlic cloves, roughly chopped
A small bunch or packet of flat-leaf parsley (28g), leaves picked
Salt and black pepper

Lightly oil a 2–3 litre square or rectangular plastic container, such as an ice-cream tub (a straight-sided container is important as it helps shape the dough). Put the olive oil and peeled whole garlic cloves into a small pan over a low heat and simmer gently for 15–20 minutes, until soft but not coloured. Remove the garlic with a slotted spoon and set aside to cool.

Put the flour into a food mixer fitted with the dough hook. Add the yeast to one side and the salt to the other and begin mixing on a slow speed. Now gradually add the water. As the dough starts to come together, add the cooled garlic cloves and continue to mix on a slow speed for 5 minutes.

Increase the speed to medium and mix for a further 10 minutes until you have a glossy, very elastic dough. When pulled, the dough should stretch so it's almost transparent without breaking. If it breaks, continue to mix for another 5 minutes.

Tip the dough into the prepared tub, cover and leave to prove in the fridge for 24 hours. Line a baking tray with baking parchment, or use a baguette tray.

Coat the work surface with a little olive oil and then carefully tip the dough onto it. Rather than knocking it back, handle the dough gently so you keep in as much air as possible. This will help to create the irregular, airy texture of a really good baguette. The dough will be wet to the touch but still lively.

Divide the dough in half. Shape each piece into an oblong by flattening the dough out slightly and folding the sides up into the middle. Turn over and carefully roll each piece of dough up into a sausage – the top should be smooth with a join underneath, running along the length of the base.

Beginning in the middle, roll out each sausage with your hands to elongate; don't force the dough to lengthen by pressing heavily. Concentrate on the backwards and forwards movement and gently use the weight of your arms to roll out the dough to a baguette shape.

Place the baguettes on the prepared tray and put it into a large, clean plastic bag. Leave to prove in the fridge for 24 hours.

Heat your oven to 220°C/Gas 7 and put a roasting tin in the bottom to heat up.

Remove the tray from the bag. Dust the baguettes lightly with flour. Use a sharp knife to make 3 or 4 long, diagonal slashes, about 2cm deep, in the top of each loaf.

Carefully pour enough hot water into the roasting tin in the oven to almost fill it – this will create steam. Slide the tray of bread into the oven and bake for 20 minutes, until the baguettes are golden brown and sound hollow when tapped on the bottom. Transfer to a wire rack to cool.

For the garlic butter, place all the ingredients in a food processor and mix until smooth.

To turn the baguettes into garlic bread, have your oven at 180°C/Gas 4. Make vertical cuts three-quarters of the way down into one baguette, at 4cm intervals (make sure you don't cut all the way through). Spread garlic butter into the gaps between the slices and then all over the surface of the baguette. Repeat with the other baguette.

Wrap each baguette in foil and bake for 15 minutes. Open the foil fully then bake for a further 5 minutes to crisp the bread.

Photographs overleaf

CARAMELISED ONION SODA BREAD

MAKES 1 LOAF

I love soda bread and I really like a good onion-flavoured loaf. The beauty of soda bread is that it's so simple to make, and with no proving required you achieve quick results. Adding extra flavours to a basic soda loaf, as I have done here, takes it to another level.

- 1 tbsp sunflower oil
- 15g unsalted butter
- 2 onions, finely sliced
- 1 tbsp soft dark brown sugar
- 2 bushy sprigs of thyme, leaves picked
- 1 tsp fine salt, plus a pinch for the onions
- 250g plain white flour, plus extra for dusting
- 250g plain wholemeal flour
- 1 tsp bicarbonate of soda
- 400ml buttermilk

Heat the oil and butter in a large frying pan. Once the butter has melted, add the onions and stir to coat. Cook slowly over a low heat, stirring occasionally, for about 20 minutes until the onions are softened. Add the sugar, thyme and a pinch of salt. Continue to cook until the onions turn golden brown, stirring occasionally to stop them burning. Tip onto a plate and leave to cool.

Heat your oven to 200°C/Gas 6 and line a large baking tray with baking parchment.

Put both flours into a large bowl with the salt and bicarbonate of soda and mix well. Make a well in the centre and add the caramelised onions and half the buttermilk. Use the fingers of one hand (or a round-bladed knife and then your fingers) to draw the flour into the buttermilk. Continue to add the buttermilk until all the flour has been incorporated and you have a sticky, malleable dough. You may not need all the buttermilk (depending on the flour – different brands absorb slightly more or less liquid).

Tip the dough onto a floured surface, shape into a ball and flatten slightly. Place on the prepared baking tray. Use a large sharp knife to mark the loaf into quarters, cutting deeply into the dough but not quite through the base. Dust the top of the loaf with flour.

Bake for 30–35 minutes until the loaf is golden brown and sounds hollow when tapped on the base. You can carefully cut along one of the seams to see if the inside is cooked through; if not, put the loaf back in the oven for 5 minutes or so.

Transfer to a wire rack to cool completely. Soda bread is best eaten on the day it is made, or at least within a day or two. It also freezes well.

STILTON & WALNUT SODA BREAD

MAKES 1 LOAF

Adding extra flavours to bread dough is popular these days but it was rare when I started out. Blue cheese works well in all types of bread and becomes even more special when combined with walnuts in this savoury soda bread.

- 500g plain white flour, plus extra for dusting
- 1 tsp fine salt
- 1 tsp bicarbonate of soda
- 100g walnut pieces
- 200g Stilton, crumbled
- 400ml buttermilk

Heat your oven to 200°C/Gas 6 and line a large baking tray with baking parchment.

Put the flour, salt and bicarbonate of soda into a large bowl and mix well. Add the walnuts and Stilton and stir gently. Make a well in the centre of the mixture and pour in half the buttermilk. Using the fingers of one hand (or a round-bladed knife and then your fingers), draw the flour into the buttermilk. Continue to add the buttermilk until all the flour has been incorporated and you have a sticky dough. You may not need all the buttermilk (different brands of flour absorb slightly more or less liquid).

Tip the dough onto a floured surface, shape into a ball and then flatten slightly. Place on the prepared baking tray. Use a large sharp knife to mark the loaf into quarters, cutting deeply into the dough but not quite through the base. Dust the top of the loaf with flour.

Bake for 30–35 minutes until the loaf is golden brown and sounds hollow when tapped on the base. You can carefully cut along one of the seams to see if the inside is cooked through; if not, put the loaf back in the oven for 5 minutes or so.

Transfer the soda bread to a wire rack and leave to cool completely. It is best eaten on the day it is made, or at least finished within a day or two. It also freezes well.

ROQUEFORT & ALMOND SOURDOUGH

MAKES 1 LARGE LOAF

I used to supply this bread to Harrods and at the time it hit the headlines as 'the most expensive bread in Britain', selling at £25 per loaf. To be fair, it was a big 2kg loaf – and the salty-sweet mix of blue cheese and nuts does turn humble bread into a star turn. A banneton – a special wicker proving basket – is especially useful for wetter doughs such as sourdoughs, to keep the shape and lift. You will need to prepare the starter a few days ahead.

For the sourdough starter
250g strong white bread flour
6 organic, seedless green grapes, chopped
250ml water

To refresh the starter (each time)
100g strong white bread flour
100ml water

For the loaf
Oil, for oiling
375g strong white bread flour, plus extra for dusting
200g sourdough starter (see above)
7g fine salt
About 175ml water
100g Roquefort, crumbled into small pieces
125g blanched almonds, chopped medium-fine
Fine semolina, for dusting

To prepare the starter, in a bowl, mix the flour with the grapes and water. Transfer this mixture to a Kilner jar, close the lid and leave to ferment at warm room temperature (ideally 20–24°C). After 2–3 days the mixture should have started to grow and look lively, with bubbles on the surface.

Once the mixture is active, discard half of it then add 100g flour and 100ml water. This process is called 'feeding' the mixture and should be repeated every few days for as long as you have your starter. (You can keep a starter dormant between loaves by storing it in the fridge, bringing it back to room temperature and starting the feeding process again before using it.)

After the starter has been fed, leave it for a day and the mixture should become thicker and have a jelly-like texture. Once at this stage it is ready to use.

For the loaf, lightly oil a 2–3 litre square or rectangular plastic container, such as an ice-cream tub. Mix the flour, starter and salt together in a large bowl then mix in just enough water to form a soft dough, using a spoon first, then your hands.

Lightly oil your work surface, tip the dough onto it and knead for at least 10 minutes until smooth and elastic.

Place the dough in the oiled plastic container and cover with cling film. Leave to rise until doubled in size. This can take up to 5 hours or longer, depending on the temperature and the vigour of your starter.

Continued overleaf

When the dough is ready, mix equal quantities of flour and semolina together in a small bowl and use to dust your work surface generously.

Gently tip the dough onto the surface and flatten into a rectangle. Scatter the cheese and chopped almonds over the surface then fold the dough in on itself a few times to incorporate them.

Flatten the dough into a rectangle again and bring the sides into the middle to meet, so you get a chunky squareish shape. Turn the dough over so the join is now on the bottom.

Shape the dough into a ball by cupping it with the sides of your hands and turning it around to create a smooth ball. (This is looser than a standard bread dough and so more difficult to handle; you can dust your hands with flour to make the task less sticky.)

Dust a round banneton basket or a medium bowl liberally with flour or the flour and semolina mix. Add the ball of dough, inverting it so that it sits smooth side down. Put inside a large, clean plastic bag and leave to prove until doubled in size. This is likely to take somewhere between 4 and 8 hours, possibly even longer. Don't rush this stage; it's important for developing the flavour and structure of the loaf.

Heat your oven to 220°C/Gas 7 and put a roasting tin in the bottom to heat up. Heavily dust a baking tray with the flour and semolina mix.

Tip the bread onto the tray and use a scalpel or sharp knife to slash a 2cm deep cross on the top.

Carefully pour enough hot water into the roasting tin in the oven to almost fill it – this will create steam.

Put the bread into the oven and bake for 20 minutes, then lower the oven setting to 200°C/Gas 6 and bake for a further 15 minutes. The loaf should be dark brown and sound hollow when tapped on the base. If not, put it back in the oven for another 5 minutes. Transfer the cooked loaf to a wire rack and leave to cool.

CRUMPETS

MAKES ABOUT 10

Crumpets get their texture from two different rising stages: first a rise with yeast, then one with bicarbonate of soda to create the characteristic holes. Slow cooking on a griddle or in a heavy frying pan gives the crumpets their brown base and flavour. They take a little practice to perfect; in particular, keep an eye on the heat throughout cooking. I've also included a tangy rarebit topping (overleaf) that turns them into a meal.

175g strong white bread flour
175g plain white flour
14g instant dried yeast
1 tsp caster sugar
350ml warm whole milk
About 200ml cold water
½ tsp bicarbonate of soda
1 tsp fine salt
Sunflower oil, for cooking

Put both flours into a large bowl and mix in the yeast. In a jug, dissolve the sugar in the warm milk, then pour onto the flour mixture. Use a wooden spoon to draw the dry ingredients into the liquid, then beat until the mixture forms a smooth batter. Beat the batter for a further 3 minutes.

Cover the bowl with a tea towel and leave to stand for 1 hour. The mixture will rise and then begin to fall – you will see marks on the side of the bowl where the batter reached before it dropped. This indicates that the yeast has created its carbon dioxide and is now exhausted. The gluten will have developed sufficiently to give the crumpets the structure to rise and hold their shape.

In a jug, mix 150ml water with the bicarbonate of soda and salt. Stir this into the batter until evenly combined, then gradually stir in as much of the remaining water as necessary to get a thick dropping consistency. Cover the bowl and leave the batter to rest for about 20 minutes. Small holes will appear on the surface and the batter will become a bit sticky.

Heat a flat griddle or heavy-based frying pan over a medium-low heat. Lightly but thoroughly grease the inside of at least four 7–8cm metal crumpet rings (ideally non-stick). Lightly grease the griddle or pan, using a crumpled kitchen paper dipped in oil.

It's a good idea to start with a trial crumpet to get used to the heat of the pan and how your batter will cook (the first one is never the best, like the first pancake). Put a greased crumpet ring on the griddle or in the frying pan. Ladle enough batter into it to come just below the top of the ring.

Continued overleaf

After 6–8 minutes, the bottom of the crumpet should be browned and the rest almost cooked through. The top of the crumpet will be drier and almost set, and most of the bubbles on the top will have burst. You can slightly speed up the cooking by popping these bubbles as they appear, with a skewer or the sharp tip of a knife; when the crumpet is ready, the bubbles will stay open rather than fill up with liquid batter.

Turn the crumpet over carefully, using a spatula and a palette knife. Leave the crumpet to cook for a few more minutes then lift it out onto a wire rack. Run a small, sharp knife around the outside of the crumpet to loosen it and remove from the ring.

Now you know the time and temperature needed for your batter, you are ready to cook the rest of the crumpets, in batches.

CRUMPETS WITH RAREBIT TOPPING

Have a batch of crumpets cooked and ready. For the rarebit topping, put 2 tbsp plain flour, 1¼ tsp mustard powder, 1 tsp Worcestershire sauce, 125ml milk or beer and 185g grated strong Cheddar into a saucepan. Bring to the boil, stirring, over a medium heat. Lower the heat and simmer until thickened and smooth, stirring constantly. Pour into a bowl and beat in 2 medium egg yolks. Cover with cling film and leave to cool, then refrigerate until needed. The rarebit will firm up once cold. Heat your grill to high. Toast the crumpets on both sides then place on a baking tray. Spread the rarebit on top of the crumpets and place under the grill until bubbling and golden brown. Eat at once.

ENGLISH MUFFINS

MAKES 8

A good English muffin – simply cut, toasted and buttered – is a thing of beauty, particularly if it's home-made. I used to make muffins for Eggs Benedict when I worked in hotels, and through doing this I discovered that the secret to good muffins is getting the heat just right and adjusting it as you cook.

300g strong white bread flour, plus extra for dusting
5g instant dried yeast
1 tsp fine salt
1 tbsp caster sugar
20g unsalted butter, cut into small pieces, softened
1 medium egg, beaten
About 200ml whole milk
Oil, for oiling
Fine semolina, for dusting

Put the flour into a large bowl and add the yeast to one side and the salt to the other. Add the sugar, butter, egg and three-quarters of the milk. Turn the mixture around with the fingers of one hand to mix then continue to add more of the remaining milk until all the flour is incorporated. The dough needs to be soft but not soggy. (You may not need all the milk or you may need a little more; it depends on the flour.)

Tip the dough out onto a lightly floured surface and knead it for 5–10 minutes, until smooth and elastic.

Place the dough in a lightly oiled bowl, cover with a clean tea towel and leave to rise for an hour or until doubled in size. Line two baking trays with baking parchment.

Mix equal quantities of flour and semolina together in a small bowl and use to lightly dust your work surface. Tip the dough onto the surface and roll out to about a 2.3cm thickness. You don't want the muffins to be too thick or they will overcook on the outside before cooking properly within.

Use an 8.5cm plain cutter to stamp out 8 rounds. Put these on the prepared tray and sprinkle the tops with a little semolina. Place each tray in a large, clean plastic bag and leave to prove for about an hour, or until risen slightly. Remove from the bags.

Heat a heavy-based frying pan or griddle over a low heat. Wipe the surface with an oiled piece of scrunched-up kitchen paper. Cook the muffins, two at a time, for 5–6 minutes on each side until golden; wipe the pan with oiled kitchen paper as necessary between batches.

Place the muffins on a wire rack and leave to cool completely. Slice in half and toast before serving with butter.

FRUIT DOUGHNUTS

MAKES 20

I like to keep doughnuts simple, without fancy icing. This version uses three kinds of fresh fruit instead of jam and is slightly less sweet than usual.

For the dough
500g strong white bread flour, plus extra for dusting
50g caster sugar
10g instant dried yeast
7g fine salt
140ml warm whole milk
5 medium eggs
250g unsalted butter, cut into small pieces, softened, plus extra for greasing

For the filling
50g raspberries
50g blueberries
1 fig, cut into small pieces

To cook and finish
Sunflower oil, for deep-frying
Caster sugar, for dredging

Put the flour and sugar into a food mixer fitted with the dough hook and add the yeast to one side and the salt to the other. Add the milk and eggs and mix for about 8 minutes until smooth.

Knead the dough on a slow speed for 5 minutes then add the butter, piece by piece, scraping down the side of the bowl from time to time. Once it is all incorporated and the dough is smooth and sticky, increase the speed and knead for a further 6 minutes. Tip the dough into a lightly greased large bowl, cover and refrigerate overnight.

Turn out the dough onto a lightly floured surface and knock back by folding the dough inwards repeatedly to expel the air.

Weigh the dough and divide it into 20 equal pieces (55–60g each). Roll each piece into a ball between the palms of your hands and flatten out a little. In the middle of each piece, place a couple of raspberries, a few blueberries or a few fig pieces. Form the dough into a ball around the fruit, making sure it is well sealed.

Roll each one lightly but firmly into a smooth ball by placing it in a cage formed by your cupped hand on the work surface and moving your hand around in a circular motion. Place the balls on a lightly floured tray, cover loosely with cling film and leave to prove for an hour, or until doubled in size.

When you are ready to cook, heat the oil in a deep-fryer, or a deep, heavy saucepan (no more than one-third full) to 180°C, or until a cube of bread dropped in browns in a minute. You will need to cook the doughnuts 2 or 3 at a time. Gently lower them into the hot oil and fry, turning with tongs every few minutes to ensure they cook evenly. The doughnuts colour quickly, but need 10–12 minutes to cook through, when they'll puff up and float. Keep the oil at a constant temperature.

Remove the doughnuts with a slotted spoon and drain on kitchen paper. Dredge with sugar while they are still hot and serve as soon as they are cool enough to eat. These doughnuts will keep for a day or two, but they are best eaten soon after they are cooked.

CHEESE CRACKERS

MAKES 14

These spicy cheese crackers are gluten-free, a way of baking that is much more in demand than when I started out, and so a useful recipe to have to hand.

- 75g strong Cheddar, finely grated
- 50g ground almonds
- 1 tbsp cornflour
- ¼ tsp baking powder
- A pinch each of celery salt, garlic salt, paprika and white pepper (less than ¼ tsp of each)
- 1 tsp Worcestershire sauce
- ½ tsp runny honey
- 2 tsp cold water

Put the cheese, ground almonds, cornflour, baking powder and dry seasonings into a bowl and mix together.

Add the Worcestershire sauce, honey and 1 tsp water. Squeeze and work the mixture until it comes together, adding the remaining water if required. You want the dough to be firm but malleable.

Place the dough on a large sheet of baking parchment paper on your work surface and press it out into a rectangle, of even thickness. Place another sheet of parchment on top. Roll out the dough between the parchment until it is about 16 x 27cm and 2–3mm thick. Remove the top piece of parchment and mark the dough into 14 rectangles with a knife, without cutting right through.

Lift the dough on its sheet of parchment onto a baking tray and place in the fridge to rest for 30 minutes. Meanwhile, heat your oven to 170°C/Gas 3½.

Bake for 12–15 minutes, until the crackers are turning brown.

Take out the tray and lower the oven setting to 100°C/Gas ¼. While the crackers are still hot, cut along the marked lines to separate them. Once the oven has cooled to the correct temperature, return the tray to the oven for 10 minutes to dry out the crackers a little.

Transfer the crackers to a wire rack and leave to cool completely. Store in an airtight container.

LAVROCHE

MAKES 30

Lavroche is a crisp wafer bread that's great with cheese at the end of a meal, or served with pre-dinner drinks, on its own or with a spread or a dip such as hummus. When I used to do big batches in hotel bakeries, we would make it in massive sheets that you'd pass through a rolling machine, but at home you can use a rolling pin to do the same job.

- 190g strong white bread flour
- 75g fine semolina
- 1 tsp fine salt
- 1 tbsp olive oil
- About 75ml water
- 40ml milk
- 1 medium egg, beaten, to glaze
- 1 tbsp linseeds (also known as flaxseed)
- 10g Gruyère, finely grated
- 10g Parmesan, finely grated
- 1 tsp fennel seeds
- 1 tsp caraway seeds

Put the flour, semolina and salt into a bowl and stir to combine. Add the olive oil, water and milk and mix to bring the ingredients together. Add a little more water if necessary; you want the mixture to be dry but pliable.

Turn the dough out onto a lightly floured surface and knead it for 5 minutes until smooth. Wrap in cling film and leave to rest in the fridge for 30 minutes. Line two baking trays with baking parchment.

Roll the dough out on a lightly floured surface to a very thin square, about 35 x 35cm. Brush off any excess flour. Trim the edges of the dough to neaten then cut into 3 strips, each about 30 x 9cm.

Brush the dough strips with beaten egg. Coat one with linseeds, another with the grated cheeses and the third with the fennel and caraway seeds. Cut each strip of dough into 10 small triangles.

Place the triangles on the prepared baking trays and rest in the fridge for 30 minutes. Meanwhile, heat your oven to 220°C/Gas 7.

Bake the lavroche triangles for about 15 minutes until they are crisp and browned.

The Chester Grosvenor
Afternoon Tea Menu
Opening Times

FIVE-STAR BAKING
HOTEL SECRETS

AS A TEENAGER, I WAS LUCKY enough to go with my dad to some good restaurants. It was at the Chester Grosvenor that I first saw a bread trolley in a Michelin-starred restaurant. I thought: this is interesting. And I also thought: the bread's okay, but it could be better.

At the age of twenty-one, I finished working for my dad and applied for a job at the Chester Grosvenor. It's a city centre hotel in a Grade ll listed, black-and-white timbered building. Beautifully decorated inside, you always feel you are somewhere really special there.

As a hotel baker, I learnt a whole new range of skills and recipes. My ingredients were more expensive, I had more time and I could experiment. There were all these dainty little things that you might find in a Paris pâtisserie – so easy to eat and gorgeous. Before working there, I'd never made Danish pastries or croissants – there was little call for croissants in a high-street bakery in the early eighties; if you wanted to eat croissants, you went to France.

The head baker taught me his recipes before he left and I've refined them over the years, partly by working with other French pastry chefs, and partly in order to make them more accessible for the home baker.

The main lesson I learnt is that a little effort can make a great difference, whether it's a plate of scones or a refined French tart. Working in high-street bakeries, you'd say, 'That'll do' and get away with it. But in hotels, everything has to be consistent and everything has to look perfect. In a normal bakery, when you make scones, say, they are probably 2–3 inches high – quite lumpy scones – because people want to get value for their money. But in a hotel, that's not the case; they want finesse.

One of the keys to a smart afternoon tea is keeping everything the same size. That was always critical – from the sandwiches to the scone to the petits fours, barquettes and meringues. Quality and presentation matter. Scones are easy to make so it's what you serve them with – good jam, butter, cream and tea – that sets a scone apart.

The standards in a hotel kitchen are rigorous. Each day, the executive chef would get the least successful breakfast dishes put onto a plate and brought into his office. If anything wasn't good enough, he'd call me in, as head baker. I'd be criticised if a roll was a touch more tanned or if a Danish pastry was slightly raw. It tended to happen because some of the ovens weren't the best, but everything had to be perfect and you couldn't just blame your tools.

At the Grosvenor, I nearly gave up my baking career. I said to the chef, 'I'm alright at baking but I've been doing it for years and I want to be a chef.' So he moved me into *hors d'oeuvres*, then veg, then sauces, and finally *mise en place*, where you plate up the food. I did that for many months, moving around the kitchen and learning from the chefs and sous-chefs. I learnt to butcher the meat, to gut and prepare a fish.

The chef wanted to make the most of my baking skills, so I ended up doing two jobs for a while and working a twelve-hour day. Finally, I said, 'I want to give up the baking and become a full-time chef.' Then he told me the salary. No chance. I went back to full-time baking.

However, the experience of working as a chef for a while gave my baking another dimension. I learnt knife skills that helped me to prepare ingredients for breads and pastries, and it really opened up the world of food, introducing me to flavours and textures I had never encountered before. I would find myself thinking that I could use this or that ingredient in a loaf or on top of a cake, and that became part of my craft. Cooking and baking are different skills but there's a crossover between them that helps a baker to be more creative.

Next came London. At the age of twenty-four, I became the youngest head baker the Dorchester Hotel had ever had. It's one of the most prestigious five-star hotels in the world, in the centre of London by Hyde Park, and guests come from all over the world to enjoy its thirties' glamour. The staff had a separate entrance down Deanery Street. You'd scan your card and go down to a beautiful kitchen the size of five tennis courts, with the latest equipment, and all of us in brand new uniforms.

I'd work ten days and have only two or three days off. I couldn't go back home all that much and I missed my friends and family. In the end I thought: 'London's not for me.' I went up North again, to work at the Chester Grosvenor for another two years.

The final chapter in my hotel years came when I worked at Cliveden. This was after I'd been working abroad in Cyprus for six years and it was a return that took me to the heart of the English countryside. You'd swear you were in the middle of nowhere but in fact you are only half an hour's drive from London. As you turn into this gravel drive you see one of the most beautiful stately homes in the country; it's been in many, many films. It takes a good five minutes to get to the top of the drive, and when you step into the hotel's grand hallway you'll be greeted by a suit of armour, tapestries on the walls and a huge formal staircase. But the thing I love about Cliveden is that it's still like being in someone's home, and you feel as though you should be there.

There was a big snooker room down in the cellar, next to the bakery. I'd go in there when I was in between bakes, or when things were proving, and my snooker improved vastly. The place was beautiful but I have to say that it was also quite creepy at night when I was up baking and everyone else was asleep – I probably looked like a ghost, covered in white flour.

Looking back, why did I make the move from the high street to hotel baking? Why did I go for the job of head baker at the

Dorchester when I reached the age of twenty-four? It's always the challenge. I knew that if I didn't go for a job, I'd kick myself later.

Stretch yourself, and you become a better baker. Some of the recipes in this chapter are straightforward but have small touches that make them 'five star'. Others are more complex, such as the seasonal Danish pastries on page 118 and the ham and cheese croissants on page 156. These require time and attention but I'd encourage any baker to give them a go.

If you can make a bread, you can make a croissant dough. On paper, the recipe seems to go on for ever and ever. But when you break it down, it's not hard. It's really just dough, with layers of butter in between – that's it. Use a good French butter and that will make all the difference. If you choose a high-quality butter and take your time with the folding, you'll end up with something that's up to professional standards. If you push yourself, you'll always find that actually it's not that difficult.

Shortcrust pastry is also a matter of practice. It's key to get the fat and sugar to a fine crumb, before adding your egg yolk or water. Once the liquid goes in, mix it together with your hands, pushing and binding it together gently. Don't be tempted to add more liquid, as you'll knead the mixture too much and make it rubbery. Bring the dough together, wrap it in cling film and rest in the fridge for 30 minutes or so. If you make the pastry well ahead, you'll need to let it soften a little at room temperature before using it, or you'll struggle to roll it out without cracking. You can also roll your pastry out between a couple of sheets of baking parchment or cling film to stop it sticking to the work surface.

If you stretch yourself then you'll always enjoy the rewards. As well as the satisfaction of making something well, you have much more control over what you're eating. Many commercial croissants and pastries use margarine rather than butter as the fat, for example. Bake them yourself and you know what goes into them. That way you'll be eating the best.

SEASONAL DANISH PASTRIES

MAKES 15

Danish pastry dough is versatile and can be used to make all kinds of breakfast pastries. To achieve the layering of the dough and butter takes time – around 12 hours of chilling between folding and rolling – but the hands-on work isn't laborious. These luxurious pastries are filled with raspberries but you can use other fruits that suit the season – blackberries or apple for autumn, apricots in the summer, or even bananas all year round.

For the dough
450g strong white bread flour, plus extra for dusting
7g instant dried yeast
7g fine salt
75g caster sugar
2 medium eggs
75ml cold water
100ml whole milk
225g unsalted butter (ideally a good-quality Normandy butter), softened

For the crème pâtissière
250ml whole milk
1 vanilla pod, split lengthways
2 medium egg yolks
50g caster sugar
1½ tbsp cornflour
20g unsalted butter, cut into small dice

To assemble
1 egg, beaten, to glaze
150g raspberries
75g apricot jam, to finish

Put the flour into a food mixer fitted with the dough hook. Add the yeast to one side and the salt and sugar to the other and begin mixing on a slow speed. Add the eggs, water and milk and mix for a couple of minutes to bring the dough together. Increase the speed and mix for a further 5 minutes. (You can make this dough by hand but I would recommend using a mixer if possible.)

Tip the dough onto a lightly floured surface and form into a ball. Wrap in cling film and rest in the fridge for 1 hour.

Press the dough out on a lightly floured surface with your knuckles, then stretch to a rough rectangle. Now roll out to a smooth rectangle, 45 x 20cm, to end up with a short side facing you. The dough can be quite hard to stretch because it wants to pull back into shape; one tip is to press the sides down onto the work surface to help hold the dough as you roll. Spread the butter out to cover the bottom two-thirds of the dough; make sure it is in an even layer and comes almost to the edges.

Fold the exposed dough down to cover half of the butter. Fold the bottom half of the buttered dough up and over, then seal the dough by gently squeezing the edges together. Wrap in cling film and refrigerate for at least an hour, until the butter has hardened.

Unwrap the chilled dough, place it on a lightly floured surface and roll again into a rectangle, 45 x 20cm, with a short side facing you. Fold the bottom third of the dough up and the top third down on top. This is called 'a single turn'. Wrap the dough in cling film and place in the fridge for an hour. Repeat this stage twice more, chilling the dough between turns. Write the number of turns on the cling film with a marker pen, as a reminder.

Continued overleaf

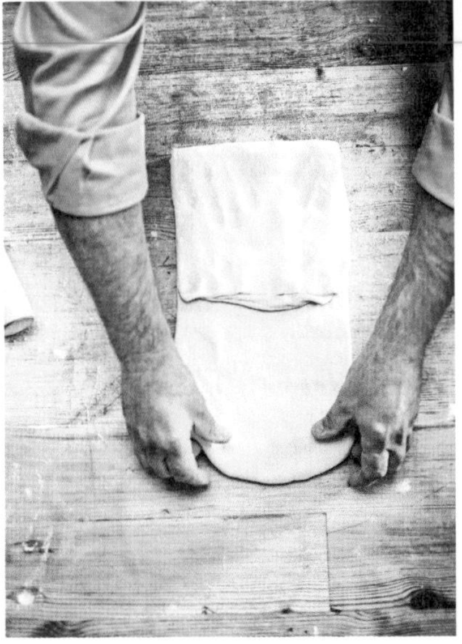

Your dough now needs to be wrapped in cling film and chilled for at least 8 hours, or overnight, to rest and rise slightly.

To make the crème pâtissière, pour the milk into a saucepan. Scrape out the seeds from the vanilla pod and add them to the milk with the empty pod. Slowly bring to the boil. Meanwhile, in a large bowl, beat the egg yolks with the sugar and cornflour. As soon as the milk comes to the boil, remove the vanilla pod and pour the milk onto the egg mix, whisking as you do so. Pour back into the pan and heat gently, stirring all the time, until the custard thickens.

Pour the crème pâtissière into a clean bowl and stir in the butter. Cover the surface closely with cling film to prevent a skin forming and leave to cool, then place in the fridge.

Line three baking trays with baking parchment. Unwrap the chilled dough and roll out on a lightly floured surface to a 35cm square. Trim the edges to straighten.

Cut the dough into 15 strips, flouring the knife from time to time to stop it sticking. Twist each strip in opposite directions from both ends and tie in a knot then tuck the ends under to form a circle.

Place the pastries on the prepared baking trays, leaving enough space in between for them to expand. Put each tray inside a large, clean plastic bag and leave to prove for 2 hours, or until doubled in size.

Heat your oven to 200°C/Gas 6. Take the trays out of the bags. Gently ease open the centre of each knot to make more space and put a spoonful of crème pâtissière in the middle. Brush the pastries with beaten egg to glaze and bake for 15–20 minutes, until risen and golden. Transfer to a wire rack to cool.

Before serving, place the fruit on top of the crème pâtissière. Warm the apricot jam and brush on the pastries to give them a final glaze.

Photographs overleaf

DOUBLE CHOCOLATE DANISH TWISTS

MAKES 6

I like to play around with different types of chocolate for Danish pastries, even putting cut-up Mars Bars and Snickers inside. Hazelnut chocolate spread, such as Nutella, is twisted inside these pastries and they are topped with white chocolate. It's breaking the rules, but it works. The technique for rolling and folding the Danish pastry dough is illustrated on page 119; remember that you'll need to allow plenty of time for chilling the dough – around 12 hours in total.

450g strong white bread flour, plus extra for dusting
7g instant dried yeast
7g fine salt
75g caster sugar
2 medium eggs
75ml cold water
100ml whole milk
225g unsalted butter (ideally a good-quality Normandy butter), softened

For the filling and topping
150g chocolate spread
100g good-quality white chocolate, cut into small pieces

Put the flour into a food mixer fitted with the dough hook. Add the yeast to one side and the salt and sugar to the other and begin mixing on a slow speed. Add the eggs, water and milk and mix for a couple of minutes to bring the dough together. Increase the speed and mix for a further 5 minutes. (You can make this dough by hand but I would recommend using a mixer if possible.)

Tip the dough out onto a lightly floured surface and form into a ball. Wrap in cling film and rest in the fridge for 1 hour.

Press the dough out on a lightly floured surface with your knuckles, then stretch it to a rough rectangle. Now roll out the dough on a lightly floured surface to a rectangle, 45 x 20cm, to end up with a short side facing you. The dough can be quite hard to stretch because it wants to pull back into shape; one tip is to press the sides down onto the work surface to help hold the dough as you roll. Spread the butter out to cover the bottom two-thirds of the dough; make sure it is in an even layer and comes almost to the edges.

Fold the exposed dough down to cover half of the butter. Fold the bottom half of the buttered dough up and over, then seal the dough by gently squeezing the edges together. Wrap in cling film and refrigerate for at least an hour, until the butter has hardened.

Unwrap the chilled dough, place it on a lightly floured surface and roll again into a rectangle, 45 x 20cm, with a short side facing you. Fold the bottom third of the dough up and the top third down on top. This is called 'a single turn'. Wrap the dough in cling film and place in the fridge for an hour. Repeat this stage twice more, chilling the dough between turns. Write the number of turns on the cling film with a marker pen, as a reminder.

Your dough now needs to be wrapped in cling film and chilled for at least 8 hours, or overnight, to rest and rise slightly.

Line two baking trays with baking parchment. Unwrap the chilled dough and roll it out on a lightly floured surface to a rectangle, 60 x 30cm. Trim the edges to straighten.

Cover the surface of the dough with chocolate spread, leaving about a 1cm clear margin along the edges. Fold the dough in half lengthways, to make a rectangle 60 x 15cm.

Cut the dough into 6 long strips, each 2.5cm wide, flouring the knife from time to time to stop it sticking. Twist each strip in opposite directions from both ends and tie in a knot then tuck the ends under to form a circle.

Place the pastries on the prepared baking trays and put each tray inside a large, clean plastic bag. Leave to prove for 2 hours, or until the pastries have doubled in size.

Heat your oven to 200°C/Gas 6. Take the baking trays out of the bags. Bake the pastries for 15–20 minutes, until risen and golden. Transfer to a wire rack to cool.

Melt the white chocolate in a heatproof bowl over a pan of barely simmering water (the bottom of the bowl must not touch the water). Drizzle the melted white chocolate over the cooled pastries and leave to set before serving.

Photograph overleaf

SULTANA & PECAN SCONE RING

MAKES 8

Scones are a hotel afternoon tea staple. Mine once got the approval of Queen Elizabeth, the Queen Mother, who used to come to Cliveden quite often and take tea in Madame de Pompadour's French dining room. I like to use strong bread flour in my scones and in this recipe I've slipped in some lard as well as butter, for a better texture and flavour – a tip I got from my nan.

- 225g strong white bread flour, plus an extra 25g for dusting
- ¼ tsp fine salt
- 2 tsp baking powder
- 20g cold unsalted butter, cut into small dice
- 20g cold lard, cut into small dice
- 40g caster sugar
- 60g golden sultanas
- 20g pecan nuts, roughly chopped
- Finely grated zest of 1 orange
- 1 medium egg
- 125ml whole milk
- 1 egg, beaten, to glaze

Heat your oven to 220°C/Gas 7. Line a baking tray with baking parchment.

Put the 225g flour into a large bowl with the salt and baking powder. Add the butter and lard and rub in with your fingertips until the mixture resembles breadcrumbs. Add the sugar, sultanas, chopped pecans and orange zest and stir to combine.

Make a well in the centre and break in the egg. Pour in half of the milk then mix with a wooden spoon until smoothly combined. Mix in the remaining milk, a little at a time, until you have a soft dough – you may not need all of it.

Dust your work surface with the 25g flour. Tip the dough onto it and gently fold it repeatedly until the flour is incorporated and the dough is smooth. If the dough is sticky, dust your hands with more flour to make it easier to handle.

Shape the dough into a round, 2.5cm thick, and place on the prepared tray. Score the scone round into 8 triangles by cutting deeply into the dough until your knife touches the baking tray. Brush the top with beaten egg.

Bake the scone round for 20 minutes, until risen and golden brown. Transfer to a wire rack to cool. Eat warm or cold, cut into 8 wedges, on the same day to enjoy at its best.

NICE BISCUITS

MAKES 12–15

I do like the classic biscuits and this is my version of one of the best. Thin, crisp and flavoured with coconut, these delicate biscuits are perfect with a cuppa.

125g plain flour, plus extra for dusting
10g cold unsalted butter, cut into small dice
50g caster sugar
20g desiccated coconut
¼ tsp baking powder
40–50ml milk
¼ tsp vanilla extract
1–2 tsp granulated sugar, for sprinkling

Put the flour into a large bowl, add the butter and rub in using your fingertips. Add the caster sugar, coconut and baking powder and mix to combine.

Add 25ml of the milk with the vanilla extract and use one hand to bring the mixture together. Add the remaining milk, 1 tsp at a time, until you have a stiff dough that forms a ball; you may not need all the milk or you may need a little more. Wrap in cling film and leave to rest in the fridge for at least 30 minutes.

Line a baking tray with baking parchment. Lightly dust your work surface with flour and roll out the dough on it to a 3mm thickness.

Using a 5cm fluted square cutter, stamp out squares. (Alternatively, you could cut straight-sided biscuits using a sharp knife.) Place on the prepared tray, leaving a small space between each one. Re-roll any trimmings and stamp out more squares.

Prick the surface of each square with a fork (this stops them rising too much). Place the tray in the fridge to chill for 30 minutes. Meanwhile, heat your oven to 190°C/Gas 5.

Just before baking, sprinkle 1 tsp granulated sugar over the surface of the dough squares. Bake for 15 minutes, until the biscuits are pale golden brown and cooked through. Remove from the oven and leave on the tray to firm up for a few minutes then transfer to a wire rack to cool. Sprinkle with a little more sugar before serving, if you wish.

JAFFA CAKES

MAKES 12

Children – and adults – love these Jaffa Cakes, which are made using a shallow bun tray as a mould. The orange is just that little bit more intense and you can use your choice of chocolate. It's a poshed up version of an all-time favourite, fit for a five-star hotel tea.

For the sponge base
Unsalted butter, for greasing
25g self-raising flour
A pinch of fine salt
⅛ tsp baking powder
1 large egg, separated
25g caster sugar
⅛ tsp cream of tartar

For the orange jelly
½ x 135g packet orange jelly
2 tsp orange marmalade
60ml boiling water

For the chocolate topping
100g dark chocolate
(60–70% cocoa solids)
40ml double cream
1 tbsp caster sugar

Heat your oven to 180°C/Gas 4 and grease a shallow 12-hole bun tray with butter.

For the sponge, sift the flour, salt and baking powder together; set aside. In a medium bowl, using a hand-held electric whisk, beat the egg yolk with half of the sugar until the mixture thickens and turns pale in colour – this will take about 5 minutes. Carefully fold in the flour mixture, using a large metal spoon or spatula.

In a clean bowl, whisk the egg white with the cream of tartar until stiff. Gradually add the remaining sugar, whisking well after each addition, then gently fold into the whisked egg and sugar mixture.

Divide the mixture evenly between the bun tray moulds and gently smooth the surface to level. Bake for 8–10 minutes until the sponges are risen and spring back when lightly touched. Leave in the tray for a few minutes then transfer to a wire rack to cool completely.

Wash and dry the bun tray then line the moulds with cling film.

Break the jelly into cubes and cut into small pieces. Place in a jug with the marmalade, pour on the boiling water and stir until the jelly has dissolved. Divide between the lined moulds then refrigerate to set.

For the topping, break the chocolate into pieces and put into a small pan with the cream and sugar. Warm gently over a low heat until melted. Stir to combine and form a thick silky sauce. Let cool slightly.

To assemble, take the jellies from the moulds. For a neat finish, cut each jelly with a small round cutter. Sit each one, rounded side up, on a sponge base and spoon on the chocolate topping to coat. (This must not be too warm or it will melt the jelly layer and slide off. If necessary, let cool for a little longer.) Mark a decorative pattern in the chocolate using a cocktail stick or skewer. Leave to set on a wire rack.

FIG ROLLS

MAKES 14

An afternoon tea is a great pick-me-up and can be made into a special treat just with a welcome pot of tea and a little plate of home-made biscuits like these. You can vary the spices and citrus zest to your taste, and the grated apple adds a little freshness to the dried fruits.

For the pastry
200g plain flour
½ tsp baking powder
120g cold unsalted butter, diced
A pinch of fine salt
1 tbsp caster sugar
1 medium egg, lightly beaten

For the filling
175g dried figs, roughly chopped
50g dates, roughly chopped
75ml water
¼ tsp bicarbonate of soda
Finely grated zest and juice of 1 orange
Finely grated zest of 1 lemon
25g dark muscovado sugar
1 small apple, peeled and coarsely grated
¼ tsp ground cinnamon
¼ tsp freshly grated nutmeg

To make the pastry, mix the flour and baking powder together in a large bowl. Add the butter and rub in with your fingertips until the mixture resemble fine breadcrumbs. Add the salt and sugar and mix well. Add the egg and bring the mixture together to form a soft dough.

Transfer to a lightly floured surface and gently knead into a smooth ball. Wrap in cling film and place in the fridge to rest.

For the filling, put the figs and dates into a small pan with the water, bicarbonate of soda, orange zest and juice, lemon zest and sugar. Heat gently until bubbling and simmer until thick, sticky and jam-like. Set aside to cool, then add the grated apple and spices and mix well.

Heat your oven to 190°C/Gas 5 and line a baking tray with baking parchment.

Roll out the rested pastry on a lightly floured surface to a rectangle, 32 x 25cm and 5mm thick. Trim the edges to straighten. Cut the pastry in half so you have two 30cm long strips.

Turn one piece of pastry so the long side is facing you. Spoon half of the sticky fruit filling in a line along this pastry strip, towards the edge closest to you but leaving a 1cm clear margin. Brush this pastry edge with water, then bring the other side of the pastry up over the filling and press the edges together to seal. Trim the ends to neaten. Repeat with the remaining strip of pastry, using the rest of the filling.

Carefully lift the filled rolls onto the prepared baking tray and score at 4cm intervals, taking care not to cut right through the pastry. Press a fork down onto the top of each roll to mark it and slightly flatten to the classic fig roll shape. Bake for 15–20 minutes, until golden.

Leave to cool on the tray for 5 minutes, then cut along the scored marks and transfer the fig rolls to a wire rack to cool completely.

CHOCOLATE & ORANGE MINI TARTS

MAKES 8

The flavour of the orange really comes through in these special little tarts. Because the chocolate is so rich, you don't want too much so I've made them small enough to eat in a couple of bites. The gold leaf decoration is a five-star hotel touch but I'd be equally happy with just the chocolate curls, or even a halved fresh orange segment brushed with a bit of apricot jam!

For the pastry
100g unsalted butter, softened
50g icing sugar
1 medium egg, beaten
125g plain flour
Finely grated zest of 1 orange

For the filling
110g dark chocolate (60–70% cocoa solids)
Finely grated zest of 1 orange
1 tsp orange blossom water
100ml double cream
20g unsalted butter

To decorate
75g dark chocolate (60–70% cocoa solids)
1 small sheet edible gold leaf (optional)

To make the pastry, beat the butter and icing sugar together in a large bowl until light and fluffy. Gradually incorporate the beaten egg, then add the flour and orange zest and stir until just combined; try not to over-mix. The dough will be very soft at this stage. Form it into a ball, wrap in cling film and chill in the fridge for at least an hour.

Heat your oven to 200°C/Gas 6. Have ready 8 fluted mini tarts tins, 6.5cm in diameter and 2cm deep. (Alternatively, you could use a shallow 12-hole bun tray and make 12 slightly smaller tarts.)

Roll out the pastry on a lightly floured surface to a 3mm thickness and cut out 8 rounds, using a 10.5cm plain round cutter (or an 8cm cutter if using a bun tray). Use to line the mini tart tins, making sure you push the pastry into the fluted edges; leave the excess overhanging the edges of the tins.

Line each pastry case with a small square of baking parchment and fill with baking beans. Bake 'blind' for 8 minutes, until the pastry is dry to the touch, then remove the parchment and beans and return the pastry cases to the oven for about 4 minutes until the base is dry and the pastry is very lightly coloured. Let cool, then use a small, sharp knife to trim away the excess pastry from the edge of the tins.

Melt 20g of the chocolate (for the filling) in a heatproof bowl over a pan of simmering water, making sure the bottom of the bowl doesn't touch the water. Brush the base of the tarts with the melted chocolate. Leave to set.

For the filling, chop the remaining 90g dark chocolate into small pieces with a large knife, or in a food processor, and place in a bowl with the orange zest. Put the orange blossom water, cream and butter into a pan and heat slowly until the mixture just comes to the boil. Pour onto the chocolate and stir until it melts to form a smooth, shiny paste. Spoon the filling into the mini tart cases and leave to set (at room temperature).

To make the chocolate curls, break the 75g dark chocolate into small pieces and melt in a heatproof bowl over a pan of simmering water (as before), stirring occasionally until smooth. Pour the chocolate onto the centre of a clean baking sheet and use a palette knife to spread it out into a smooth, thin layer. Place in the fridge for about 5–10 minutes, until set but not brittle. Press gently with your fingertip – it should leave a mark but not an indentation.

Use the edge of a large, sharp knife to scrape the chocolate away from you: it should curl. If it breaks, the chocolate is too cold so leave it to soften on the work surface for a few minutes then try again. Store the chocolate curls in an airtight box between layers of baking parchment until required. (You will have more than you need, but the excess can be frozen.)

Before serving, decorate each mini chocolate and orange tart with a few chocolate curls and a little crumpled gold leaf, if you like.

Photographs overleaf

JAPONAISE MERINGUES

MAKES 12

If you've never come across a Japonaise meringue before, it's a meringue mix that includes nuts, usually ground almonds or hazelnuts. The trick is to whip the meringue properly, so it can hold the nuts well even when they release some of their oils. These meringue fingers are piped, baked, then sandwiched with cream and decorated with chocolate and toasted almonds. In a luxury hotel such as the Grosvenor, they would have been piped perfectly, of course.

---

4 medium egg whites
¼ tsp cream of tartar
170g caster sugar
75g ground almonds
1 tbsp cornflour

For the filling and decoration
75g dark chocolate (60–70% cocoa solids), cut into small pieces
400ml double cream
50g chopped toasted almonds

Heat your oven to 140°C/Gas 1 and line two baking trays with baking parchment.

In a clean bowl, whisk the egg whites with the cream of tartar until stiff. Gradually add 120g of the sugar, a spoonful at a time, whisking well between each addition until you have a thick, glossy meringue.

In a small bowl, mix together the remaining 50g caster sugar, ground almonds and cornflour. Gradually and carefully fold this into the meringue, until evenly combined.

Put the mixture into a piping bag fitted with a 1cm star nozzle and pipe 24 fingers, about 9cm long and 3cm wide, onto the prepared baking trays.

Bake for 20 minutes, then turn off the oven and leave the meringues inside for a couple of hours until they are set and cooled.

For the decoration, put the chocolate into a heatproof bowl set over a pan of gently simmering water, making sure the bottom of the bowl doesn't touch the water, and leave until melted and smooth.

For the filling, whip the cream until it is fairly stiff but still easy to pipe, and place in a piping bag fitted with a large plain nozzle. Place pairs of meringues side-by-side, flat-side up, to form a V-shape. Pipe cream between the meringues to sandwich them together.

Scatter chopped nuts over the cream filling and drizzle the melted chocolate decoratively over the meringues to finish.

INDIVIDUAL LEMON MERINGUE PIES

MAKES 4

The French have dominated high-end baking because of the finesse of their pâtisserie. But I think that's wrong! Here's a recipe for a British classic, made on a smaller scale so you can eat it for tea or as a dessert. Take a little bit of care and it will look and taste great. You will have more lemon curd than you need – keep the rest in the fridge in a sealed jar to use as you like – to fill tartlet cases, top pancakes, spread on wholemeal bread etc.

For the base
150g gingernut biscuits
75g unsalted butter, melted

For the filling
Finely grated zest of 3 lemons
Juice of 6 large lemons
50ml water
2 tbsp cornflour
175g caster sugar
3 large egg yolks
25g unsalted butter

For the meringue
3 large egg whites
175g caster sugar
1 tsp cornflour

Crush the ginger biscuits to fine crumbs in a food processor (or use a rolling pin to smash them in a plastic bag) and mix with the melted butter. Divide between four individual 10cm loose-based tart tins, 3cm deep, and press the mixture onto the base and sides to line them. Place in the fridge to set.

For the filling, put the lemon zest and juice, water, cornflour, sugar and egg yolks in a small heavy-based saucepan. Heat gently, stirring continuously, until the mixture thickens. Be patient, as this will take 10–15 minutes. Stir in the butter to make a thick, glossy lemon curd. Spoon a layer over the biscuit bases and leave to cool. (Keep the rest of the lemon curd in a sealed jar in the fridge to use as required.)

Heat your oven to 190°C/Gas 5.

Whisk the egg whites in a large, clean bowl until stiff, then add the sugar a spoonful at a time, whisking well between each addition, until you have a thick, glossy meringue. Fold in the cornflour, using a large metal spoon or spatula.

Spoon or pipe the meringue generously over the lemon layer and bake for 15 minutes, until the meringue is lightly browned on top. Serve hot, warm or cold, with pouring cream.

PRUNE & ARMAGNAC TART

SERVES 8

This is a great tart and the Armagnac's the killer ingredient – it brings a special quality to the flavour. Here I've made a large tart to cut up and share out for afternoon tea or dessert but you can make individual tarts, or bake it in a long tranche tin to slice into fingers if you prefer.

For the pastry
200g plain flour, plus extra for dusting
2 tbsp icing sugar
100g cold unsalted butter, cut into small dice
1 medium egg
1 tsp lemon juice
2–3 tsp cold water

For the prunes
175g dried prunes (ideally Agen)
3 tbsp Armagnac (or other brandy)

For the filling
100g unsalted butter, softened
100g caster sugar
2 large eggs
50g plain flour
75g ground almonds
100g plum jam
20g flaked almonds

For the glaze
50g caster sugar

For the pastry, mix the flour and icing sugar together in a large bowl and rub in the butter with your fingertips until the mixture resembles fine breadcrumbs. Mix the egg with the lemon juice and 2 tsp water, then stir into the rubbed-in mixture, using a table knife. Add the extra 1 tsp water to bring the dough together if necessary. Gently knead the dough into a smooth ball, wrap in cling film and chill for 30 minutes.

Meanwhile, in a small bowl, soak the prunes in the Armagnac.

Roll out the pastry on a lightly floured surface to a 30cm circle and use to line a 23cm loose-based tart tin, 3.5cm deep, leaving a little excess overhanging the edge. Prick the base with a fork, then chill in the fridge for 15 minutes. Meanwhile, heat your oven to 200°C/Gas 6.

Line the pastry case with baking parchment and fill with baking beans. Bake 'blind' for 12–15 minutes, until the pastry is dry to the touch, then remove the paper and beans and return the pastry case to the oven for 5 minutes, until the base is dry and the pastry is lightly coloured. Use a small knife to trim away the excess from the edge.

To make the almond filling, beat the butter and sugar together in a bowl until light and fluffy, then beat in the eggs, one at a time. Stir in the flour and ground almonds.

Spread the jam over the base of the pastry case. Spoon the almond filling on top and spread to level. Drain the prunes, reserving the juice. Carefully press the prunes into the almond mixture and scatter the flaked almonds on top. Bake for 25–30 minutes, until the filling is risen and golden.

For the glaze, in a small pan, heat the reserved prune soaking liquor with the 50g caster sugar. Bring to the boil and let bubble to reduce until it thickens. Brush the surface of the tart with the syrup. Serve warm or at room temperature, with crème fraîche or cream.

STAUB

APRICOT & ALMOND CLAFOUTIS

SERVES 4

If it is made well, a clafoutis is gorgeous. I'd have it with a cup of tea but it's also good with a glass of Cognac or port. It has to be moist and you need to use flavourful fruit, whether it's blackberries, strawberries, raspberries or, as here, apricots.

For the apricots
100g caster sugar
100ml amaretto liqueur
4 apricots, stoned and each cut into 6 wedges

For the batter
2 large eggs, plus an extra 2 yolks
3 tbsp caster sugar
A pinch of fine salt
2 tbsp plain flour
125ml double cream
75ml milk
Finely grated zest of 1 lemon

To finish
15g flaked almonds, lightly toasted
Icing sugar, for dusting

For the apricots, put the sugar and liqueur into a saucepan. Bring to the boil, then lower the heat and simmer for 5 minutes. Place the apricot wedges in the syrup and remove from the heat. Leave to cool.

To make the batter, in a bowl or large jug, whisk together the whole eggs, extra yolks, sugar, salt and flour. Add the cream, milk and lemon zest and whisk again until evenly combined. Leave to stand for about 30 minutes. Meanwhile, heat your oven to 160°C/Gas 3.

Drain the apricots and place them in a shallow ovenproof dish, about 25 x 17cm (saving the syrup for poaching or eating with other fruit).

Pour the batter over the apricots and bake for 20–25 minutes, until risen, golden and just set. Scatter over the flaked almonds, dust with icing sugar and serve straight away.

LEMON BRIOCHE À TÊTE

MAKES 1 LARGE BRIOCHE

A brioche is one of those classic French bakes you have to learn when you're working in a smart hotel. This brioche is shaped so it has a tête, or head. One of the difficulties is to keep this bobble balanced. The trick is not to make the top part too heavy or it will crush the lower one. There's also a special technique in this recipe for joining the two balls together in a way that keeps the tête right on top. You will need to allow plenty of time for the long, slow rise.

350g strong white bread flour, plus extra for dusting
7g instant dried yeast
5g fine salt
35g caster sugar
About 100ml warm whole milk
3 medium eggs
Finely grated zest of 1 lemon
170g unsalted butter (ideally a good-quality Normandy butter), cut into small pieces, softened, plus extra for greasing
Egg wash (1 egg, lightly beaten with a little milk), to glaze

For the filling and glaze
2 tbsp apricot jam
2 tbsp pearl sugar
200g lemon curd

As this is a wet dough with lots of butter, I'd highly recommend using a food mixer if possible.

Put the flour into a food mixer fitted with the paddle attachment. Add the yeast to one side of the bowl and the salt and sugar to the other. Now add the milk, eggs and lemon zest and mix on a slow speed for 2 minutes, then on a medium speed for a further 6–8 minutes until you have a soft, glossy, elastic dough.

Add the butter pieces and continue to mix for a further 4–5 minutes, scraping down the bowl periodically to ensure that the butter is fully incorporated. The dough will be very soft.

Tip the dough into a plastic bowl, cover with cling film and chill for at least 7 hours, or overnight, until it has firmed up and you are able to shape it.

Grease a 22cm brioche tin with butter.

Take the brioche dough from the fridge. Tip it onto a lightly floured surface and fold it in on itself a few times to knock out the air.

Tear off a piece of the dough (about 125g in weight) and shape it into a smooth ball by placing it in a cage formed by your cupped hand on the work surface and moving your hand around in a circular motion, rotating the ball rapidly.

Take the larger piece of dough and form it into a smooth, tight ball by cupping it with the sides of your hands and turning it around to create a smooth ball. Press gently to flatten slightly.

Continued overleaf

Dust your middle finger and forefinger with flour and push them through the centre of the larger ball of dough to make a hole (or use the end of a wooden spoon). Now stretch the hole so the ball looks like a tall ring doughnut.

Shape the smaller ball into a cylinder and taper one end. Using a knife, slice the bottom half of the tapered end vertically in two, keeping the top half intact. Pull the two ends apart then insert these tapered ends through the hole in the large ball and tuck them outwards underneath the large ball. Form the top of the cylinder into a ball. (This technique keeps the small ball of dough in place when it's baked, otherwise it can tip to the side and won't stay in the middle.)

Push the handle of a wooden spoon down through both balls right to the base. This will help the brioche to cook all the way through.

Place the brioche in the prepared tin and stand it on a baking tray. Place inside a large, clean plastic bag and leave to prove for 2–3 hours, or until doubled in size. Meanwhile, heat your oven to 190°C/Gas 5.

Remove the tray from the plastic bag. Brush the brioche with egg wash and bake for 25–30 minutes, until risen and golden brown. Note that the sugar and butter will make the brioche colour before it is fully baked. To check it is cooked, carefully tip the brioche out of its tin and tap the bottom: it should sound hollow. If not, return it to the tin and bake for a further 5 minutes. But keep a close eye – if you overcook the brioche, it will become dry.

Leave the brioche in its tin for 5 minutes. Meanwhile, gently heat the apricot jam with a little water, then press through a sieve. Brush the top of the brioche with the apricot glaze and sprinkle with the pearl sugar. Remove the brioche from the tin and place on a wire rack. Leave to cool.

Spoon the lemon curd into a piping bag fitted with a bismarck nozzle (for filling doughnuts) and inject the brioche from the top with the lemon curd to fill the centre with it. Cut into wedges to serve.

SALMON IN BRIOCHE

SERVES 4

This is one of the dishes I created at the Dorchester for our special guests. The combination of tastes and textures is amazing: the crispness of the crust on the outside, the softness of the brioche beneath and the gorgeous salmon with a hint of dill in the middle. Allow plenty of time for the lengthy, slow rise.

For the dough
375g strong white bread flour
7g instant dried yeast
7g fine salt
3 tbsp caster sugar
5 tbsp milk
3 medium eggs
185g unsalted butter (ideally a good-quality Normandy butter), cut into small pieces, softened
1 medium egg, beaten, to glaze

For the filling
4 sprigs of dill
4 salmon fillets (about 175g each), skinned and pin-boned
Finely grated zest of 1 lemon
Salt

Put the flour into a food mixer fitted with the paddle attachment and add the yeast to one side and the salt and sugar to the other. Now add the milk and eggs and mix on a medium speed for about 8 minutes until smooth. (If you don't have a freestanding mixer, use a hand-held mixer fitted with dough hooks – the dough is too loose to knead easily by hand.)

With the motor running, gradually add the butter pieces, scraping down the bowl periodically. Once all the butter is incorporated and the dough is smooth and sticky, increase the speed and knead for a further 6 minutes.

Tip the dough into a large bowl (it will almost double in size), cover with cling film and place in the fridge overnight, or for at least 7 hours.

Heat your oven to 200°C/Gas 6 and line a baking tray with baking parchment.

Tip the brioche dough out onto a lightly floured surface and roll out to a 36cm square, about 5mm thick. Cut into 4 even squares. Place a sprig of dill in the centre of each square and sit a portion of salmon on top. Season the salmon lightly with salt and sprinkle with a little lemon zest.

Brush the edges of the pastry with beaten egg. Enclose the salmon in the pastry by bringing the two sides along the length of each fillet together and sealing, then folding the two ends up and over. Trim away any excess pastry so it isn't thick where the seams join. (If the pastry is too thick, the fish won't cook properly.)

Carefully turn the parcels over and very lightly score the pastry to mark a criss-cross pattern. Brush the surface with more beaten egg and bake the parcels in the oven for 15–20 minutes, or until golden brown. Serve hot or warm.

PEA, PANCETTA & PARMESAN TART

SERVES 6

This is a lovely, light, refreshing summer tart that is perfect for a more substantial but refined savoury tea. Little chunks of salty pancetta sit alongside sweet peas within a Parmesan and lemon flavoured custard.

For the pastry
225g plain flour, plus extra for dusting
A pinch of fine salt
60g cold unsalted butter, cut into small dice
60g cold lard, cut into small dice
3–5 tbsp ice-cold water

For the filling
195g pancetta, cut into 5–6mm dice
½ red onion, finely diced
5 medium eggs, plus an extra 3 egg yolks
200ml double cream
75g Parmesan, finely grated
A pinch of white pepper
A pinch of fine salt
100g ricotta
100g frozen peas
Finely grated zest of 1 lemon

To make the pastry, mix the flour and salt together in a bowl, add the butter and lard and rub in lightly with your fingertips until the mixture resembles fine breadcrumbs. Gradually add the water and mix until the dough begins to come together. Gently knead into a smooth ball, wrap in cling film and chill for at least 30 minutes.

Roll out the pastry on a lightly floured surface to a 3mm thickness and use to line a 25cm loose-based round tart tin, 3.5cm deep, leaving a little excess overhanging the edge. Prick the base all over with a fork, then chill for 15 minutes. Meanwhile, heat your oven to 200°C/Gas 6.

Line the pastry case with baking parchment and fill with baking beans. Bake 'blind' for 12–15 minutes, until the pastry is dry to the touch, then remove the paper and beans and return the pastry case to the oven for about 5 minutes, until the base is dry and the pastry is lightly coloured. Use a small, sharp knife to trim away the excess pastry from the edge. Lower the oven setting to 180°C/Gas 4.

To make the filling, cook the pancetta in a dry frying pan over a medium heat until golden and the edges begin to crisp, then remove. Lower the heat under the pan slightly, add the red onion and cook gently in the pancetta fat until softened.

In a bowl, beat the eggs, extra yolks and cream together until evenly combined. Add the grated Parmesan, pepper and a small pinch of salt (the pancetta and Parmesan are salty).

Scatter the diced pancetta and onion in the pastry case. Dollop the ricotta in heaped teaspoonfuls over the top and scatter over the peas and lemon zest. Carefully pour in the creamy egg mixture. Bake for 35–45 minutes, until the filling is just set and golden. Leave in the tin for 5 minutes, then carefully unmould the tart. Serve warm or cold.

HAM & CHEESE CROISSANTS

MAKES 12

For a sensational brunch dish that everyone will remember, it really is worth making your own croissants. The recipe looks long but once you understand the process, it's just a matter of repeating stages that don't take much time. A croissant is all about the layers. Make sure you chill the dough well and roll it out to exactly the same level each time so you don't get more butter in some parts and end up with bread rather than a properly flaky croissant. You'll need to allow around 20 hours in total for chilling the dough.

350g strong white bread flour, plus extra for dusting
150g plain flour
10g instant dried yeast
10g fine salt
80g caster sugar
280ml water
300g unsalted butter (ideally a good-quality Normandy butter), softened
120g ham, thinly sliced
200g mature Cheddar, grated
1 egg, beaten, to glaze

Put both flours into a food mixer fitted with the dough hook. Add the yeast to one side and the salt and sugar to the other and begin mixing on a slow speed. Add the water and mix for a couple of minutes to bring the dough together. Increase the speed and mix for a further 6 minutes. The dough should be fairly stiff. (You can make this dough by hand but I'd recommend using a mixer if possible.)

Lift the dough onto a lightly floured surface and form into a ball. Put into a greased bowl, cover with cling film and leave to rest in the fridge for at least 8 hours, or overnight.

Roll out the dough on a lightly floured surface to a rectangle, 60 x 20cm, to end up with a short side facing you. The dough can be quite hard to stretch because it wants to pull back into shape; one tip is to press the sides down onto the work surface to help hold the dough as you roll. Spread the butter out to cover the bottom two-thirds of the dough; make sure it is in an even layer and comes almost to the edges.

Fold the exposed dough down to cover half of the butter. Fold the bottom half of the buttered dough up and over, then seal the dough by gently squeezing the edges together. Wrap in cling film and refrigerate for at least an hour, until the butter has hardened.

Unwrap the chilled dough, place it on a lightly floured surface and roll again into a rectangle, 45 x 20cm, with a short side facing you. Fold the bottom third of the dough up and the top third down on top. This is called 'a single turn'. Wrap the dough in cling film and place in the fridge for an hour. Repeat this stage three more times, chilling the dough in between turns. Write the number of turns on the cling film with a marker pen, as a reminder.

After the final turn, wrap the dough in cling film and chill for at least 8 hours, or overnight, to rest and rise slightly.

When you are ready to shape the croissants, line two or three baking trays with baking parchment.

Place the chilled dough on a lightly floured surface and roll into a rectangle, 42 x 30cm, with a short side facing you. Trim the edges to neaten. Cut the rectangle in two lengthways, then cut triangles along the length of each strip (a pizza wheel is a good tool for this job). The base of each triangle should be about 12cm wide and it should be about 15cm high. You will get 6 triangles from each strip (you'll need to trim off a small triangular piece from each end).

Cut the ham into pieces that are roughly the same size as the dough triangles. Place a piece of ham on each triangle and sprinkle over some grated cheese. Hold the wide base of the triangle and gently tug the pointed opposite end to cause slight tension in the dough. Starting at the thick end, roll up into a croissant shape.

Place the croissants on the prepared trays, leaving space in between for them to expand. Place each tray in a large, clean plastic bag and leave to prove at room temperature for 2 hours, or until the croissants have doubled in size. (If you want to make these in advance, wrap each croissant in cling film before it proves, and freeze. Thaw and prove in the morning for a mid-morning brunch.)

Heat your oven to 200°C/Gas 6. Take the trays of croissants out of the bags. Just before baking, brush the croissants with egg wash. Bake for 15 minutes, then lower the oven setting to 180°C/Gas 4 and bake for a further 5 minutes, until risen and golden. Transfer to a wire rack to cool. The croissants are best eaten warm.

Photographs overleaf

BAKES OF THE WORLD
CYPRUS & TRAVELS

WHEREVER I TRAVEL, I meet bakers and gather ideas, tips and recipes. The bakes of other countries expand your repertoire. In recent years, the range of ingredients available in this country has exploded, making exotic recipes much more accessible. Most of what you need can be found in supermarkets and delis, or else is easily available online.

My travels in baking really began in my late twenties, when I was approached about working as a head baker for a hotel in Cyprus. The guests at the time were mainly from Europe and the hotel needed someone to show the Cypriot guys how European baking worked. Most bakers who went out there stayed six months. I fell in love with the place and stayed for six years.

Going to Cyprus was a massive change from life in the north of England. It was very hot in the bakery so we just wore shorts. I got on with the lifestyle and the people, and I made a lot of new friends. Most importantly, I met my wife Alex out there – she was working in the hotel – and we got married in the oldest Christian church on the island.

The hotel where I worked is called the Annabelle and it's like something out of a dream: swimming pools, the view of the sea, the heat. Even in winter, it's 25°C when the sun's out.

I soon started to pick up the Cypriot way of baking. They still make bread at home in the beehive ovens you see all over the island; every family has one in the garden. They're like the outdoor ovens you find in Italy, with an arched opening and a domed interior. They fire the oven up with loads of wood and once the brick starts turning white, you push the wood and ash to one side, mop it out, get a big bunch of oregano tied to a stick and brush the inside of the oven, so the herbs infuse the oven and all your breads.

Cypriot families get together on a Sunday – the teenagers, the grandparents, everyone. They might work in the city but at the weekend they go back to their village to see their *yayas* – grandmothers – and their mothers. It's all about food, and bread baked in the oven is the centre of that. Like olives, halloumi and feta, it's a celebration of their area.

Cyprus has got a Greek aspect, obviously, but it also has a great influence from the Middle East. When I lived in Cyprus, it wasn't part of the EU and I had to leave the country every six months to go and get a stamp on my visa, so I did a lot of travelling in the Middle East, finding out about different ways of baking.

First I travelled to Jordan to check out their flatbreads. I remember going to the walled city of Petra and coming across a Bedouin woman squatting down on the ground next to a fire, making breads on a small metal dome. As she demonstrated how to make bread in this very basic way I realised that, essentially, nothing in this method had changed for thousands of years.

Then I went to Egypt, and there I was fascinated by the tarts and puddings made with set milk or cream. They've often got mastika, or mastic, in there. This is a dried tree resin with the aniseed flavour that runs through many of the bakes in the Middle East, and also Cyprus, and it is one of the more unusual ingredients that I've included in this chapter. The ovens were similar to the ones in Cyprus, except a bit more square and longer, in order to get more into them.

Being abroad is about digging around to discover why people eat what they do. In the Middle East, how do you bake when the temperatures are so extreme? You have to adapt your recipes to make them work. What flours do they have? The soils of the Middle East mean the flour is less strong – with less protein to make it rise – and so they make flatbreads.

Because many people in the Middle East used to be nomadic, they didn't stay in one place for long enough to build an oven, and kept the bread-making pretty simple. When they did build ovens, they were more like furnaces than our Western ovens.

It's all about getting very high temperatures when it comes to flatbreads – the thinner the bread, the faster you want to cook it to stop it drying out.

When I travel, I try flavours, I try techniques. I think about the bakes people ate historically and then see how that leads up to what they eat today. There are the differences between countries, and then there are the connections. Just look at the variations on the same ingredients: you think of fruit cake and hot cross buns in Britain but you also find fruited buns and loaves in Italy, France, Norway, Sweden. The methods have changed slightly but the basic recipe is instantly recognisable. Some of these connections go way back. Archaeologists have found sourdough spores in the large ceramic pots they used for bread-making in Ancient Egypt; this style of baking, so popular again these days, has long roots.

Back in this country, London is one of the world's most important centres of food, thanks to the city's diversity and the huge number of chefs. It's a melting pot of food cultures and top-quality cooking – from Mexican to Indian to Middle Eastern. You can take all these flavour combinations into baking, both savoury and sweet. You can also learn different techniques, though they're not always easy. I once had a go at cooking naan bread in a tandoor in an Indian restaurant and nearly scalded my eyebrows off it was so hot!

When I went to work in the Mediterranean, I fell in love with baking all over again. I still travel and bake today. You always discover another approach to food in other countries and different slants on the familiar – flavours, methods, proving, baking. It keeps you learning.

FIG & WALNUT BREAD STICKS

MAKES 16

Simple to make, these are delicious eaten on their own. They also make a great accompaniment to blue cheese, gooey ripe Brie or an oozy baked Camembert. Make sure that you chop the figs and walnuts quite finely; if they are too chunky, it makes rolling the sticks more difficult.

250g strong white bread flour, plus extra for dusting
5g instant dried yeast
½ tsp fine salt
1 tbsp olive oil, plus extra for oiling
About 175ml cold water
75g dried figs, cut into small pieces
50g walnuts, finely chopped

Tip the flour into a large bowl. Add the yeast to one side and the salt to the other. Add the olive oil and three-quarters of the water and mix together using the fingers of one hand. Add as much of the remaining water as you need to incorporate all the flour and form a kneadable dough (it doesn't need to be as soft as a typical bread dough).

Tip the dough onto a lightly oiled surface and knead for 5–10 minutes, until smooth and elastic. Place the dough in an oiled bowl, cover with cling film and leave to stand for 1 hour. (The dough should rise but it doesn't need to double in size.)

Heat your oven to 220°C/Gas 7 and line two baking trays with baking parchment.

Tip the dough onto a lightly floured surface and fold it in on itself repeatedly until all the air is knocked out. Shape into a rectangle then scatter over the chopped figs and walnuts. Fold the dough over itself a few times to incorporate the fruit and nuts. The figs can make the dough sticky so flour your hands and work surface if necessary.

Divide the dough into 16 equal pieces and roll each one into a thin stick, about 25–30cm in length. Lay the dough sticks on the prepared trays and bake for 12–15 minutes, until crisp and golden brown. Transfer to a wire rack to cool.

CYPRIOT VILLAGE BREAD

MAKES 1 LOAF

This loaf, called 'kalouri', is the typical round bread of Cyprus. Mastika is the aromatic dried resin of the mastic tree and has a slightly aniseed flavour, and mahleb is made from the kernels of a type of cherry and has a sweet-sour almondy flavour. The recipe works without these ingredients but, for an authentic bread, you can source them online, or from a good continental deli or Middle Eastern shop.

¼ tsp mastika resin (mastic)
¼ tsp mechlebe seeds (mahleb)
A pinch of sugar
450g strong white bread flour, plus extra for dusting
7g instant dried yeast
5g fine salt
3 tbsp olive oil, plus extra for oiling
About 300ml cold water
2 tbsp sesame seeds
1 tbsp black sesame seeds (or nigella seeds)

Using a pestle and mortar, grind the mastika and mechlebe seeds with a pinch of sugar to a powder.

Put the flour into a large bowl. Add the yeast to one side and the salt to the other. Add the ground spices and olive oil. Pour three-quarters of the water into the bowl and turn the mixture around with the fingers of one hand, mixing the water into the flour.

Continue to add the remaining water, a little at a time, until all the flour is incorporated and you have a rough dough. The dough needs to be soft but not soggy. (You may not need all the water or you may need a little more; it depends on the flour.)

Coat the work surface with a little olive oil then carefully tip the dough onto it and knead for 5–10 minutes until soft and smooth.

Place the dough in a lightly oiled bowl, cover with a clean tea towel and leave to rise until doubled in size. This will take at least an hour and can take 3 hours or longer, depending on the room temperature.

Meanwhile, put all the sesame seeds into a bowl, pour on enough hot water to cover and leave to soak and swell while the dough is rising. Line a large baking tray with baking parchment.

Tip the risen dough onto a lightly floured surface and fold it inwards repeatedly until all the air is knocked out.

Now shape the dough into a ball. To do this, first flatten the dough into a rough rectangle then roll it up into a thick oblong. Turn the dough so that the longer edge is running away from you and flatten it slightly. Now fold the two ends in towards the centre and press them down, so you end up with a chunky, squarish shape.

Turn the dough over, so the join is underneath. With your palms turned upwards, put your hands on each side, slightly under the dough. Turn the ball around, tucking the dough neatly under itself as it turns. You are gently forcing the sides of the dough down and underneath, to create a smooth, taut top and a rough underside. Try to avoid using too much extra flour during shaping if you can.

Coat the top and sides of the loaf with the damp sesame seeds, gently pressing them on with your hands. Put the loaf on the prepared tray, then place in a large, clean plastic bag and leave to prove for an hour, or until doubled in size. Meanwhile, heat your oven to 220°C/Gas 7.

Remove the proved loaf from the bag. Just before baking, score the bread about 1cm deep around its circumference about halfway down. Also make a couple of 2cm deep slashes on top of the loaf. Bake for 30–35 minutes until golden brown and cooked through. Transfer to a wire rack to cool.

Photograph overleaf

FETA & CHIVE BREAD

MAKES 1 LARGE LOAF

There's a strong Cypriot influence in this bread. You need little pockets of feta within so don't break up the cheese too much, and use fresh chives, chopping them finely. It's particularly good with grilled halloumi and fresh mint.

- 500g strong white bread flour, plus extra for dusting
- 7g instant dried yeast
- 7g fine salt
- 4 tbsp olive oil, plus extra for oiling
- About 300ml water
- 100g feta
- 2 tbsp chopped chives

Put the flour into a large bowl and add the yeast to one side and the salt to the other. Add the olive oil and three-quarters of the water. Turn the mixture around with the fingers of one hand to mix and add the remaining water, a little at a time, until all the flour is incorporated. The dough needs to be soft but not soggy. (You may not need all the water or you may need a little more; it depends on the flour.)

Coat the work surface with a little olive oil then carefully tip the dough onto it and knead for 5–10 minutes until smooth. Place in a lightly oiled bowl, cover and leave to rise until doubled in size. This will take at least an hour, possibly 2–3 hours or longer.

Tip onto a lightly floured surface and fold inwards repeatedly until all the air is knocked out. Push down on the dough with your knuckles to shape it into a rectangle, about 25 x 20cm. Crumble the cheese over the surface and scatter over the chives. Fold the dough in on itself a few times, until the cheese and chives are evenly distributed.

Flatten the dough into a rectangle again, with a long side facing you. Fold the long side furthest from you into the middle of the rectangle. Then fold the long side closest to you into the middle, on top of the other fold. Turn the loaf over, so you have a smooth top with a seam running along the base. Tuck the ends of the loaf under to create a rough oval shape. Roll the dough firmly but gently so the ends are tapered and you have a fat torpedo shape. Place on the prepared tray with the join underneath.

Put the tray inside a large, clean plastic bag and leave the loaf to prove until it has risen and doubled in size. This will take at least an hour and may take up to 3 hours, depending on the room temperature.

Heat your oven to 220°C/Gas 7. Take the tray from the bag. Using a sharp knife, make 3 diagonal slashes, about 2cm deep, in the top of the loaf. Bake for 30–35 minutes, until golden brown. Cool on a wire rack.

PITTAS

MAKES 4 LARGE OR 6 MEDIUM PITTAS

The key to a good pitta is to get your oven as hot as possible but at the same time not to over-bake the breads – you don't want them crispy. They're ready when a fleck of colour appears on the top. If your oven is glass-fronted, keep an eye on them without opening the door.

- 300g strong white bread flour, plus extra for dusting
- 7g instant dried yeast
- 5g fine salt
- 1 tbsp dried oregano
- About 200ml cold water
- 1 tbsp olive oil, plus extra for oiling

Tip the flour into a large bowl. Put the yeast to one side and the salt to the other. Add the oregano, then pour in three-quarters of the water and add the olive oil. Mix the ingredients together using the fingers of one hand, making sure you gather in all the flour from the side of the bowl. Add the remaining water a little at a time until all the flour is incorporated and you have a smooth, soft dough. (You may not need all the water or you may need a little more; it depends on the flour.)

Coat the work surface with a little olive oil then tip the dough onto it. Knead for 5–10 minutes until the dough is smooth and elastic.

Put the dough into a lightly oiled bowl. Cover and leave to rise until the dough has doubled in size. This will take at least an hour and can take 2–3 hours or longer, depending on the room temperature.

Meanwhile, heat your oven to 250°C/Gas 10 (or as high as it will go) and put a baking stone or a large heavy-duty baking tray on the top shelf to heat up.

Tip the dough onto a lightly floured surface and knock back by folding the dough in on itself repeatedly until all the air is knocked out.

Divide the dough into 4 or 6 equal pieces and shape each one into a ball. Roll out each ball to an oval, 1cm thick.

Carefully take the hot trays from the oven and dust with flour. Lay the pittas on the trays and bake for 5–10 minutes until the breads begin to puff up and just start to colour. Wrap in a clean cloth to help keep them soft. Best eaten warm.

NO-KNEAD BREAD

MAKES 1 LOAF

Travelling the world and meeting like-minded enthusiastic bakers is one of the most enjoyable parts of my work. This recipe originates from celebrated New York City baker Jim Lahey, who came up with the idea of an amazing bread that requires no kneading. He baked it in a Dutch oven, giving the bread its characteristic thick crust. I bake mine in a tin instead. It has a great flavour, good structure with large air pockets and an artisan look. It's a loaf to be proud of – and one that anyone can make. You just need to allow plenty of time for the long, slow rise.

400g strong white bread flour, plus extra for dusting
8g fine salt
2g instant dried yeast (½ tsp)
About 300ml cold water
Fine semolina, wheat bran or extra flour, for dusting the surface

Tip the flour into a large bowl. Put the yeast to one side and the salt to the other. Add the water and use a wooden spoon or your hand to mix everything together until you have a wet, sticky dough; this will only take around 30 seconds. The dough should be very sticky to the touch; if it isn't, add another 1–2 tbsp water.

Cover the bowl with cling film and leave at room temperature (but out of direct sunlight), until the dough has more than doubled in size and the surface is dotted with bubbles. This will take at least 8 hours.

Once the dough is risen, generously dust your work surface with flour. Use a plastic dough scraper or a spatula to scrape the dough out of the bowl in one piece onto the floured surface. As you pull the dough away from the edge of the bowl, it will cling in long, thin strands and will be quite loose and sticky. Don't be tempted to add more flour.

Dust your hands with flour and lift the edges of the dough in towards the centre. Tuck the edges in to form a round shape.

Place the dough, smooth side uppermost, in a 20cm springform tin and dust the surface with flour, semolina or wheat bran. Cover and leave to rise for 8 hours.

Heat your oven to 220°C/Gas 7. Bake the loaf for about 20 minutes, then lower the oven setting to 200°C/Gas 6 and bake for a further 40 minutes, until the crust is a deep chestnut colour.

Remove the loaf from the tin and place on a wire rack to cool. Don't be tempted to cut or tear the bread until it has cooled completely; this will take at least an hour.

PESHWARI NAAN BREAD

MAKES 6

This is a recipe for a classic Peshwari naan, suitable for the home cook. Once you've mastered the recipe, you can play around with flavours for your naan, adding black cumin, caraway or poppy seeds, or brushing them at the end with different flavoured oils, such as a garlic-infused oil or walnut oil.

450g strong white bread flour, plus extra for dusting
½ tsp baking powder
5g instant dried yeast
1 tsp fine salt
2 tsp caster sugar
About 150ml warm whole milk
About 150ml natural yoghurt
2 tbsp sunflower or vegetable oil, plus extra for oiling
25g desiccated coconut
25g sultanas
25g flaked almonds
25g unsalted butter

Mix the flour and baking powder together in a bowl and add the yeast to one side and the salt and sugar to the other.

Heat the milk in a pan over a low heat until warm, then remove from the heat and mix with the yoghurt. Pour three-quarters of this liquid into the flour and mix together using the fingers of one hand. Add as much of the remaining liquid as you need to gather in all the flour and form a rough dough that comes away from the side of the bowl.

Coat the work surface with a little oil then tip the dough out onto it. Knead for 5–10 minutes until the dough is smooth and elastic. Place in a lightly oiled bowl, cover and leave to rise for 1 hour.

Tip the dough onto a lightly floured surface and knock back by folding it in on itself repeatedly until all the air is knocked out. Roll out into a rough rectangle and scatter the coconut, sultanas and flaked almonds over the surface. Fold the dough over repeatedly to incorporate the filling then roll into a ball.

Divide the dough into 6 pieces and shape each one into a ball. Flatten each ball then roll into a teardrop shape, about 3–5mm thick.

Heat a large frying pan over a medium-high heat and add 1 tsp oil and 1 tsp butter. Once the butter has melted, lay one piece of dough in the pan. Cook for 3–4 minutes, or until the underside is turning golden and speckled with brown patches. Turn over and cook the other side for 2 minutes, or until it is speckled with brown and cooked through.

Remove the naan from the pan and wrap it in a clean tea towel (this helps to keep it soft); keep warm. Cook the remaining naan in the same way, adding a little more oil and butter to the pan as required. Enjoy with your favourite curry.

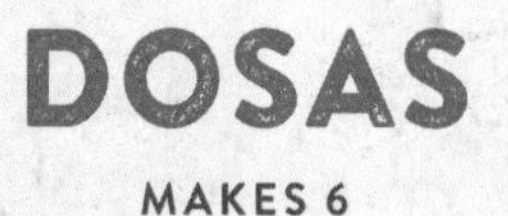

DOSAS

MAKES 6

You need to plan ahead when making these South Indian pancakes as the rice and lentils need soaking. They are then ground and the batter is left to ferment. It's not difficult but practice and patience are required. You need the right consistency for the batter, to cook it at the right temperature and to get the dosas as thin as possible. Buy skinned, split lentils for this recipe. My optional filling is a tasty dry potato curry to spread on the dosas.

For the dosas

250g basmati rice
75g urid dal (skinned and split black lentils)
½ tsp fenugreek seeds
500ml water
½ tsp fine salt
Sunflower oil, for cooking

For the filling

Potato masala (see opposite) and/or a small jar of your favourite chutney

Wash the rice and lentils in a sieve then place in a large bowl with the fenugreek seeds. Cover with the water and leave to soak for at least 6 hours, or overnight.

Drain the rice and lentils, saving 250ml of the liquid. Put the soaked rice and lentils into a blender and pour in 175ml of the liquid. Blitz thoroughly, scraping down the sides occasionally. Add the remaining liquid and blend to a completely smooth batter.

Pour the batter into a bowl, cover with a clean tea towel and leave to stand and ferment overnight.

The batter should be slightly risen and have small bubbles on the surface. The consistency should be slightly thicker than pancake batter, so add a little more water if it is too thick. Stir in the salt.

Heat a 20cm frying pan over a medium heat and wipe the surface with an oiled wad of kitchen paper. Using a ladle or large spoon, pour enough batter into the centre of the pan to coat the base as thinly as possible, using the bottom of the ladle or spoon to spread it out.

Cook for about 2 minutes until the underside is golden, then use a palette knife to turn the dosa. Cook for a minute on the other side, then remove to a warmed plate. Repeat until all the batter is used, stacking the dosas interleaved with greaseproof paper; keep them warm in a low oven. Wipe the pan with more oil as necessary to stop the batter sticking.

Spread the cooked dosas with a thin layer of potato masala and/or chutney, roll up and eat straight away.

POTATO MASALA

Peel 2 large potatoes (about 500g), cut into large chunks and cook in boiling salted water until tender. Drain, return to the pan and shake to roughen the surface. Heat a large sauté pan and add 3 tbsp sunflower oil. When hot, add 2 tsp urid dal, ½ tsp mustard seeds and ½ tsp cumin seeds. Stir to coat in the oil. Cook for 1 minute, until the lentils darken in colour and the seeds begin to pop. Add 15 small curry leaves and 1 chopped onion, lower the heat and cook for 7–8 minutes or until the onion begins to soften.

Add 100ml water, cover and cook for 10 minutes or until the onion is very soft and the liquid has reduced down. Add 2 sliced green chillies (deseeded for less heat, if preferred), a finely grated 2cm piece of ginger, ½ tsp ground turmeric and ½ tsp fine salt. Stir and cook for a few minutes until the liquid has evaporated. Add the potato chunks and stir to coat them in the spices – don't worry if they break down; this is a dry curry that is intended to be spreadable. Stir through 2 tbsp chopped coriander or flat-leaf parsley, then taste and adjust the seasoning before serving.

Photograph overleaf

SPICY SAUSAGE SCACCIA

MAKES 1 LOAF

Scaccia is a traditional Sicilian stuffed and layered bread that I came across when filming there once. Sicily is very different to other parts of Italy and I could see similarities between Sicilians and Cypriots as Mediterranean islanders with strong family bonds that relate a lot to foods, including bakes such as this one. Serve it with salad for lunch or supper.

150g strong white bread flour, plus extra for dusting
100g fine semolina
5g instant dried yeast
½ tsp fine salt
1 tbsp olive oil, plus extra for oiling
About 175ml cold water

For the filling
2 tbsp olive oil
1 large onion, diced
1 garlic clove, finely chopped
¼ tsp dried chilli flakes
½ tsp fennel seeds
400g good-quality sausages
½ tsp fine salt
A large bunch of flat-leaf parsley, roughly chopped
200g ricotta, drained if necessary
10g Parmesan, finely grated

To finish
Olive oil, for brushing
1 tsp fennel seeds
½ tsp dried chilli flakes

Mix the flour and semolina together in a large bowl. Add the yeast to one side and the salt to the other. Make a well in the middle and pour in the olive oil and three-quarters of the water. Turn the mixture around with your fingers, adding more of the water, until all the flour is incorporated and you have a rough dough. The dough needs to be soft but not soggy. (You may not need all the water or you may need a little more; it depends on the flour.)

Coat your work surface with a little olive oil, then tip the dough onto it and knead for 5–10 minutes until the dough is smooth and silky.

Place the dough in a clean bowl, cover and leave to rise until doubled in size. This will take at least an hour and can take 2–3 hours or even longer, depending on the room temperature. The longer it takes, the more flavour the dough will develop; ideally, leave it somewhere cool, but not the fridge.

To make the filling, heat the olive oil in a pan, add the onion and fry gently until soft but not coloured. Add the garlic, chilli flakes and fennel seeds and cook, stirring occasionally, for 2–3 minutes. Remove from the pan with a slotted spoon and set aside.

Remove the sausages from their skins and add them to the pan with the salt. Cook over a medium-high heat, using a wooden spoon to break the sausages down into small pieces. Cook until the pieces of sausage are brown and a little crisp on the outside. Remove from the heat, return the onion mixture to the pan and stir to distribute evenly. Once cooled, stir through the chopped parsley.

Continued overleaf

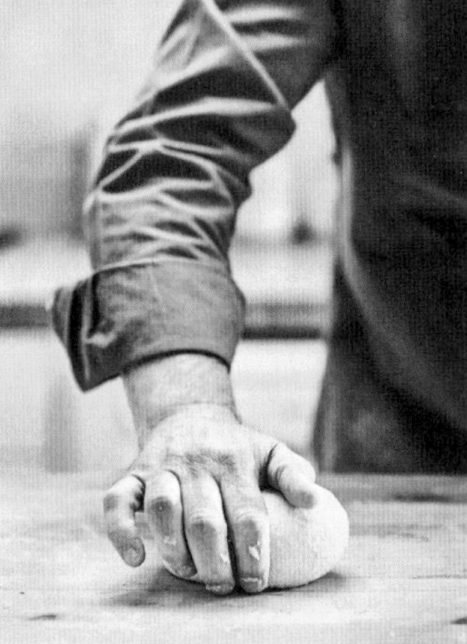

Heat your oven to 200°C/Gas 6 and line a baking tray with baking parchment.

When the dough is ready, tip it onto a floured surface. Roll it out into a rough rectangle, about 40 x 30cm. Turn the dough 90° if necessary, so you have a long side facing you. Take a third of the meat and place it in a line along the bottom, leaving a 3cm clear margin at the edge. Dot a third of the ricotta over the meat then sprinkle with a third of the Parmesan.

Roll the dough up from the bottom, enclosing the filling in the dough (rather like a Swiss roll). As soon as the filling is encased, stop rolling and add another line of meat, ricotta and Parmesan. Roll the dough up again to enclose the filling. Continue with a third layer of filling, which will lie towards the top edge of the dough. Now roll up again so you have a large cylinder of filled dough. Trim the ends.

Pull the cylinder of dough to straighten and make sure it is even all the way along. Rotate the cylinder of dough 90° on the work surface so that it extends away from you then, starting at the top, coil the dough into an upwards spiral.

Place the loaf on the baking tray, brush with olive oil and scatter over the fennel seeds and chilli flakes. Bake for 25–30 minutes until crisp and golden. Transfer the loaf to a wire rack to cool slightly and serve hot or warm.

SPANAKOPITA

SERVES 6

Spanakopita is a celebrated dish in Cyprus, and naturally everyone thinks that they make the best one. The flavour, the flakiness, the bake, all make this special. It's a great dish that can be made in advance for gatherings of family and friends – it even appeals to those kids who think they don't like spinach.

1 tbsp olive oil
2 garlic cloves, finely chopped
500g frozen spinach
200g feta, crumbled
150g ricotta
25g Parmesan, finely grated
2 tbsp chopped dill
½ tsp freshly grated nutmeg
2 medium eggs
100g unsalted butter, melted
7 sheets of filo pastry (270g)
Salt and white pepper

Heat the olive oil in a large frying pan over a low heat. Add the garlic and cook until it just begins to colour, then remove from the pan with a slotted spoon and place in a bowl.

Add the spinach to the pan and increase the heat to high. Cook, stirring continuously, until the spinach is soft and all the liquid has evaporated. Add to the garlic and leave to cool.

Put the feta, ricotta, Parmesan, dill, nutmeg and eggs into another bowl and mix together until evenly blended, seasoning with a little salt and a pinch of white pepper. Add the cooled spinach and garlic and stir to combine.

Heat your oven to 200°C/Gas 6. Brush a 25 x 20cm baking tin with melted butter. Lay 7 sheets of filo on a clean work surface and cut each one in half (the pieces will be slightly bigger than your tin).

Brush one piece of filo with melted butter and lay, buttered-side up, in the prepared tin to line the base and sides. Repeat with another 6 pieces of filo, brushing each one with butter before placing in the tin.

Pack the filling into the filo-lined tin. Layer the remaining pieces of filo on top, brushing each layer with melted butter and tucking the sides in around the edges of the pie.

Brush the top of the pie with melted butter then, using a sharp knife, mark into 6 portions, cutting through the top few layers of filo.

Bake for 35–40 minutes, until the pastry is a rich golden brown colour and crisp. Serve hot, warm or at room temperature.

COURGETTE PIZZA WITH RICOTTA & THYME

MAKES 2 LARGE PIZZAS

This is a light, summery pizza with fresh flavours. The dough uses a small amount of yeast and has a lengthy prove to develop an amazing flavour. I once worked with a guy called Enzo, one of the best pizza makers in Naples, who was particular about details. He even claimed you've got to mix the dough in a clockwise direction... that's how myths and legends start!

For the dough
300g strong white bread flour, plus extra for dusting
2g instant dried yeast (½ tsp)
1 tsp fine salt
About 220ml cold water
Oil, for oiling

For the topping
1 courgette
2 tbsp olive oil
30g Parmesan, finely grated
30g Gruyère, finely grated
125g ball of buffalo mozzarella, torn or cut into chunks
125g ricotta
Finely grated zest of ½ lemon
A small handful of thyme sprigs
Sea salt and black pepper

For the dough, put the flour into a bowl and add the yeast to one side and the salt to the other. Add three-quarters of the water and mix with the fingers of one hand. Gradually add more water to form a very soft dough that comes away from the side of the bowl. (You may not need it all or you may need more. I like pizza dough to be as wet as possible.)

Turn the dough onto an oiled surface and knead for 5–10 minutes, until smooth and elastic. To check it's kneaded sufficiently, cut off a small piece and stretch part of it as thinly as you can. If it doesn't tear and the light shines through, it's ready. If not, keep going. Shape into a ball, place in a clean bowl, cover and leave to rest for 10–12 hours.

Divide the dough in half and form each piece into a ball. Stretch or roll each ball into a thin circle, about 26cm in diameter, and place on a floured baking tray. Heat your oven to 220°C/Gas 7 and put a pizza stone or flat baking tray on the top shelf to heat up for 30 minutes.

For the topping, using a swivel vegetable peeler, cut the courgette into ribbons. Toss in a bowl with 1 tbsp olive oil and some salt and pepper.

Place one pizza dough base on the hot stone or tray and bake for 3–4 minutes. Take it out and switch the oven to grill setting. Scatter half the grated cheeses and mozzarella over the pizza base. Trickle over ½ tbsp olive oil then lay half the courgette ribbons on top. Dot with teaspoonfuls of ricotta, using half of it. Slide the pizza into the oven, placing it 10cm or so from the grill. Cook for 4–5 minutes, until the topping is bubbling; watch closely to ensure the crust doesn't burn.

Repeat the process to cook the other pizza. Just before serving, sprinkle with the grated lemon zest and thyme sprigs.

JULE VÖRTBRÖD

MAKES 1 LOAF

This yeasted fruit bread comes from Scandinavia, where it's traditionally made with the local non-alcoholic fruit beer. Fruit breads and cakes are found in many countries and this one is akin to the tea bread that I remember eating as a child.

- 500g strong white bread flour, plus extra for dusting
- 50g cold unsalted butter, cut into small dice
- 60g caster sugar
- 10g instant dried yeast
- 1 tsp ground star anise (or 2 whole star anise, ground)
- ½ tsp ground cloves
- ½ tsp ground cinnamon
- ½ tsp ground cardamom (or seeds from 15 pods, ground)
- ½ tsp ground pepper
- 1 tsp fine salt
- 150ml fruit beer
- 150ml whole milk, plus extra to glaze
- 400g raisins
- Icing sugar, sifted, for dusting

Put the flour into a large bowl, add the butter and rub in using your fingertips until the mixture resembles breadcrumbs. Stir in the sugar and yeast, then the ground spices and salt, making sure they are evenly distributed.

Add the beer and begin to mix, then gradually incorporate the milk and mix to form a rough dough.

Tip the dough out onto a lightly floured surface and knead it for 5–10 minutes until smooth and elastic. Flatten into a rough rectangle, scatter a quarter of the raisins over the surface, then fold the dough over itself a couple of times to disperse the fruit. Repeat this three times until all the raisins are incorporated and evenly distributed through the dough.

Place the dough in a bowl, cover and leave to rise until doubled in size. This will take at least 3 hours and may take longer; the quantity of fruit makes this loaf take longer to rise.

Line a baking tray with baking parchment. Tip the risen dough out onto a lightly floured work surface and knock out the air by folding it in on itself repeatedly.

Flatten the dough into a rectangle and fold the long sides into the middle. Roll up so the top is smooth and you have a join running along the middle of the underside. The loaf should be an oval shape.

Place on the lined baking tray and put the tray inside a large, clean plastic bag. Leave to prove for about 2 hours – it is ready when the dough springs back when lightly pressed.

Heat your oven to 180°C/Gas 4. Remove the tray from the bag and brush the loaf with milk to glaze. Bake for 40–50 minutes, until risen and the crust is dark brown. Transfer to a wire rack to cool. Dust with sifted icing sugar before serving sliced, with butter.

LOUKOUMADES

SERVES 6

These light and fluffy Greek doughnuts are soaked in an orange-infused honey syrup and taste fantastic. I've watched them being made with great skill in Cyprus, where they are a traditional treat.

275g plain flour
10g instant dried yeast
A pinch of fine salt
1 tbsp runny honey
275ml tepid water
Sunflower oil, for deep-frying

For the orange syrup
75g caster sugar
150g runny honey
Finely grated zest and juice of 1 orange
100ml water

To finish
50g walnuts, chopped
1 tsp ground cinnamon

Tip the flour into a large bowl. Put the yeast to one side and the salt to the other. Add the honey to the tepid water in a jug and stir to dissolve.

Gradually add the honey liquid to the flour and stir, then beat with a wooden spoon until you have a thick batter with no lumps.

Cover and leave to stand for an hour until the batter has risen to double in volume and is very lively with lots of bubbles on the surface.

Meanwhile, to make the orange syrup, put all the ingredients into a saucepan and slowly bring to the boil, then simmer for 10–15 minutes until the syrup reduces and thickens slightly but is still pourable (it will thicken further as it cools). Leave to cool.

Pour enough oil into a deep, heavy saucepan to fill it by no more than a third (or use a deep-fryer and more oil). Heat the oil to 180°C, or until a cube of bread dropped into the hot oil turns brown in about 1 minute. You will need to cook the doughnuts in batches, ideally 5 or 6 at a time, to avoid overcrowding the pan.

Carefully drop large teaspoonfuls of the batter into the hot oil. They will puff up and begin to turn golden. Cook for about 2–3 minutes on each side, turning them with tongs to ensure they cook evenly. Try to maintain the oil at a constant temperature. Remove the doughnuts from the oil using a slotted spoon and drain on kitchen paper.

Once all the doughnuts are cooked, pour half the orange syrup into a large bowl, add the hot doughnuts and walnuts and toss to coat in the syrup, adding more syrup if needed.

Sprinkle with the ground cinnamon and serve hot, with Greek yoghurt and the rest of the orange syrup in a small jug on the side.

BAKLAVA SPIRALS

MAKES ABOUT 35

I was taught to make baklava by Kokos, one of the pastry chefs at the hotel I worked at in Cyprus, who was a master of the craft. His were stuffed with pistachios and brushed with ghee. Once you've mastered the recipe, you can vary the nuts and use honey, rose water or other flavourings in the syrup.

150g unsalted butter, melted
200g walnuts, finely chopped
2 tbsp caster sugar
10 sheets of filo pastry (380g)

For the syrup
100g caster sugar
Finely grated zest of 1 lemon
Juice of ½ lemon
50g runny honey
100ml water

Heat your oven to 170°C/Gas 3½ and use some of the melted butter to grease the base of a 25cm springform tin.

Mix the walnuts with the caster sugar. Lay a sheet of filo on your work surface and brush with butter. Lay another sheet of pastry on top and brush with butter. Spread out one-fifth of the walnut filling (about 3½ tbsp) along the long edge nearest you. Roll up tightly, as if you were rolling a Swiss roll. Trim the ends that contain little filling.

Form the roll into a spiral and place it in the middle of the prepared tin. Repeat the process to make another 4 rolls, coiling each one and arranging them in the tin around the central spiral to form a ring. You don't want the spirals to be too tight – the edges of each roll need to get the chance to cook.

Brush the top and outside edges of the spirals with melted butter, then bake for 30–35 minutes, or until the baklava is golden brown.

Meanwhile, make the syrup: place all the ingredients in a pan and bring to the boil. Lower the heat and simmer for about 10 minutes, or until reduced and thickened to a pourable syrup.

Slice the baklava into 5cm pieces, leaving them in the tin, then pour on the syrup while the pastry is still hot. Let the baklava sit and soak up the syrup for an hour before serving. Store any that won't be eaten straight away in a non-metallic container.

BLUEBERRY CHEESECAKE

MAKES 12 SLICES

The perfect cheesecake is slightly under-set and the Americans make the best. I fell for this particular one when filming in Miami at a restaurant specialising in seafood. After eating fish all day, it tasted especially good.

For the base
150g unsalted butter, softened
75g caster sugar
150g plain flour
A pinch of fine salt
50g semolina (or ground rice)
100g blueberry jam

For the filling
400g full-fat cream cheese
1 tbsp custard powder
50g caster sugar
2 medium eggs
1 tsp vanilla extract
125ml double cream
125g blueberries

Heat your oven to 150°C/Gas 2. Grease a 27 x 18cm baking tin, about 4cm deep, and line with baking parchment.

For the base, beat the butter and sugar together in a large bowl until light and fluffy. Add the flour, salt and semolina (or ground rice) and bring everything together to form a dough; try not to overwork it.

Press the mixture onto the base of the baking tin. Lay a sheet of baking parchment on top, press evenly to level the base, then remove. Prick the base all over with a fork. Bake for 35–40 minutes until cooked but still pale. Leave to cool in the tin. Turn the oven up to 175°C/Gas 3½.

To make the filling, in a large bowl, slowly beat 100g cream cheese with the custard powder and 1 tbsp of the sugar, using a hand-held electric whisk, until smooth. Add another 100g cream cheese with 1 tbsp sugar and whisk again on a low speed, scraping down the sides of the bowl every so often as you go. Repeat twice more, until all the cream cheese and sugar are incorporated. Don't be tempted to rush this stage; this careful process creates the velvety smooth texture.

Whisk in the eggs, one at a time, on a medium speed then incorporate the vanilla and cream. Finally, carefully fold in the blueberries.

Spread the jam over the cooled base. Spoon on the filling and spread out in an even layer. Stand the tin in a large roasting tray and pour in enough cold water to come halfway up the sides of the tin. Bake for 35–40 minutes, or until the edges of the cheesecake are lightly golden and the centre has a slight wobble. Lift out of the roasting tin.

Carefully lift the cheesecake in its parchment from the tin and transfer to a wire rack to cool. Once cold, peel away the parchment and place the cheesecake on a plate. Refrigerate for at least 4 hours to firm up.

Cut the cheesecake into slices, using a knife dipped into just-boiled water. Eat just as it is, or serve with extra berries.

CHERRY TART

SERVES 8

Here's a fabulous tart that I came across on a trip to Paris. There's the shortbread-like pastry, the soft creamy filling, then the fruit: it all comes together and melts in your mouth.

For the pastry
200g plain flour
2 tbsp icing sugar
100g cold unsalted butter, cut into small dice
1 large egg yolk
2–3 tbsp cold water

For the custard filling
400ml whole milk
4 large egg yolks
100g caster sugar
3 tbsp cornflour
1 tsp vanilla extract
1 tbsp kirsch
125ml whipping cream

For the topping
350g cherries, pitted and halved
4 tbsp cherry jam
1 tbsp kirsch

To make the pastry, mix the flour and icing sugar together in a large bowl and rub in the butter using your fingertips until the mixture resembles fine breadcrumbs. Mix the egg yolk with 2 tbsp water, then stir into the rubbed-in mixture, using a round-bladed knife. Add the extra water if needed to bring the dough together. Gently knead into a smooth ball, wrap in cling film and chill for at least 30 minutes.

To make the custard, slowly heat the milk in a pan until it just comes to the boil. Meanwhile, in a large bowl, whisk together the egg yolks, sugar and cornflour. As the milk comes to the boil, pour it onto the egg mixture, whisking as you do so. Pour back into the pan and heat gently, stirring constantly, for about 5 minutes until the custard thickens. Take off the heat and stir in the vanilla and kirsch. Pour into a clean bowl and cover the surface closely with cling film to prevent a skin forming. Leave to cool (then refrigerate if making well in advance).

Roll out the pastry on a lightly floured surface to about a 30cm circle and use to line a 23cm loose-based fluted tart tin, 3.5cm deep, leaving a little excess pastry overhanging the edge. Prick the base all over with a fork, then chill in the fridge for 15 minutes. Meanwhile, heat your oven to 200°C/Gas 6.

Line the pastry case with baking parchment and fill with baking beans. Bake 'blind' for 12–15 minutes until the pastry is dry to the touch, then remove the paper and beans and return to the oven for 5 minutes or so, until the base is dry and the pastry is lightly coloured. Let cool, then use a small, sharp knife to trim the excess pastry from the edge.

To assemble the tart, whip the cream to soft, firm peaks and fold into the cold custard. Spoon into the cooled pastry case then spread out to level the surface. Starting from the outer edge, arrange the cherry halves in concentric circles on top of the tart to cover it completely. Warm the cherry jam with the kirsch, press through a sieve, then brush this glaze over the cherries. Refrigerate until ready to serve.

MARZIPAN & APPLE TART

SERVES 4–6

This is my spin on a Normandy apple tart. Making your own marzipan is crucial; shop-bought doesn't have such a high proportion of almonds and will melt. The flavour of the apples balances the flavour of the nuts beautifully.

For the marzipan
110g ground almonds
50g icing sugar, sifted, plus extra for dusting
50g caster sugar
A few drops of almond extract
¼ tsp lemon juice
2 medium egg yolks

For the frangipane
40g unsalted butter, softened
40g caster sugar
1 medium egg
20g plain flour
30g ground almonds

For the apple layer
1 large or 2 medium eating apple(s)
2 tbsp apricot jam
1 tbsp water

To make the marzipan, mix the ground almonds and both sugars together in a large bowl. Add the almond extract, lemon juice and egg yolks and mix to combine. At first, the mixture will feel dry and crumbly but keep squeezing and kneading and it will come together.

When it starts to form a ball, lightly dust your work surface with icing sugar and knead the marzipan on it to form a smooth paste. Wrap in cling film and chill in the fridge for at least 30 minutes.

To make the frangipane, beat the butter and sugar together until the mixture is light and fluffy, then add the egg and combine well. Add the flour and ground almonds and mix to a smooth, thick paste.

Heat your oven to 190°C/Gas 5 and line a baking tray with a sheet of baking parchment.

Dust the work surface with icing sugar again and roll out the marzipan to an 18cm circle, about 5mm thick (use a plate as a template). Lift it onto the prepared baking tray.

Spread the frangipane over the marzipan in a thick layer, leaving a 5mm clear margin around the edge.

Quarter and core the apple(s) then cut into 3mm slices. Arrange the apple slices over the frangipane in concentric circles. Bake for 12–15 minutes, until the frangipane is risen and golden brown.

Heat the apricot jam with the water and press through a sieve. Brush the apricot glaze over the top of the warm tart. Serve with cream, or just as it is.

FIG, PECAN & CHEESE TART

SERVES 6

I first saw this impressive tart in France and loved the way it plays around with flavours, mixing the sweet and the savoury. Serve as a dessert, or at the end of the meal as an alternative to cheese and biscuits.

For the pecan pastry
25g pecan nuts
85g unsalted butter, softened, plus extra for greasing
75g caster sugar
1 large egg yolk
100g plain flour
¼ tsp baking powder
¼ tsp fine salt

For the filling
100g mascarpone
150g full-fat cream cheese
100g soft, creamy blue cheese, such as Yorkshire Blue
1 tbsp runny honey

To serve
6 figs, each cut into 8 wedges
15g pecan nuts, roughly chopped
1½ tsp runny honey

Butter a 20cm loose-based fluted tart tin.

For the pastry, blitz the nuts in a food processor until finely chopped. Using an electric whisk, beat the butter and sugar together in a bowl until pale and fluffy. Add the egg yolk and mix until just combined. Add the flour, baking powder, salt and ground pecans and fold in, using a large metal spoon, until evenly incorporated.

The pastry will be very soft at this stage, so scrape it together to form a ball, then place between two sheets of greaseproof paper. Roll out the pastry thinly between the paper to a 20cm circle, 1–2cm thick. Remove the top sheet of paper and invert the pastry onto the base of the greased tin. Remove the other sheet of paper.

Push the dough into the fluted edge of the tin and press the base to level the surface. Prick all over with a fork. Cover loosely with baking parchment and place in the fridge to rest for 6–8 hours, or overnight.

Heat your oven to 170°C/Gas 3½. Remove the parchment covering the pastry base then bake in the oven for 20–25 minutes, until golden brown. Leave it to firm up and cool down completely.

For the filling, using a hand-held electric whisk, beat the mascarpone, cream cheese, blue cheese and honey together until smooth. Put into a piping bag fitted with a 1cm nozzle, or use a paper piping bag and snip 1cm off the tip. (Alternatively, the filling can be spread rather than piped onto the base.)

To assemble the tart, carefully remove the pastry case from the tin and place on a serving plate. Pipe peaks of the whipped cheese filling in concentric circles over the base (or spread it evenly using a metal spoon). Arrange the fig wedges on top of the filling and finish with the chopped pecans. Drizzle over the honey just before serving.

SHOWSTOPPING PIES, PUDS & CAKES

A RETURN TO BRITISH BAKING

TELEVISION IS A DIFFERENT WAY of teaching. People like to be entertained as they learn – you know that from back at school and the teachers who made you want to listen. I want viewers to get little nuggets that they can take back to the kitchen and use.

When I came back to live in Britain in 1999, I started to run my own bakeries and at the same time began to appear on TV. I'm not quite sure why but being in front of a camera came naturally. The advice is always to be yourself. I'm not an actor so it was straightforward to do just that.

It was 2010 when I got a call from Love Productions telling me about a new programme they were making. Would I be interested in auditioning? Someone from the production team came to my house, tipped out a bag of bakes and said: judge them. Then I met my fellow presenters and it all fell into place. You cannot fake chemistry; it happens from day one.

The programme really started to take shape in the first series. In the original *Bake Off* line up, Mary was everyone's grandma, including mine. She was from the tradition of home baking. I was used to dealing in 20kg of flour for making batches of bread, while Mary thinks in grams. She was the comforting arm around the shoulder while I was more the teacher who said, 'I think you should do this, see me afterwards.' My job was to be a straight, honest and fair judge. You have to give constructive criticism so the contestants learn. *Bake Off* is a journey for them, just as baking has been for me in my own life. Mel and Sue were the gel between us all who kept us sane. They lightened the mood and everyone was happier for it.

But *Bake Off* is not about the hosts and the judges, it's about the bakers – they are the stars of the show. It's important for them to manage their time properly in order to succeed – and the same thing is true in a professional bakery. A bakery has to be working at all levels, immediately, because if your ovens are on and not being used, you're wasting money. So you plan your time carefully. That's also true at home, when you want to be efficient as you bake, and make the most of your time.

The bakers need two other qualities to do well: technique and artistic flair. Most have a bit of one aspect, and a lot of the other. Some might be talented and artistic, but have more style than substance. The skill is to marry the two together. When you get both, it's magical. The ones who do well in the competition tend to develop over time. And sometimes they're lucky, because another baker just happens to have done worse that day.

The challenges we set for contestants show off and test their skills, and encourage people at home to bake. The Showstopper is the 'wow factor'. It's most often a highly decorated bake and this is where a baker's creativity shines through. What viewers get from this is ideas – how to create three-tiered cakes, how to make something look good.

Some of the recipes in this chapter, such as the Swiss roll and the roulade, are more of a technical challenge that you can learn and then adapt to your own tastes. I've also given recipes for some of my favourite pies, a British tradition that we feature in the programme. Then there are the recipes that take technique to perfect, such as a mirror glaze on a cake. And there are some impressive pudding recipes, including soufflés, that aren't that difficult to make once you've learnt a few tricks.

People watching an elaborate cake being prepared may think, 'I don't think I could make that.' But there are also ways to make a bake special with the minimum amount of work and fuss. Part of this is flavour. But be careful – stick with flavours that you like and know work well together. There are lots of trendy and strange tastes out there. In reality you'll probably prefer coconut, banana, strawberry to Earl Grey or lavender. If you're dealing with flavours such as lavender, rosemary or rose then be sparing. Don't go crazy because the taste will kill everything.

When I first started doing television, baking was seen as niche. But *Bake Off* has had far more people watching it than any other cookery show. Sales of bakeware, food mixers and different kinds of flours have soared and I can even see its impact in my day-to-day life. Everybody and anybody asks me about baking: 'My bread's too tight'; 'My cake's dropped in the middle'; 'How do I make a decent soufflé?' The questions I get asked are many and varied. Builders shout out to me at the traffic lights – 'I burnt me cakes, mate, what am I doing wrong?' I get grandmas and kids coming up to me in supermarkets about their brownies.

Why is this? It's because we're a nation of bakers and we'd forgotten about that. We went through twenty years of buying stuff rather than making it. Now we've come back to making again. Some of the bakes in mainland Europe are complicated, but in this country we have some great basic bakes with good flavours. We've got a plethora of ingredients from all over the world to use. We've got some of the best flours. We've also got great bakers. No wonder people want to bake and learn more than ever before.

BREAKFAST PIE

SERVES 6

This delicious pie takes its name from a filling that contains many of the ingredients of a classic English breakfast. The lattice top looks good and the crust is robust enough to enable the pie to be taken on a picnic.

For the pastry
275g plain flour, plus extra for dusting
A pinch of fine salt
135g cold unsalted butter, cut into small dice
1 medium egg, beaten
2–3 tbsp cold water
1 medium egg, beaten, to glaze

For the filling
3 traditional pork or Lincolnshire sausages
1 tbsp sunflower oil
1 large onion, finely chopped
150g unsmoked streaky bacon, diced
50g mushrooms, sliced
150g full-fat cream cheese
5 medium eggs
100g mature Cheddar, grated
1 tbsp roughly chopped flat-leaf parsley
Salt and white pepper

To make the pastry, mix the flour with the salt in a large bowl. Add the butter and rub in lightly with your fingertips until the mixture looks like fine breadcrumbs. Make a well in the centre, add the egg with 2 tbsp water and mix with a round-bladed knife. Bring the dough together with your hand, adding the extra water if necessary. Gently knead to form a smooth ball, wrap in cling film and rest in the fridge for 30 minutes.

Preheat your grill to medium-high and grill the sausages until golden and cooked through. Leave to cool, then cut each one into 4 pieces.

Heat the oil in a wide frying pan over a medium heat. Add the onion and cook gently for about 8 minutes until soft. Add the bacon and mushrooms, increase the heat and cook for 8–10 minutes until the mushrooms are tender and any liquid they release has evaporated. Leave to cool completely.

Heat your oven to 200°C/Gas 6. Roll out two-thirds of the pastry on a lightly floured surface and use to line a 20cm loose-based tart tin, 5cm deep, leaving a little excess overhanging the edge of the tin. Roll out the rest of the pastry and cut into 12–14 strips, each 1cm wide and 22cm long.

On a board covered with a sheet of baking parchment, use the pastry strips to create a lattice, with 6–7 strips going each way, weaving them under and over each other. Place in the fridge while you make the filling.

In a large bowl, beat the cream cheese with 2 eggs until smooth. Add the grated cheese and chopped parsley and season with a little salt and a pinch of pepper. Stir in the cooled onion and bacon mixture, along with the sausage pieces.

Spoon the filling into the pastry case and make 3 evenly spaced depressions in the surface. Crack the remaining eggs into them. Dampen the pastry rim with water and invert the lattice from the parchment onto the pie. Press the ends of the strips onto the pastry rim, then trim to neaten.

Brush the pastry lattice with beaten egg to glaze. Bake the pie for 35–40 minutes, until golden brown. Leave to stand for 15 minutes before cutting. It can be eaten hot, warm or cold.

HAGGIS PASTIES

MAKES 5

Haggis is packed with flavour, making it an ideal pie filling. I've paired it with two typical accompaniments – neeps and tatties – and put them all in a pasty.

For the pastry
450g plain flour, plus extra for dusting
½ tsp fine salt
115g cold lard, cut into small dice
75g cold unsalted butter, cut into small dice
About 90ml cold water
1 egg, beaten, to glaze

For the filling
1 onion
100g peeled swede
1 large potato, peeled
400g haggis
50g unsalted butter
Salt and white pepper

Line two baking trays with baking parchment. To make the pastry, mix the flour with the salt in a large bowl. Add the lard and butter and rub in lightly with your fingertips until the mixture resembles fine breadcrumbs. Using a round-bladed knife, stir in just enough water to make a firm dough. Knead gently into a ball, wrap in cling film and place in the fridge to chill for at least 30 minutes.

For the filling, thinly slice the onion and cut the swede and potato into small, thin pieces. Place each vegetable in its own bowl. Remove the uncooked haggis from its casing and crumble into another bowl.

Heat your oven to 200°C/Gas 6. Dust your work surface with flour and divide the pastry into 5 equal pieces. Roll out each piece to a round, about 3mm thick, and cut out a 24cm circle, using a plate as a guide.

To fill and shape each pasty, scatter a thin layer of swede over half of the circle, leaving a 1cm clear margin. Add a similar layer of potato, season lightly with salt and pepper, then top with some onion. Repeat the swede and potato layers, seasoning as you go and checking that the pastry will still go over the top to encase the filling. Top with a layer of crumbled haggis. Add a final layer of onion, season once more and dot with butter.

Brush the pastry border with beaten egg, then fold the pastry over the filling, so the edges meet. Press these together firmly and crimp by pinching the pastry edge all round between the thumb and forefinger.

Put the filled and sealed pasties on the prepared baking trays. Cut 2 slits in the centre of each pasty and brush the top with beaten egg.

Bake the pasties for 20 minutes, then lower the oven setting to 160°C/Gas 3 and bake for a further 30 minutes until golden brown. These pasties are best eaten warm.

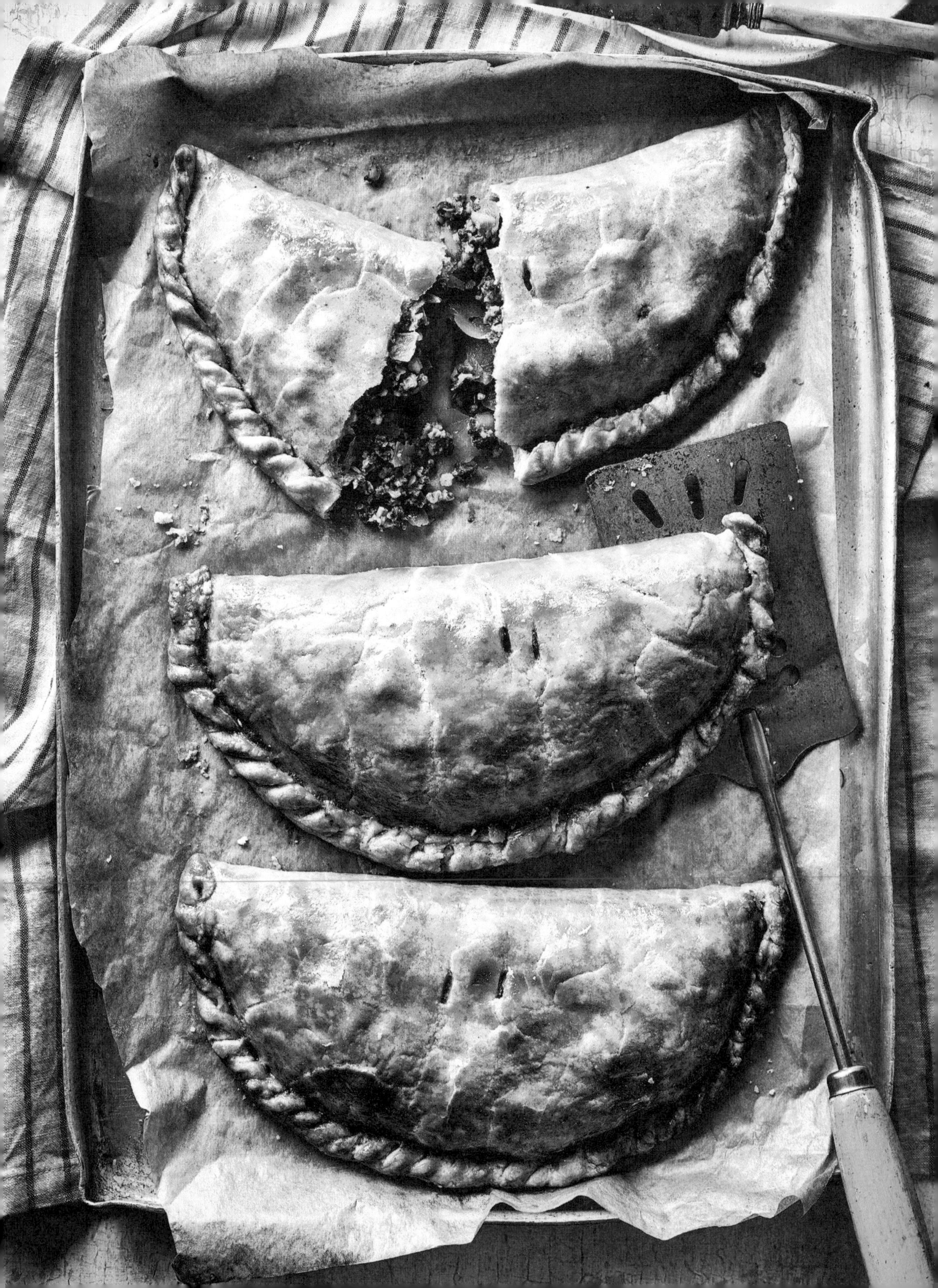

BEEF & ALE PIE

SERVES 4

This is comfort food at its best, with the beer giving the sauce both depth of flavour and richness. I'd recommend using bitter or stout.

For the filling

2 tbsp plain flour
2 tsp English mustard powder
A pinch of fine salt
700g chuck or other stewing steak, cut into 4cm chunks
2–4 tbsp sunflower oil
2 large onions, sliced
2 celery sticks, cut into 1cm chunks
2 carrots, cut into 5cm chunks
300ml beer (a good bitter or stout is best)
300ml rich beef stock
A dash of Worcestershire sauce
1 tsp dark brown sugar
1 bay leaf
2 sprigs of thyme
Salt and black pepper

For the suet pastry

375g self-raising flour, plus extra for dusting
175g shredded beef suet
200–250ml cold water

To make the filling, put the flour and mustard into a bowl, season with a little salt and mix together. Add the pieces of meat and toss in the seasoned flour until evenly coated.

Heat 2 tbsp oil in a large, flameproof casserole. When it is hot, quickly brown the meat in small batches on all sides, removing the pieces with a slotted spoon to a plate as soon as they are coloured, and adding more oil to the pan as necessary.

Once all the meat is browned and set aside, add a little more oil to the pan if needed and cook the onions, celery and carrots over a medium-low heat, stirring occasionally, for about 5 minutes.

Return the meat to the pan and stir, then pour in the beer and stock. Add the Worcestershire sauce, sugar, bay leaf, thyme and a little salt and pepper. Bring to the boil, then lower the heat to a simmer and cook gently, covered, for at least 2 hours, until the beef is tender.

Tip the filling into a 1.2 litre pie dish and leave to cool completely. Meanwhile, heat your oven to 200°C/Gas 6.

To make the suet pastry, put the flour and suet into a large bowl, add some salt and pepper and stir to mix. Add 200ml water and mix to a soft sticky dough with one hand, adding more water to bring the dough together if required.

On a lightly floured surface, roll out the dough to a large oval, about 5cm bigger than the top of your pie dish all round and 5–7mm thick. Cut a 2cm wide strip of pastry from around the outside. Dampen the rim of the pie dish with water, position the pastry strip on the rim and brush this with a little water. Lay the pastry oval over the top and press down the edges onto the pastry strip to seal. Crimp the edges to seal, then trim off the excess pastry.

Bake the pie for 30–40 minutes until the pastry is golden brown. Let the pie stand for 10 minutes before serving.

TOAD IN THE HOLE

SERVES 4

This British classic is simple but special. In recent years, 'toad in the hole' has become part of fine dining, not just a family dish. Either way, I want good pork sausages or spicy Lincolnshire bangers. One of the keys to achieving the best batter is to use good eggs; get the freshest you can for the best results.

8 sausages
60g beef dripping, in small pieces

For the batter
125g plain flour
1 tsp fine salt
2 large eggs
80ml milk
About 40ml cold water

Heat your oven to 220°C/Gas 7.

First make the batter. Put the flour and salt into a bowl, make a well in the middle and add the eggs. Using a wooden spoon, beat the mixture to a thick paste, incorporating the flour from the sides of the well.

Gradually add the milk and continue to mix until the batter is smooth and lump-free. Leave to rest for at least 30 minutes.

Place the sausages and dripping in a 30 x 20cm roasting tray and cook for 15–20 minutes, until browned.

Stir the cold water into the batter. It should now be the consistency of pouring cream; add a little more water if necessary.

Remove the hot tray of sausages from the oven, turn the sausages over then pour in the batter mix – take care as the fat may spit.

Return the roasting tray to the oven and cook for 20–25 minutes, until the batter is risen and crisp. Don't be tempted to open the oven door before the batter is cooked as this will cause it to sink. Serve with mashed potatoes and gravy.

RAISED PIE

SERVES 4

A pork pie is one of my favourite foods – eaten with mustard and a pickled onion or tomato. Make your own and you can vary the seasoning and flavours to your taste. To mould your pie crust, you can use a wooden structure called a dolly, as I have here, or alternatively a baked bean tin or a pie tin.

For the hot water crust pastry
250g plain flour, plus extra for dusting
50g strong white bread flour
40g cold unsalted butter, cut into small dice
50g cold lard, cut into small pieces
100ml water
¼ tsp fine salt
1 egg yolk, beaten, to glaze

For the filling
150g good-quality sausage meat
150g minced pork
100g pork loin, cut into 1cm dice
2 shallots, finely chopped
½ tsp ground mace
¼ tsp fine salt
A good pinch of white pepper
2 tbsp chopped flat-leaf parsley

For the jelly
½ chicken stock cube
150ml just-boiled water
3.2g leaf gelatine (2 sheets Costa brand)

Preheat your oven to 200°C/Gas 6 and line a baking tray with baking parchment.

To make the hot water crust pastry, combine the flours in a large bowl and rub in the butter using your fingertips until the mixture resembles breadcrumbs.

Put the lard, water and salt into a saucepan and place over a medium heat until the mixture just begins to boil, then immediately pour onto the flour and mix with a wooden spoon. Once cool enough to handle, gather the dough, tip onto a lightly floured surface and knead to form a smooth ball.

Cut off a quarter of the dough for the lid and set aside (ideally in the still-warm pan used to heat the lard mix as this will help to keep it pliable). Working quickly (while the pastry is still warm), flatten the larger ball of dough with the palm of your hand.

Take a 9.5 x 11cm wooden pie dolly, dust with flour and sit it in the middle of the dough. Use your hands to raise the pastry up the sides of the dolly.

Once you are almost halfway, turn the dolly upside down and work the pastry down the dolly until the pastry covers about three-quarters of it. Trim the edge to neaten and leave the pastry to set slightly.

To make the filling, mix all the ingredients together in a large bowl until well combined and shape into a cylinder, a bit smaller than the pie case on the dolly. Roll out the remaining pastry to a 12cm circle for the pie lid.

Continued overleaf

Use a small knife to ease the pastry case from the dolly then fill the cavity with the meat filling. (If the pastry falls down when it comes off the dolly just mould it up again over the meat.) Brush the edge of the pastry with beaten egg yolk and place the lid over the filling. Press the edges together to seal and trim off the excess pastry. Pinch the edges together to crimp decoratively.

Carefully lift the pie onto the prepared baking tray and cut a small hole in the pastry lid to let the steam out. Brush the top and sides of the pie with the beaten egg, taking care to get the brush into the crimped edge. Bake for 50 minutes until the pastry is golden brown. Leave to cool slightly.

In the meantime, to make the jelly, dissolve the stock cube in the boiling water in a bowl. Soak the gelatine leaves in a dish of cold water for a few minutes to soften. Lift out the gelatine, squeeze out any excess water, then add to the stock, stirring to dissolve.

Insert a funnel into the hole in the top of the pie and gradually add the gelatine mixture to fill the cavity between the meat and the pastry – add it a little at a time and let the liquid seep down before pouring in more. Once the pie is cool enough, place it in the fridge to set the jelly for a few hours, or overnight.

CHORIZO & CHILLI SCOTCH EGGS

MAKES 4

I love a Scotch egg and whenever I am working away and on the road it is one of my go-to snacks, along with a sausage roll. This is a modern variation and a world away from the ones you buy at a service station.

---

4 medium eggs
½ tsp cumin seeds
275g minced pork
80g unsliced chorizo, skin removed and cut into small dice
½ tsp smoked paprika
A pinch of dried chilli flakes
¼–½ tsp fine salt

For the coating
75g plain flour
3 medium eggs
150–200g white breadcrumbs
Oil, for deep-frying

Place the unshelled eggs in a pan, cover with water and bring to the boil. Boil for 7 minutes, then remove the eggs with a slotted spoon and immerse in cold water to cool quickly.

Toast the cumin seeds in a dry frying pan for a couple of minutes until fragrant but not burnt, then grind coarsely, using a pestle and mortar.

In a large bowl, mix the minced pork, chopped chorizo, toasted cumin, smoked paprika and chilli flakes together and add some salt. (To check the seasoning, break off a small piece of the mixture and fry in a little oil until cooked then taste it.)

Remove the boiled eggs from the water, tap to break the shells, then peel. Take three bowls and tip the flour into one, lightly beat the eggs in another and place the breadcrumbs in the third. Divide the meat mixture into 4 equal portions.

Lay a piece of cling film on your work surface, place a portion of the meat mixture on it and press down evenly to flatten. Take a boiled egg and dust with flour then sit on the flattened meat mixture. Bring the sides of the meat up around the egg, using the cling film to help wrap the egg; this also prevents the meat sticking to your hands.

Dip the meat-wrapped egg in the beaten egg, then coat thoroughly in breadcrumbs. Dip in the egg and crumbs once more, giving it two coats for a crisper outside. Repeat with the other 3 boiled eggs. Refrigerate for at least 30 minutes.

Heat your oven to 180°C/Gas 4. Heat the oil into a deep-fryer or in a large, heavy saucepan, filling it is no more than one-third full. Heat the oil to 170°C, or until a cube of bread dropped in turns brown in just over a minute. Deep-fry the eggs, two at a time, for 6–8 minutes until the outside is a deep golden brown colour, turning them over halfway through. Remove with a slotted spoon and drain on kitchen paper.

To ensure the meat is cooked through, place the Scotch eggs on a baking tray in the oven for a further 8 minutes. Eat hot or cold.

PUMPKIN PIE

SERVES 12

This traditional American pie has now become popular here as an autumnal dessert. I love the crisp base and the rich, spiced taste of the filling.

For the pastry
200g plain flour, plus extra for dusting
2 tbsp icing sugar, sifted
1 tsp ground cinnamon
100g cold unsalted butter, cut into small dice
1 medium egg, beaten
About 2 tsp very cold water

For the filling
450g pumpkin or butternut squash
2cm piece of root ginger, peeled and sliced
2 tbsp maple syrup
275ml double cream
1 medium egg, plus an extra 2 yolks
4 tbsp dark muscovado sugar
1 tsp ground cinnamon
½ tsp finely grated nutmeg, plus extra to finish

For the pastry, mix the flour, icing sugar and cinnamon together in a large bowl then add the diced butter and rub in with your fingertips until the mixture looks like fine breadcrumbs. Make a well in the centre and add the beaten egg mixed with the water. Using one hand, mix the liquid into the flour to bring the pastry together, adding a splash more water if needed. Gently knead the dough into a ball, wrap in cling film and leave to rest in the fridge for 30 minutes.

Roll out the pastry on a lightly floured surface to about a 30cm circle and use to line a 23cm loose-based tart tin, 3.5cm deep, leaving a little excess overhanging the edge. Prick the base all over with a fork, then refrigerate for 15 minutes. Meanwhile, heat your oven to 200°C/Gas 6.

Line the pastry case with a sheet of baking parchment and fill with baking beans. Bake 'blind' for 15 minutes, or until the pastry is dry to the touch and golden around the edge. Remove the beans and parchment and bake for a further 5–8 minutes, until the pastry case is crisp and golden all over. Let cool, then use a small, sharp knife to trim away the excess pastry from the edge.

For the filling, peel and deseed the pumpkin or squash and cut into roughly 2cm chunks. Place in a roasting tin with the ginger, trickle over the maple syrup and toss the pumpkin to coat. Cover with foil and bake at 200°C/Gas 6 for 25 minutes, or until tender. Remove from the oven and leave to cool. Turn the oven down to 180°C/Gas 4.

Tip the pumpkin, ginger and any syrup from the roasting tin into a food processor and blitz to a smooth purée. In a bowl, lightly beat the cream with the egg, extra yolks and muscovado sugar. Add the cinnamon and nutmeg then pour the mixture into the processor. Blend with the pumpkin until evenly combined.

Tip the filling into the pastry case and bake for 30–35 minutes, or until just set. Leave in the tin to cool, before cutting and serving. Dust with grated nutmeg to finish.

PECAN & PEAR TARTE TATIN

SERVES 6

As well as being impressive to look at, a tarte tatin is pretty straightforward to make, once you've got the knack. In this one, the pecans take on a lovely praline taste from being cooked in the caramel. Don't be afraid to cook the colour into the caramel, but don't let it go too far – there's a gap between caramelised sweetness and burnt. And make sure you tuck the pastry in well around the outside.

Plain flour, for dusting
350g ready-made all-butter puff pastry

For the filling
4 ripe dessert pears
Juice of ½ lemon
100g granulated sugar
50g unsalted butter
25g pecan nuts, roughly chopped

Lightly dust your work surface with flour and roll out the pastry on it to a circle, 5mm thick and 28cm in diameter. Trim to neaten. Lift the pastry round onto a baking sheet and place in the fridge to rest for 30 minutes. Meanwhile, heat your oven to 220°C/Gas 7.

For the filling, peel and halve the pears, then carefully remove the core from each half. Place the pears in a bowl and toss in the lemon juice.

Sprinkle the sugar in an even layer over the base of an ovenproof 24cm frying pan and set over a medium heat to melt and caramelise. Keep a close eye as the sugar will turn suddenly and, once it starts to colour, stir or move the pan around to ensure it caramelises evenly. When it is a golden caramel colour, remove the pan from the heat and stir in the butter, taking care as it is very hot and liable to splutter.

Sprinkle the chopped pecans over the caramel then arrange the pear halves, cut side down, on top. Lift the chilled pastry over the top and tuck the edges around the pears inside the edge of the pan. Cut off any excess pastry. Bake for 25–30 minutes, until the pastry is crisp and golden brown.

Leave the tarte tatin to stand for 5 minutes after removing from the oven, then run a knife around the edge of the pan. Protecting your hands with oven gloves, invert the tarte tatin onto a large, lipped serving plate (to hold the juices) then lift off the pan.

Serve with vanilla ice cream or cream.

CHOCOLATE SOUFFLÉ

SERVES 4–6

Making a soufflé is all down to timing. If the bake is perfect, this soufflé will hold from the oven for as long as 7 minutes. The smell of the chocolate is potent as you bring it to the table and dig in a spoon, and the texture is beautifully light and airy.

- 10g unsalted butter, softened, to grease the dish
- 1 tbsp cocoa powder, plus 2 tbsp to coat the dish
- 280ml whole milk
- 225g dark chocolate (60–70% cocoa solids)
- 2 tbsp caster sugar
- 2 tbsp cornflour
- 3 large eggs, separated, plus an extra egg white
- Icing sugar, sifted, for dusting

Butter a 1.4 litre soufflé dish then dust the inside with cocoa powder, rotating the dish on its side to coat evenly. Turn the dish upside down and tap out any excess.

Heat 250ml milk in a pan over a low heat until it is just simmering. Meanwhile, chop the chocolate into small pieces and place in a bowl. In another bowl, mix together the sugar, cornflour, 1 tbsp cocoa powder and remaining 2 tbsp milk.

Pour the hot milk onto the chocolate, stirring as you do so, and continue to stir until it has melted. Pour the chocolate milk onto the cornflour and cocoa mixture and stir until evenly blended. Return to the pan and heat, stirring, until it comes to the boil. Lower the heat and cook, stirring, for a further 2–3 minutes.

Put the 3 egg yolks into a medium bowl and pour on the chocolate mixture, whisking as you go. Cover the surface with cling film and leave to cool slightly (you can do this slightly in advance and let it cool to room temperature but it shouldn't be cold). Heat your oven to 190°C/Gas 5.

Whisk the 4 egg whites to fairly stiff peaks. Stir a spoonful of the egg white into the chocolate mixture to loosen it, then gently fold in the rest of the egg white.

Carefully tip the chocolate mixture into the prepared dish. Bake in the oven for 40–45 minutes until the soufflé is risen. Dust with icing sugar and serve immediately, with single cream.

QUEEN OF PUDDINGS

SERVES 4

Invitingly soft and unctuous, this is an indulgent pudding that looks wonderful yet is easy to make. It's thought to date back to the eighteenth century and is one of the best of British puds. The base of vanilla and lemon flavoured custard-and-breadcrumbs is covered with jam and then crowned with meringue.

Unsalted butter, for greasing
100g white breadcrumbs (preferably 1–2 days old)
100g raspberry jam

For the custard
600ml whole milk
Finely pared zest of 1 lemon
1 large egg, plus an extra 2 yolks
50g caster sugar
1 tsp vanilla paste, or the seeds from 1 vanilla pod

For the meringue
4 large egg whites
100g caster sugar

Heat your oven to 180°C/Gas 4. Butter a 1 litre pie dish and spread the breadcrumbs evenly over the base.

To make the custard, heat the milk slowly in a pan with the pared lemon zest until it just comes to the boil. Meanwhile, in a bowl, beat the whole egg and extra yolks with the caster sugar and vanilla paste or seeds. Remove the lemon zest from the hot milk, then pour it onto the egg mixture, whisking as you go.

Carefully pour the custard over the breadcrumbs in the dish and leave to stand for about 10 minutes, then bake for 25–30 minutes or until the custard is just set. Remove from the oven.

Warm the jam gently in a small pan (or in a bowl in the microwave), then spread over the set custard.

For the meringue, whisk the egg whites in a clean bowl until stiff. Gradually add the sugar, a spoonful at a time, whisking well between each addition, to make a smooth, glossy meringue.

Spoon the meringue on top of the pudding and return it to the oven for 15 minutes or until the meringue topping is golden brown. Serve straight away, with cream.

CHEAT'S MANGO & PASSION FRUIT SOUFFLÉ

SERVES 4

The beauty of this recipe is that it uses some store-cupboard ingredients to create a restaurant-looking dessert. The shortcut is to use ready-made custard, which works beautifully as the base for a sweet soufflé, along with tinned mango purée and ripe passion fruit.

Unsalted butter, for greasing
20g caster sugar, plus an extra 2 tbsp to coat the ramekins
100ml ready-made custard (tinned or carton)
75ml tinned mango purée
3 ripe passion fruit
4 large egg whites
Icing sugar, sifted, for dusting

Heat your oven to 200°C/Gas 6 and butter four ramekins. Put ½ tbsp caster sugar in each ramekin and rotate the dish so the sugar coats the base and the sides evenly. Tap out any excess.

Tip the custard and mango purée into a bowl. Cut the passion fruit in half, then scoop out the seeds and juice into the bowl. Mix with the custard and mango purée until evenly combined.

Whisk the egg whites in a clean bowl until stiff. Gradually add the 20g sugar, a spoonful at a time, whisking well between each addition, to make a smooth, glossy meringue. Gradually fold the meringue into the passion fruit and mango custard, using a large, metal spoon or spatula, until it is all incorporated.

Divide the mixture between the prepared ramekins. Use a palette knife to gently smooth and level the surface of each soufflé, then run your finger around the edge to lift the mixture away from the side slightly (this helps it to rise evenly).

Bake for 12–15 minutes until the soufflés are risen. Dust with icing sugar and serve immediately.

FLOATING ISLANDS

SERVES 6

This classic French dessert was first shown to me by my mother-in-law and is simply delicious, with fluffy clouds of meringue in a pool of creamy custard.

For the custard
600ml whole milk
1 vanilla pod, split lengthways
6 medium egg yolks
150g caster sugar

For the poaching liquid
500ml milk
500ml water
2 tbsp caster sugar

For the meringues
6 medium egg whites
150g caster sugar

For the caramel
100g granulated sugar

To make the custard, pour the milk into a pan. Scrape the seeds from the vanilla pod, using the tip of a knife or teaspoon, and add them to the milk along with the scraped-out pod. Heat gently until the milk is about to boil. Meanwhile, beat the egg yolks and sugar together in a bowl. Slowly pour the hot milk onto the egg yolk mix, whisking as you do so.

Pour the custard back into the pan and cook, stirring constantly, over a low heat until it is thick enough to coat the back of a spoon; this takes about 6–7 minutes. Remove from the heat and discard the vanilla pod. Cover the surface of the custard closely with cling film to prevent a skin forming and set aside.

For the poaching liquid, pour the milk and water into a sauté pan, add the sugar and bring to a simmer, stirring to help dissolve the sugar.

Meanwhile, for the meringues, whisk the egg whites until stiff. Add the caster sugar, a spoonful at a time, whisking well between each addition, until you have a thick, glossy meringue.

Use 2 big serving spoons to shape 6 large quenelles of meringue. To do so, take a heaped spoonful of meringue and pass it repeatedly between the spoons, turning and smoothing the sides as you do so. Add the meringue quenelles to the gently simmering liquor and poach gently for 8–10 minutes, turning once, until just firm to the touch. Remove the meringues from the poaching liquid with a slotted spoon, place on a tray or plate and set aside.

To make the caramel, scatter the granulated sugar evenly over the base of a clean pan and heat gently until it melts and turns a golden caramel colour.

Meanwhile, pour the warm custard into warmed serving bowls and sit a meringue in each portion. As soon as the caramel is ready, drizzle it over the meringues using a metal spoon, working quickly so the caramel doesn't set in the pan. Serve at once.

SWISS ROLL

SERVES 8

Once you've mastered this recipe, you can play around with the sponge and filling – rolling it up with praline cream or hazelnut chocolate spread such as Nutella, pouring over chocolate sauce, piping stripes into the sponge. As a child in the Northwest, I had Swiss roll as a pud with custard – give it a go!

Vegetable oil, for oiling
3 large eggs
100g caster sugar, plus an extra 2 tbsp for dusting
100g self-raising flour
1 tbsp warm water

For the filling
185g good-quality raspberry jam

Heat your oven to 200°C/Gas 6. Line a 32 x 22cm Swiss roll tin with baking parchment and oil this very lightly.

Using a hand-held electric whisk or food mixer fitted with the whisk attachment, whisk the eggs and sugar together in a large bowl until the mixture turns pale, increases in volume and is mousse-like in texture. This takes about 8–10 minutes. The mixture should be thick enough to hold a trail on the surface when the whisk is lifted. Sift the flour over the surface and carefully fold in. Finally, fold in the warm water.

Carefully pour the mixture into the prepared tin, tilting the tin so it spreads out evenly and gently easing it right into the corners. Bake for 10–12 minutes, until golden and firm to the touch.

Cut a sheet of baking parchment larger than the Swiss roll tin, place on a wire rack and sprinkle with the 2 tbsp sugar. Invert the sponge onto the paper, cover with a damp tea towel and leave to cool for 5 minutes.

Remove the tea towel and carefully peel the paper from the sponge. Lightly score a line along the short side nearest to you, about 1cm from the edge. Carefully roll up the sponge, folding along the score mark to make the first roll and using the paper to help. This initial roll, while the sponge is warm (before the jam is added), helps to prevent cracking.

Gently unroll the sponge, cover with the damp tea towel and leave to cool a little more, until just slightly warm. Trim the edges of the sponge to neaten. Spread the jam on the sponge, leaving a 2cm margin at the edges. Roll up the sponge again, starting at the short end along the score mark again. Roll up tightly, using the paper and both hands, patting gently as you go to keep the roll compact but still airy.

Trim the ends off the sponge to neaten then place the Swiss roll on a serving plate or board, with the seam underneath.

Photographs overleaf

PISTACHIO & ROSE PETAL ROULADE

SERVES 8

Swiss rolls shouldn't crack but roulades are allowed to. This roulade is filled with sweet buttercream and jam; if you'd prefer a less sweet version, replace the buttercream with 200ml cream, whipped until thick. I've used pistachios and rose here, for a hint of the Middle East.

Vegetable oil, for oiling
75g pistachio nuts
4 large eggs, separated
225g caster sugar, plus extra for dusting
¼ tsp cream of tartar

For the filling
75g unsalted butter, softened
150g icing sugar
120g rose petal jam

To finish
1–2 tsp food-grade dried rose petals

Heat your oven to 180°C/Gas 4. Line a 32 x 22cm Swiss roll tin with baking parchment and oil this very lightly. Finely chop the pistachios with a sharp knife or blitz in a small food processor.

Using a hand-held electric whisk or food mixer fitted with the whisk attachment, whisk the egg yolks and sugar together in a large bowl until the mixture turns pale, increases in volume and is thick and mousse-like in texture. This takes about 8–10 minutes. The mixture should be thick enough to hold a trail on the surface when the whisk is lifted. Carefully fold in 50g of the finely chopped pistachios.

In a clean bowl, whisk the egg whites with the cream of tartar until stiff. Now gently fold into the whisked pistachio sponge mixture, a spoonful at a time.

Carefully pour the mixture into the prepared tin, tilting the tin so it spreads out evenly, and gently easing it right into the corners. Scatter the remaining pistachios over the surface. Bake for 15–20 minutes until golden and firm to the touch.

Cut a sheet of baking parchment larger than the Swiss roll tin and place on a wire rack. Sprinkle the parchment with sugar. Invert the cooked sponge onto the parchment, cover with a damp tea towel and leave to cool completely.

Meanwhile, for the filling, beat the butter in a bowl until very soft then gradually beat in the icing sugar to make a smooth, fluffy buttercream.

Peel away the baking parchment from the sponge then trim the edges to neaten. Spoon the jam onto the sponge and spread it out evenly, leaving a 2cm margin around the edges. Dot over the buttercream then spread this out carefully, using a palette knife.

Score a line along one of the short sides of the roulade, 1cm in from the edge, making sure you don't cut right through. Carefully roll up the sponge quite tightly, folding along the incision to make the first roll and using the paper to help turn the sponge over. The roulade will crack a bit; this is normal.

Carefully transfer the roulade to a serving plate or board with the seam underneath. Scatter over a few edible rose petals to decorate and serve with fresh berries to cut through the richness, if you like.

CHOCOLATE & SALTED CARAMEL MACARONS

MAKES 30

It's a technical challenge to get perfect macarons but they'll taste good even if they don't look immaculate. The key, as with so many bakes, is to be patient. Leave the piped macarons to rest so that a slight skin forms on the top. You then bake them off, pipe your filling on the base and sandwich them together.

For the chocolate paste
3 large egg whites
240g ground almonds
240g icing sugar
40g cocoa powder

For the meringue
3 large egg whites
240g caster sugar
1 tbsp finely chopped cocoa nibs, to finish

For the salted caramel filling
150g granulated sugar
90ml double cream
½ tsp fine sea salt
30g unsalted butter

Line three baking trays with baking parchment. Using a 4.5cm cutter as a guide, draw circles on the paper, leaving 2cm space in between them. Turn the paper over and place on the baking tray (so you can see the circles but the lines won't mark the macarons).

To make the chocolate paste, put the egg whites into a bowl with the ground almonds, then sift over the icing sugar and cocoa powder. Mix together to form a thick paste.

To make the meringue, put the egg whites and sugar into a heatproof bowl and set over a pan of simmering water (making sure the water is not touching the bowl). Using a balloon whisk, beat the mixture thoroughly until the sugar dissolves and the mixture reaches a temperature of 65°C (as registered on a cook's thermometer).

Remove the bowl from the heat. Either transfer the mixture to a food mixer fitted with the whisk attachment or use a hand-held electric whisk to whisk until cooled and you have a stiff, glossy meringue; this will take at least 5 minutes.

Gradually fold the meringue into the chocolate paste, a spoonful at a time. The mixture is stiff so this will take some effort.

Spoon the mixture into a piping bag fitted with a 1cm nozzle, or snip the end off a paper piping bag to create an aperture of this size. Pipe the mixture evenly within the marked circles on the parchment. Sprinkle half of them with the chopped cocoa nibs.

Leave the macarons to stand, uncovered, for at least 30 minutes, or until a skin forms. Meanwhile, heat your oven to 150°C/Gas 2.

Bake the macarons for 15 minutes, until risen and set. Leave to cool completely on the baking trays before assembling.

To make the caramel, place the sugar in a small heavy-based saucepan or frying pan. Over a low heat and without stirring, gently melt the sugar until it turns a golden caramel colour. As soon as it has changed colour, slowly pour in the cream and stir, protecting your hand with an oven glove as the mixture will bubble ferociously. Keep stirring until the cream is incorporated, then add the salt and butter. Remove the pan from the heat and stir vigorously with a wooden spoon until the butter has melted. Leave to cool in the pan.

To assemble, transfer the caramel to a small paper piping bag and snip off the end. Pipe a little salted caramel onto the plain macaron bases, leaving a clear margin around the edge. Sandwich together with the cocoa-nib-topped macarons and place on a serving plate.

MATCHA MIRROR GLAZE GÂTEAU

SERVES 8

Matcha, a special Japanese powdered green tea, gives this sponge a modern flavour and brilliant colour; you can find it in health food shops. Once mastered, a mirror glaze turns a home-made cake into something beautiful. It's all about the shine and you have to be careful to get rid of all the crumbs, as every little bump will show. As the white chocolate glaze is very sweet, it is balanced with mascarpone cream between the layers, rather than a sweeter buttercream.

For the Genoise sponge
125g plain flour
2 tbsp premium-grade matcha powder
4 large eggs
125g caster sugar
30g unsalted butter, melted

For the filling
350g mascarpone
40ml double cream

For the white chocolate mirror glaze
5g leaf gelatine (3 sheets Costa brand)
175g white chocolate (inexpensive Milky Bar works particularly well)
75ml water
150g caster sugar
100g condensed milk

For the decoration
A handful of raspberries
10g white chocolate, grated
1 tsp food-grade dried rose petals
Small scrapes of gold leaf (optional)

Heat your oven to 180°C/Gas 4. Grease two 18cm loose-based cake tins and line the bases with baking parchment.

To make the Genoise sponge, sift the flour with the matcha and set aside. Place the eggs and sugar in a large heatproof bowl and set over a pan of barely simmering water, making sure the bowl isn't touching the water. Using a hand-held electric whisk, beat until the mixture is pale, tripled in volume and thickened to a mousse-like consistency. This will take around 7–8 minutes.

Remove the bowl from the heat and gently fold the flour mix into the whisked mixture, a couple of tablespoonfuls at a time, using a rubber spatula or a large metal spoon. Run the spatula (or spoon) around the outside of the mixture and then through the middle to incorporate the flour and keep in as much air as possible. Pour the melted butter around the side of the bowl and carefully fold in.

Divide the mixture between the prepared cake tins and bake for 15–20 minutes, until risen and the cake springs back when lightly pressed with your fingertips. Leave to cool in the tins for 5 minutes then remove and transfer to a wire rack. Leave to cool completely.

To make the filling, whisk the mascarpone and cream together in a bowl until thick.

To assemble the cake, use a large serrated knife to cut each sponge in half horizontally, turning the cake as you go (shown overleaf).

Continued overleaf

Place one sponge on a cake board and spread a thin layer of cream over the surface, starting in the middle and spreading outwards, then cover with another sponge disc. Repeat until you have all 4 sponge layers sandwiched together.

Spread the remaining cream over the top and sides of the cake to cover it completely, then use a palette knife and plastic scraper to smooth the surfaces. Any imperfections will show up once the mirror glaze is applied so take your time over this – turn the cake around as you spread the cream with the edge of the palette knife or a scraper and wipe the blade with a clean, damp cloth to keep it free of crumbs.

Place the cake in the fridge for 30 minutes to chill and firm up the cream. (You want the cream to be set firm but not too cold or the mirror glaze might crack.)

To make the mirror glaze, soak the gelatine leaves in a shallow dish of cold water to soften for a few minutes. Chop the white chocolate into small pieces and place three-quarters in a medium bowl. Put the water, sugar and condensed milk in a saucepan and heat, stirring occasionally, until the sugar has dissolved. Squeeze the excess water from the gelatine sheets then add them to the pan and immediately remove from the heat. Stir until the gelatine has dissolved.

Pour the gelatine mixture onto the chocolate and whisk until the chocolate has melted. Add the remaining chocolate and stir to melt. Strain through a fine sieve into a jug (this helps to remove any air bubbles). Leave the glaze to cool until it is almost the consistency of condensed milk but still pourable (at about 25–27°C, but the exact temperature varies according to the brand of chocolate). To cool the mixture quickly, place the bowl in a larger bowl filled with iced water.

Sit the cake on its board on a wire rack with a tray placed underneath. Carefully pour the glaze over the cake, starting at the outside edge so that it runs down over the sides and then pouring in a circular motion towards the middle. Some of the glaze will run off the sides but if it is too fluid leave it to cool for a little longer. Make sure the sides of the cake are covered, as well as the top. Leave for a few minutes to allow the glaze to set on the cake then chill in the fridge for an hour.

Decorate the top of the cake with raspberries, grated white chocolate, dried rose petals and, if you like, some scrapes of gold leaf.

CELEBRATIONS
TREATS FOR FAMILY & FRIENDS

WHENEVER YOU THINK OF A CELEBRATION – a birthday, wedding, anniversary or Christmas – it has symbols attached. These always include a bake.

Birthdays mean birthday cake, with everyone sitting round and the candles to blow out. I've made many cakes for my lad Josh growing up. He likes chocolate cake and some years it is covered in his favourite sweets. I make sure the cake is good, make a lovely ganache and cover it in Milky Bars or whatever he wants. It's fine to go out and buy a novelty cake, but a cake made by family or friends is always best.

Or take Easter. It makes me think of hot cross buns and Simnel cake. I love the marzipan on a Simnel cake, but in some ways it's the tradition of making that cake at that time which matters. Then there's Christmas cake. I like heavily fruited cakes with the crunch of royal icing, even though I'm full after dinner.

The story of a wedding cake goes back hundreds of years. When Queen Victoria married Albert, they had a big tiered cake covered in white icing and that is when it became known as 'royal icing'. Such special cakes have always been about showing off skills and, most of all, sharing. If you can get people around a table with a bake central to that – a bread, a cake or pastries, it's a way of communicating, enjoying what you eat and share.

Celebration cakes and bakes are often nostalgic because they are rooted in tradition and that's something we're very good at in this country. We have a long history of baking that has been passed down generation to generation. Every family has a go-to cake and with a bit of effort, even an everyday bake can be turned into something special – by decorating it and making it personal to you. If you know how to make a simple tea loaf, then you can make a round one and cover it with marzipan; decorate it with icing and put a bride and groom on the top and you'll have a straightforward wedding cake.

One of the first cakes that most people ever make is a Victoria sandwich. Mix it together, bung it in a tin and bake it. I like to put cream in the filling – this goes against the rules for some, I know, but cream and cherry jam it is for me. I put the jam in first and pipe cream on top of the jam in concentric circles. I also like to put plenty of icing sugar on top of the cake. You can heat skewers over a gas flame and press them on to burn the icing sugar and make a criss-cross pattern. Or decorate the cake with a pile or raspberries or cherries, the same flavour as the jam. All such ideas take the cake to another level.

Decoration needn't be elaborate. You can make a simple ganache (using a decent amount of chocolate and cream and a little bit of butter), pour it on and leave it to set. Melt some white chocolate and spin that over, then fan some strawberries over the top to finish. You've gone from a £5 to a £25 cake, with the minimum of effort and outlay. Always remember that a cake at a celebration can be the main event or the finale at the end of the meal; it's often what you remember, so make it good.

People can go overboard when it comes to decoration; I, for one, don't know when to stop. I love manipulating sugar paste. One year, I made a Christmas cake featuring mice in bed. The Christmas cake was the bed and the marzipan was the duvet and then I put sugar paste around the outside. There were twelve mice in the bed and I set the whole cake in a box, painting the walls with chocolate and making chocolate floorboards marked with toothpicks to get little knots. I put a sugar paste rug next to the bed and twelve pairs of slippers. Then I used sugar paste for Father Christmas's footprints to a fireplace, which I'd filled with chocolate sticks. I painted a picture of mice on the walls. There were stockings hanging on the bed post and toys spilling out from them onto the floor, all made with coloured sugar paste. By the time I'd finished, I'd set up a scene that wouldn't be out of place in *Wallace and Gromit*.

Imagination is key. Take inspiration from things you like. If you can model something in Plasticine, you can do it in sugar paste. It's like sculpture – you just have to think in a three-dimensional way. There are lots of templates you can buy these days, or draw your own, copying or tracing over an image to help.

I generally recommend baking a Madeira sponge for novelty cakes and large scale celebration cakes – so I've given a recipe in this chapter. It tastes good, is easy to cut and acts as a great base for other flavours and for your decorations. A whisked sponge would concertina down under even a slight amount of weight, but a Madeira will take icing, fruit, whatever you want. It's also important to use ingredients that will keep. Such cakes take time to make and you need to do them in advance of a big occasion, so use buttercream rather than fresh cream, for example.

For big occasions, I have created two stunning celebration cakes. Royal icing has fallen from fashion, in terms of home baking, but I love this tradition and show you how to ice a cake in this way on pages 286–9, giving the tips of a professional. When you are piping, don't overfill the icing bag. Hold the bag at the top, rolling it down as you go so you don't get air bubbles. Keep the nozzle close to the cake, for more control, and don't push out the icing too fast – work smoothly and steadily.

As well as a royal iced cake, I've given a recipe for a naked celebration cake, using a meringue-based icing that is scraped away to reveal part of the cake. The style is informal but the cake is modern and beautiful.

The recipes in this chapter are for celebrations with family and friends, when we want to push the boat out. Some are more straightforward, and some are my personal take on classics such as crème brûlée. Others, like the gingerbread house, take time. But, of course, you can simplify the decorations if you like; that applies to the other recipes in this chapter too. Whether you go to town or keep it simple, these bakes will lift a special occasion.

ICED BISCUITS

MAKES 25

To turn a simple biscuit into a gift, flood the top with a layer of thin icing then pipe your own designs in the centre using thicker icing.

225g plain flour
¼ tsp fine salt
100g icing sugar, plus extra for dusting
150g cold unsalted butter, cut into small dice
1 medium egg, beaten

For the icing and decoration
5 tbsp cold water
450g royal icing sugar
Food colourings of your choice
Edible silver balls (optional)

Sift the flour, salt and icing sugar into a large bowl. Add the butter and rub in with your fingertips until the mixture resembles breadcrumbs. Gradually add just enough beaten egg to bind, bringing the dough together with one hand.

Tip the dough onto a surface lightly dusted with icing sugar and knead lightly until smooth. Wrap in cling film and refrigerate for at least 30 minutes to firm up. Meanwhile, heat your oven to 180°C/Gas 4 and line two baking trays with baking parchment.

Dust your work surface with a little more icing sugar and roll out the dough to a 3mm thickness. Using biscuit cutters of your choice, stamp out shapes and place them on the prepared baking trays. Re-roll any trimmings and cut out more shapes to use all of the dough.

Bake for 12–15 minutes until the biscuits are pale golden in colour. Leave to cool and firm up on the tray for 5 minutes, then transfer to a wire rack to cool completely. Turn down the oven to its lowest setting.

To make the icing, put the water into a bowl, add the icing sugar and whisk using an electric whisk on a low speed until fully incorporated. Increase the speed and beat until the icing is thick but still pliant enough to pipe.

To make the 'flood icing', divide half of the icing between 2 or 3 bowls, according to the number of coloured icings you want to use. Add a little more water (1–2 tsp) to make them slightly runnier, then add food colouring, drop by drop, to each bowl to achieve the required colour, mixing well.

Put the thicker white icing into a small disposable piping bag fitted with a size 3 plain nozzle (or snip off the end to give a 2mm opening) and draw an outline or design on each of the biscuits. Spoon some flood icing within the outline and spread it out carefully using a cocktail stick.

Place the biscuits back on the baking trays and put into the cool oven for 30 minutes to allow the biscuits to dry out and the icing to set. Decorate some of the biscuits with silver balls too, if you like.

CHRISTMAS COOKIES

MAKES 20

Cookies are about texture and flavour. Get the basic mixture right for these sablé biscuits, then you can play around with the spicing and dust them with icing sugar or pipe on decorations.

150g unsalted butter, softened
75g icing sugar, sifted, plus extra for dusting
250g plain flour
½ tsp ground cinnamon
¼ tsp ground nutmeg
A pinch of ground cloves
A pinch of ground cardamom
¼ tsp ground ginger
¼ tsp fine salt
1 medium egg, beaten
Finely grated zest of 1 lemon
Finely grate zest of 1 orange

For the icing and decoration
1 egg white, lightly beaten
Icing sugar, sifted, for dusting

Beat the butter and icing sugar together in a large bowl until pale and fluffy. In another bowl, mix the flour with the ground spices and salt.

Gradually beat the beaten egg into the creamed butter and sugar, then add the grated citrus zests. Now add the flour mixture and stir until just combined; try not to overwork the dough – it will be very soft at this stage. Form it into a ball, wrap in cling film and place in the fridge to rest for at least 1 hour.

Heat your oven to 170°C/Gas 3½ and line two large baking trays with baking parchment.

Dust your work surface with icing sugar and roll out the dough to a 5mm thickness – keep it moving and add more icing sugar to your surface as necessary to prevent it sticking.

Using Christmas biscuit cutters of your choice, stamp out shapes and place on the prepared baking trays. Re-roll any trimmings and cut out more shapes to use all the dough.

Bake for 10–12 minutes until golden brown. Leave to cool and firm up on the trays for a few minutes, then transfer to a wire rack and leave to cool completely.

To decorate, using a fine brush, paint the edges of the cookies with egg white, then dust generously with icing sugar. Shake off the excess icing sugar to leave a decorative outline.

GINGERBREAD HOUSE

SERVES 15

Every Christmas we go away to France for a family holiday and do a chalet baking competition with other families. Each team gets a gingerbread house to decorate in an hour and I'm the judge, of course! The house will last about a week or so, over Christmas. You find the roof tiles – chocolate buttons or Smarties – tend to get eaten first; then the Flake chimney goes, and then people start snapping bits and pieces off all over the place.

For the dough

- 500g plain flour, plus extra for dusting
- 2 tsp bicarbonate of soda
- 2 tsp ground cinnamon
- 2 tsp ground ginger
- 1 tsp ground cloves
- 200g cold unsalted butter, cut into small dice
- 175g caster sugar
- 2 medium eggs
- 150g golden syrup
- 150g black treacle

For the decoration

- 9 boiled sweets (ideally red or yellow), crushed using a pestle and mortar (or a spice or coffee grinder or small food processor)
- 500g royal icing sugar, plus extra for optional icicles
- 6 tbsp water
- 200g giant chocolate buttons
- 75g apricot jam
- 75g desiccated coconut
- 9 chocolate Flake bars

To assemble

- A rectangular cake board, at least 25 x 18cm

Start by cutting out the templates for your gingerbread house. You will need to make three paper or card templates: a rectangular side wall (18 x 10cm); a rectangular roof (19 x 12cm); and a main wall with a triangular gable top (base 18cm, sides 18cm and then sloping into a triangular gable 29cm from base to apex). You will use these to make two side walls, two roof pieces, a front wall and a back wall.

To make the dough, in a large bowl, mix the flour, bicarbonate of soda and spices together. Add the butter and rub in with your fingertips until the mixture resembles fine breadcrumbs, then stir in the sugar.

In another large bowl, mix the eggs with the golden syrup and treacle. Add the flour mixture and mix to combine and form a soft dough. Transfer the dough to a lightly floured work surface and knead until smooth. Wrap in cling film and refrigerate for at least 1 hour.

Heat your oven to 180°C/Gas 4 and line four baking trays with baking parchment.

Halve the dough, then divide one half into one-third and two-thirds. Roll out each piece on a lightly floured surface to a 4mm thickness. Using the templates, cut out a front wall and a back wall from the largest piece, two side walls from the smallest piece, and two roof pieces from the other (medium) piece. Cut out two 4cm square windows from the side walls. Cut an 8 x 5cm door and a 5cm circular window in the front wall. (Keep the cut-out door.)

Lift the pieces onto the prepared baking trays, placing the front and side walls on two trays, and the roof pieces, back wall and cut-out door on the other two trays. Bake for 8 minutes, then take out the trays containing the front and side walls. Trim the windows with a knife, or use a cutter, to remove the dough that has spread, then fill with crushed sweets. Return to the oven for 7 minutes until the sweets have melted to resemble coloured glass and the gingerbread is firm.

Remove the trays containing the roof pieces, back wall and door after they've been in the oven for 15 minutes, or when they are firm. Leave the pieces of gingerbread to cool on the baking trays for 5–10 minutes to firm up, then transfer to wire racks to cool completely.

Mix 250g of the royal icing sugar with 3 tbsp water to make a thick pipeable icing and put into a piping bag fitted with a writing nozzle. Pipe the decoration of your choice onto the walls. Pipe parallel lines of icing on the roof and stick on the chocolate buttons, overlapping them slightly to resemble tiles. You can also pipe semi-circles of icing on each button for extra 'snow'. Leave the walls and roof to set for at least 10 hours, or overnight.

To assemble the house, have your cake board ready. Heat the apricot jam with a little water, then brush over the cake board. Cover with the desiccated coconut so it looks like snow.

Mix the remaining royal icing sugar and water to a thick paste. Pipe icing on the base and sides of the front wall. Use a mug as a prop and stand the front wall against it so that it remains upright and sticks to the cake board. Pipe icing along the sides and base of the other three walls. Place them firmly on the cake board and join the edges together to make a house, using more icing as needed to fill any gaps. As you go, use icing to stick 3 Flakes on the inside base of the house, against each wall (except the front wall with the door); also stick 4 Flakes upright on the corners to act as supports. Attach the front door with icing.

Leave to set for at least 10 hours or overnight before attaching the roof, storing the spare icing in an airtight container.

You can attach both roof pieces at once but it is easier to do this in two stages, leaving time for setting in between. Pipe a generous amount of icing on the top edge of one side wall and the front and back gable on the same side of the house. Use icing to attach a Flake to the top inside of that side wall to act as a support. Pipe icing on the edge of one roof piece and attach it to the house. Use a large glass (such as a pint glass) to prop it up until the icing sets. Leave to set for at least 5 hours, ideally overnight; store the spare icing in an airtight container.

Attach the other roof piece in the same way and leave to set.

To finish, pipe icicles along the roof edges, using more icing, if you like.

Photographs overleaf

SIDE WALL
RECTANGULAR ROOF
RECTANGULAR ROOF

GLUTEN-FREE VICTORIA SANDWICH

SERVES 8

I do baking demos around the country these days, and I've found that someone will always ask about gluten-free alternatives. The key to the best gluten-free flour is to mix different kinds together as they all have different qualities. The texture of this cake isn't quite as soft as a regular Victoria sandwich; it's more like a Madeira cake and tastes great.

225g unsalted butter, softened, plus extra for greasing
80g white rice flour
50g quinoa flour
50g tapioca flour
50g coconut flour
2 tsp baking power
1 tsp xanthan gum
225g caster sugar
4 medium eggs

To finish
100g raspberry jam
150g whipping cream
Icing or caster sugar, for dusting

Heat your oven to 180°C/Gas 4. Grease the base and sides of two 20cm loose-based cake tins and line the bases with baking parchment.

Sift all the flours together with the baking powder and xanthan gum into a bowl.

In another large bowl, beat the butter and sugar together until light and fluffy. Add the eggs, one at a time, beating well after each addition and scraping down the sides of the bowl with a spatula. Add the flour mixture and fold in, using the spatula or a large metal spoon until just fully incorporated.

Divide the mixture between the prepared cake tins and gently smooth the surface with a palette knife to level.

Bake in the centre of the oven for 25–30 minutes, or until the sponges are risen, golden and slightly shrunk from the sides of the tins. Leave in the tins for a few minutes, then remove and place on a wire rack to cool completely.

Choose the best-looking sponge for the top layer and then lay the other one, top side down, on your serving dish. Spread the jam over this bottom layer.

Whip the cream in a bowl to soft peaks and spread on top of the jam then place the other cake layer on top. Dust with sifted icing or caster sugar to finish.

CHOCOLATE CAKE

SERVES 12

This is my go-to chocolate cake recipe, perfect for birthdays, with a rich chocolate flavour – a great crowd-pleaser and a favourite of my wife Alex.

For the sponge
250g unsalted butter, softened, plus extra for greasing
250g caster sugar
3 large eggs
200g self-raising flour
1 tsp baking powder
50g cocoa powder
50g dark chocolate (60–70% cocoa solids), grated
125ml milk

For the filling
50g unsalted butter, softened
50g cocoa powder
120g icing sugar
1–2 tbsp milk

For the ganache topping
200g dark chocolate (60–70% cocoa solids)
15g unsalted butter
100ml double cream

Heat your oven to 180°C/Gas 4. Grease the base and sides of two 20cm loose-based cake tins and line the bases with baking parchment.

In a large bowl, beat the butter and sugar together until pale and fluffy. Add the eggs, one at a time, beating well between each addition. Sift the flour, baking powder and cocoa powder together over the surface of the mixture, add the grated chocolate and fold in until just evenly combined. Fold in the milk.

Divide the mixture between the prepared tins and gently smooth the surface with a palette knife to level.

Bake for 20 minutes, or until the cakes are risen and spring back when lightly pressed with the fingers. Leave in the tins for 5 minutes, then remove and place on a wire rack to cool completely.

To make the ganache topping, chop the chocolate into small pieces and place in a bowl with the butter. Gently heat the cream in a pan until it just begins to boil, then pour onto the chocolate and butter and stir until they have melted to form a smooth, shiny chocolate ganache. Leave to cool and thicken, until set but still spreadable.

To make the filling, beat the butter, cocoa powder and icing sugar together in a bowl, adding enough milk to make a smooth chocolate buttercream with a spreadable consistency.

To assemble, choose the best-looking sponge for the top layer and then lay the other one, top side down, on your serving plate. Spread with the chocolate buttercream then place the other sponge on top to sandwich the two layers together.

Using a palette knife, spread the chocolate ganache over the top of the cake, starting in the middle and working out towards the edges. Serve for tea, or with cream or ice cream as a birthday dessert.

CARROT CAKE

SERVES 8–10

My version of carrot cake uses more natural sugars – carrots, coconut, orange and agave syrup – for a less sweet flavour than you might be used to, but with a good balance.

Unsalted butter, for greasing
200g wholemeal self-raising flour
1 tsp baking powder
1 tsp ground cinnamon
¼ tsp fine salt
250g carrots, peeled and coarsely grated
75g walnuts, roughly chopped
Finely grated zest of 1 orange
Juice of ½ orange
150ml agave syrup
225ml melted coconut oil
2 large eggs

For the topping
75g unsalted butter, softened
150g full-fat cream cheese
1 tsp vanilla extract
Juice of ½ orange
1 tbsp desiccated coconut, lightly toasted, to finish

Heat your oven to 160°C/Gas 3. Grease the base and sides of a 20cm springform cake tin and line the base with baking parchment.

In a large bowl, mix together the flour, baking powder, cinnamon and salt. Add the grated carrots, chopped walnuts, orange zest and juice, and mix together well.

In a jug, whisk the agave syrup with the coconut oil and eggs until evenly blended, then pour onto the carrot mixture and stir until thoroughly combined.

Pour the mixture into the prepared tin and bake for 1 hour, or until a skewer inserted into the centre of the cake comes out clean. Leave to cool in the tin for 5 minutes then remove and place on a wire rack. Allow to cool completely.

For the topping, beat the butter until very soft, then add the cream cheese, vanilla extract and orange juice and beat until smooth. Cover and refrigerate to firm up until ready to use.

Place the cake on a plate or cake stand and spread the topping evenly over the surface. Sprinkle with the desiccated coconut to finish.

CHOCOLATE & MINT BUNDT CAKE

SERVES 12

I've used royal icing for the finish on this as it sets better than regular icing and stays in the grooves of the bundt cake. This recipe is for my mum, to make up for the time I ate all the After Eights I bought her as a present when I was a kid. I still love the chocolate and mint combination just as much as ever.

275g unsalted butter or margarine, softened, plus extra for greasing
275g caster sugar
2 large eggs
225g self-raising flour
50g cocoa powder

For the mint icing
100g royal icing sugar
½ tsp peppermint extract
4–5 tsp water
6 After Eight mints, halved on the diagonal

Heat your oven to 180°C/Gas 4. Butter a 2.4 litre bundt tin.

Place the butter or margarine and sugar in a food mixer fitted with the whisk attachment and beat together until pale and fluffy (or use a hand-held electric whisk and a large bowl). Add the eggs, one at a time, beating well.

Mix the flour and cocoa powder together, then add to the mixer on a slow speed and continue to mix for 2 minutes until evenly combined. Use a spatula to scrape down the sides of the bowl a couple of times as you go.

Spoon the cake mixture into the bundt tin and smooth the surface to level. Bake for 45–50 minutes, or until a skewer inserted into the deepest part of the cake comes out clean.

Leave the cake to cool in the tin for 10 minutes, then turn it out and place on a wire rack to cool completely.

For the mint icing, put the icing sugar into a bowl, add the peppermint extract and 1 tbsp water and mix together, then beat with a hand-held electric whisk until smooth and glossy. The icing should only just be able to run off a spoon: it must not be too thin; if it is too thick, add another 1–2 tsp water if necessary.

Place a tray under the wire cooling rack. Pour the mint icing along the grooves of the cake. Decorate with halved After Eight mints to finish.

HAZELNUT CAPPUCCINO CAKE

SERVES 12

I love hazelnuts in different dishes, whether it's nocciola ice cream or this luscious cake. Inspired by a cup of cappuccino, the coffee-syrup-soaked hazelnut sponge is layered up with more chocolate and coffee in the filling. It's a special cake – great for a celebratory pudding or tea.

250g unsalted butter, softened, plus extra for greasing
100g skinned hazelnuts
250g soft light brown sugar
4 large eggs
150g self-raising flour
2 tsp Camp coffee essence (or very strong coffee)
3 tbsp milk

For the coffee syrup
1 tsp instant coffee powder
3 tbsp soft light brown sugar
3 tbsp water

For the mocha filling
300g dark chocolate (60–70% cocoa solids)
20g unsalted butter
150ml double cream
2 tsp instant coffee powder

For the topping
100g mascarpone
50ml double cream
1 tsp Camp coffee essence (or very strong coffee)
1 tbsp icing sugar

To finish
1 tbsp cocoa powder
30g chopped toasted hazelnuts

Heat your oven to 180°C/Gas 4. Grease the base and sides of two 20cm loose-based sandwich tins and line the bases with baking parchment.

Put the hazelnuts in a food processor with 1 tbsp of the brown sugar and blitz until finely chopped.

In a large bowl, beat the butter and the rest of the sugar together until pale and fluffy. Add the eggs, one at a time, beating well between each addition. Add the flour and chopped nuts and fold in until just evenly combined. Fold through the coffee essence and milk.

Divide the mixture between the prepared tins, spreading it out gently. Bake for 20 minutes, or until the cakes are risen and spring back when lightly pressed with the fingers. Leave in the tins for 5 minutes, then remove and place on a wire rack to cool completely.

To make the coffee syrup, put the coffee powder, sugar and water into a small pan and bring to the boil, then immediately remove from the heat and leave to cool.

To make the filling, chop the chocolate into small pieces and place in a bowl with the butter. Gently heat the cream with the coffee powder in a saucepan until the coffee dissolves and the cream just begins to boil. Immediately pour onto the chocolate and butter and stir continuously until the chocolate has melted and you have a smooth, shiny mixture. Leave to cool and thicken, until set but still spreadable.

To make the topping, in a bowl, beat the mascarpone with the cream, coffee essence and icing sugar until smooth.

To assemble, carefully slice each cake in half horizontally, using a large, serrated knife. (To help keep the knife horizontal and cut in a straight line, move the cake around as you cut and keep one hand lightly on top.) Dampen each sponge layer with a little of the coffee syrup, using a pastry brush to apply it.

Place one sponge disc, cut side up, on a plate or stand. Spread a thin layer of chocolate filling, about 5mm thick, over the sponge. Repeat with two more layers of cake and chocolate filling, then place the final sponge disc on top, cut side down. Use a palette knife to spread the mascarpone topping over the top and sides of the cake.

Dust the top with a little cocoa powder and gently press the chopped hazelnuts around the outside of the cake.

BLACK FOREST GÂTEAU

SERVES 12

In Germany, you can't become a *konditor meister*, or master pâtissier, until you can make a Black Forest gâteau correctly. For me it's all about the chocolate, the cherries and the kirsch.

For the sponge
200g unsalted butter, softened, plus extra for greasing
200g caster sugar
6 large eggs, separated
130g self-raising flour
70g cocoa powder
3 tbsp milk

For the filling and topping
3 tbsp kirsch
4 tbsp cherry jam
900ml double cream, whipped
400g tin pitted black cherries, drained and halved (about 260g drained weight)

To decorate
60g dark chocolate (60–70% cocoa solids), finely grated
A handful of fresh cherries

Heat your oven to 180°C/Gas 4. Grease the base and sides of a 23cm springform cake tin and line the base with baking parchment.

Beat the butter and sugar together in a large bowl, using a hand-held electric whisk, until the mixture is pale and fluffy. Beat in the egg yolks one at a time. Sift the flour and cocoa powder together into another bowl, then fold into the whisked mixture, using a large metal spoon. Finally fold in the milk.

In a clean bowl, whisk the egg whites to soft peaks. Gradually fold into the chocolate mixture, a spoonful at a time, until fully incorporated.

Pour the mixture into the prepared tin and gently level the surface. Bake in the centre of the oven for 45–50 minutes, or until a skewer inserted into the middle comes out clean. Leave the cake in the tin for 5 minutes, then turn out and place on a wire rack to cool completely.

When you are ready to assemble the gâteau, using a large, serrated knife, carefully cut the cake horizontally into three even layers. (Keep the knife horizontal and straight, moving the cake around as you cut and keeping one hand lightly on top.)

Place one sponge disc on your serving plate and sprinkle evenly with 1½ tbsp kirsch. Spread half of the cherry jam over the sponge, then apply a layer of whipped cream, dolloping it on the cake and spreading it out with a palette knife. Scatter over half of the cherries. Place the middle layer of sponge on top, sprinkle with the rest of the kirsch, then repeat the jam, cream and cherry layers. Place the third sponge disc on top.

Load a palette knife with cream. Starting from the middle and working outwards, spread cream all over the top and the sides to cover the entire cake in a thin layer of cream. Press grated chocolate around the sides and dust the top with more chocolate. Pipe rosettes of cream around the edge of the cake and sit whole cherries on the rosettes.

LIQUORICE CRÈME BRÛLÉE

SERVES 4

Crème brûlée was the first thing I made for my mum when I was around seventeen, along with roast chicken. She thought it was very smart. I love that moment when you crack through the caramel and get to the soft, creamy custard. This one is flavoured with liquorice, one of my favourite sweets from a local shop in Wallasey when I was growing up.

350ml double cream
250ml whole milk
1 vanilla pod, split lengthways
125g soft natural liquorice
5 large egg yolks
3 tbsp caster sugar

For the brûlée topping
4 tbsp caster sugar
4 tbsp icing sugar

Heat your oven to 160°C/Gas 3. Stand four shallow ramekins, about 200ml capacity and 10cm in diameter, in a roasting tin.

Pour the cream and milk into a pan. Scrape the seeds from the vanilla pod, using the tip of a knife or teaspoon, and add them to the milk along with the scraped-out pod. Chop the liquorice into small pieces and add to the pan. Heat gently until the creamy milk is just coming to the boil, stirring so the liquorice partially melts, infusing the liquid with flavour and adding colour. Remove from the heat.

In a bowl, whisk the egg yolks with the caster sugar for 2–3 minutes, until the mixture is smooth and turns a little paler in colour. Strain the hot infused milk onto the whisked mixture, stirring as you do so.

Pour the custard mixture into the ramekins, dividing it equally. Pour water into the roasting tin until it comes halfway up the side of the ramekins. Cook in the oven for 40–45 minutes, or until the custards are set but still have a slight wobble in the middle.

Remove the ramekins from the roasting tin, cover with cling film and leave to cool completely. Refrigerate until required.

When you are ready to serve, sprinkle the surface of each brûlée with 1 tbsp caster sugar and then sift 1 tbsp icing sugar on top (the icing sugar gives shine and the sugar lends crunch).

Caramelise the surface using a cook's blowtorch. Alternatively, place under a preheated hot grill, about 5cm from the heat source, until the sugar melts and turns a deep golden colour (about 7–9 minutes, depending on your grill). Leave the caramel to set and harden for about 5 minutes before serving.

BAKED ALASKA

SERVES 8

I was introduced to baked Alaska by my mother-in-law, who is really good at making it. There's a cold ice-cream interior with a coating of meringue, and it's flashed in the oven to colour the meringue. It shouldn't work but it does.

For the sponge base
125g unsalted butter, softened, plus extra for greasing
125g caster sugar
2 medium eggs
100g self-raising flour
25g cocoa powder

For the ice cream filling
500g chocolate brownie ice cream
300g salted caramel ice cream

For the meringue
3 medium egg whites
¼ tsp cream of tartar
175g caster sugar

Heat your oven to 190°C/Gas 5. Grease the base and sides of a 20cm loose-based cake tin and line the base with baking parchment.

In a large bowl, beat the butter and sugar together until pale and fluffy. Add the eggs, one at a time, beating well after each addition. Sift the flour and cocoa powder together over the mixture and fold in, using a large metal spoon.

Spread the mixture in the prepared tin – this is a stiff mixture to make a firm sponge base. Bake for 20–25 minutes until the sponge is risen and springs back when lightly pressed.

Leave the cake in the tin for 10 minutes, then remove and place on a wire rack to cool completely. Take the chocolate ice cream out of the freezer so it softens slightly while the cake cools (about 30 minutes).

Line a 900ml pudding basin with cling film. Beat the chocolate ice cream with a spoon until soft, to make it easier to manipulate. Spread the ice cream over the base and sides of the basin to form an even layer. Cover with cling film and sit a smaller bowl in the centre (to create a hollow in the middle). Place in the freezer just long enough for the ice cream to set – about 1–1½ hours, depending on your freezer. Meanwhile, take the salted caramel ice cream out of the freezer so it softens slightly (about 30 minutes).

Take the chocolate ice cream from the freezer and remove the smaller bowl and cling film around it. Beat the softened salted caramel ice cream with a spoon, then spoon into the hollow in the centre of the chocolate ice cream. Cover with cling film, return to the freezer and leave to freeze completely – about 1–1½ hours.

Heat your oven to 220°C/Gas 7. To make the meringue, whisk the egg whites in a clean bowl to stiff peaks. Add the cream of tartar, with a spoonful of the sugar, and whisk to combine. Continue to whisk in the sugar a spoonful at a time, until it is all incorporated and you have a thick, glossy meringue.

Place the chocolate sponge in the middle of a baking sheet. Remove the ice cream bombe from the bowl, pulling on the cling film lining to help ease it out. Sit the ice cream, flat side down, on the sponge and remove the cling film. Spread the meringue over the ice cream to cover it and the sponge base completely. Place in the oven for 3–4 minutes until the meringue is just beginning to brown.

Slide the baked Alaska onto a large plate and serve immediately.

BASIC MADEIRA CAKE

MAKES 40–60 SLICES (ONCE ICED)

Madeira has more of a chew than a Victoria sandwich sponge and is the best cake to use as the basis for a celebration cake. Cakes for special occasions are often decorated beautifully but the cake inside can often be disappointing. This recipe delivers every time. When making large cakes it is much easier to use a stand mixer fitted with the paddle attachment, if you have one. The following recipe is used to make the two tiered celebration cakes on the pages that follow.

For the 15cm cake
165g self-raising flour
110g caster sugar
110g soft tub margarine, plus extra for greasing
2 medium eggs
1 tbsp milk

For the 23cm cake
450g self-raising flour
400g caster sugar
400g soft tub margarine, plus extra for greasing
7 medium eggs
3 tbsp milk

Heat your oven to 150°C/Gas 2. Grease the base and sides of a 15cm and a 23cm deep loose-based cake tin and line the base and sides of both tins with baking parchment.

Put all the ingredients for the 15cm cake in a food mixer fitted with the paddle attachment and start mixing on the lowest speed to combine the ingredients. Then increase the speed and mix for about 1 minute until the mixture is smooth and pale in colour. Pour into the lined tin and smooth the top to level. Use the same method to prepare the larger cake.

You can cook the cakes together, ideally on the same shelf in the centre of the oven. Allow about 1 hour for the smaller cake, about 1¾ hours for the larger cake; do not open the door to check the smaller cake before 55 minutes. The cakes should be risen, lightly golden and spring back when pressed gently. To test, insert a skewer into the centre of the cake: it should come out clean. If not, continue baking for a further 5–10 minutes.

When each cake is ready, remove from the oven and leave to cool in the tin for 5 minutes, then turn out and place on a wire rack. Leave to cool completely.

CLASSIC ICED CELEBRATION CAKE

MAKES ABOUT 60 SLICES

This simple, elegant cake is ideal for a wedding, christening or other celebration. For a professional finish, invest in a few items of equipment from a specialist cake supplier – a turntable, a plastic scraper, an icing smoother and a straight-edge rule. You'll also need a non-stick rolling pin, small piping bags and 2mm and 3mm piping nozzles (i.e. sizes 3 and 5). As for timing, if the celebration is on a Saturday, bake the cake on the Monday, marzipan it on the Tuesday and royal ice on the Wednesday. Apply the sugar paste on the Thursday and pipe the finishing touches on the Friday. Position any fresh flowers at the last minute.

1 x 15cm Madeira cake
1 x 23cm Madeira cake (see page 281)

For the royal icing
50ml cold water
2 tsp dried egg white powder
260g icing sugar (regular not royal), sifted

For the buttercream
250g unsalted butter, softened
400g sifted icing sugar (regular, not royal)
About 1 tbsp rose water, to taste

To assemble and decorate
1.5kg natural marzipan
1.75kg sugar paste or ready-to-roll icing (in your chosen colour)
Gel food colouring (in your chosen colour)
Fresh flowers (optional)

To make the royal icing, put the water into a bowl, add the egg white powder and whisk until dissolved to form to a milky, lump-free liquid. (Using powdered instead of liquid egg white gives the icing lightness.)

Pour the egg white liquid into a food mixer fitted with the paddle attachment and add half the icing sugar. Mix on a slow speed to combine and then add the remaining icing sugar, a spoonful at a time, until you have the consistency of soft whipped cream.

Increase the speed to medium and beat until the mixture doubles in volume and turns glossy; this will take about 5 minutes. Now beat on the fastest setting for 2 minutes until the icing is fluffy. Transfer to a bowl, cover with a clean damp cloth and set aside until ready to use.

To make the buttercream, beat the butter using a hand-held electric whisk until very soft. Gradually add the icing sugar, mixing on a slow speed until it is all incorporated. Then increase the speed and beat until fluffy and paler in colour. The buttercream needs to be quite stiff otherwise the cake layers will move. Flavour with rose water, to taste.

To assemble, place the cakes on a work surface and, using a large serrated knife, carefully trim off the top of each so they are level. Cut each cake in half horizontally, using the knife. Spread a thin, even layer of buttercream (about 5mm thick) over the bottom half of the 23cm cake, then position the other half on top. Sandwich the 15cm cake together with buttercream in the same way.

Continued overleaf

Items for assembly
Two 30cm round cake drum boards
13cm round single-thickness card
1.7 metres ribbon (to go around the 23cm cake and 30cm board)
Double-sided tape (to stick the ribbon on)

TO APPLY THE MARZIPAN

Knead 500g marzipan into a smooth ball and roll out on a surface lightly dusted with icing sugar to a circle, about 27cm in diameter, turning it as you roll to prevent it sticking and using just enough icing sugar to keep it moving. Make sure the marzipan is an even thickness and that it moves freely and is not sticking to the work surface.

Spread a fine, even layer of buttercream over the top of the larger cake (to stick the marzipan to the cake). Invert the cake onto the centre of the marzipan round. Push the edge of the marzipan towards the edge of the cake then trim away all but 2mm marzipan. Using the straight edge of the scraper, push the excess 2mm marzipan so it is flush with the sides of the cake. Slide the cake to the edge of the work surface, turn it over and place on a 30cm drum board so the marzipan is on top and level. Clean the work surface.

Take another 500g marzipan to cover the sides and knead to soften then shape into a cylinder. Dust the work surface with icing sugar to prevent sticking and roll the marzipan out to a rectangle, 75 x 12cm and 5mm thick. Trim the short ends and one long side to straighten.

Spread the sides of the cake with a thin layer of buttercream, wiping the palette knife clean as you go to prevent crumbs going into the buttercream. Lift the cake from the board, easing it up with the palette knife. Place the cake on its side so the straight edge of the marzipan is at the top. Roll the cake along the marzipan strip to cover the side.

Lightly dust the work surface with icing sugar and place the cake on it, marzipan-covered top down. Push the two ends of the marzipan strip together and rub to smooth the join. Using a sharp knife and a short, sawing motion, trim off the excess marzipan from the uppermost bottom edge of the cake, making sure the blade is flat onto the cake, not at an angle. Put a blob of royal icing in the centre of the drum board (to help the cake stay in position). Slide the cake to the edge of your work surface, turn it over and place back on the drum board. Brush away any excess icing sugar. You should have a level, smooth cake.

Spread a thin layer of buttercream on top of the smaller cake and cover with marzipan in the same way, but roll out 250g marzipan to a 19cm circle for the top and 250g marzipan into a 45 x 12cm strip, 5mm thick, for the side.

Spread a thin layer of buttercream on the base of the smaller cake and stick on the 13cm piece of card. Turn the cake over so the base is on the bottom and the marzipan on top. Place the cake on the loose base of a cake tin slightly larger than the cake (this helps when moving it).

Continued overleaf

TO APPLY THE ROYAL ICING

Place the larger cake on a turntable. Load one side of the palette knife with royal icing and spread on top of the cake from the centre outwards to form a smooth layer, rotating the turntable as you go. Transfer the cake on its board to the work surface. Wipe a straight-edge rule with a damp cloth and hold it at a 45° angle, sloping towards you. Starting at the far side and keeping the tool level on the top of the cake, in one movement pull the straight edge across the cake towards you, then turn it so that it slopes away from you and repeat, this time pushing the straight edge to the back of the cake until the icing is smooth. It can take two or three goes to get the icing smooth and level. Wipe the palette knife with a damp cloth and hold the blade flat against the icing to scoop off any excess in small sections, wiping the knife clean between each stroke.

Load one side of the palette knife with royal icing and spread it around the sides of the cake, keeping the knife upright and flat against the cake. Try not to overlap with the top of the cake. Wipe the scraper with a damp cloth. Return the cake to the turntable. Holding the turntable with the other hand and starting at 12 o'clock, smooth the icing around the side in sections. Keep turning the cake towards your position at 6 o'clock, keeping the scraper flat against the sides at all times.

Now, in one movement, use a clean scraper to give a smooth finish on the side, starting at 12 o'clock and rotating and scraping the side as the cake goes around 360°. Use a palette knife to gently scrape off the icing where the sides meet the top. Remove any excess from the base.

Repeat to coat the smaller cake with royal icing. Leave, uncovered, overnight to dry and set. Store any spare icing in an airtight container.

TO COVER THE BOARD WITH SUGAR PASTE

To cover the (unused) drum board, take 250g sugar paste and knead on a clean surface until smooth. Roll out on a surface lightly dusted with icing sugar until slightly larger than the board. Use your icing smoother to rub the surface of the paste and give it a shine. Wipe the drum board with a damp cloth (this is enough to stick on the sugar paste). Slide your fingers under the sugar paste and in one movement lift it onto the drum board. Trim any excess from the edge. Smooth the edges with your fingers where the paste meets the edge of the board. Leave, uncovered, overnight to set.

TO COVER THE CAKE WITH SUGAR PASTE

Take the larger cake and trim the edge of the top icing, using a sharp knife. Take 1kg sugar paste and knead into a smooth ball. Lightly dust

Continued overleaf

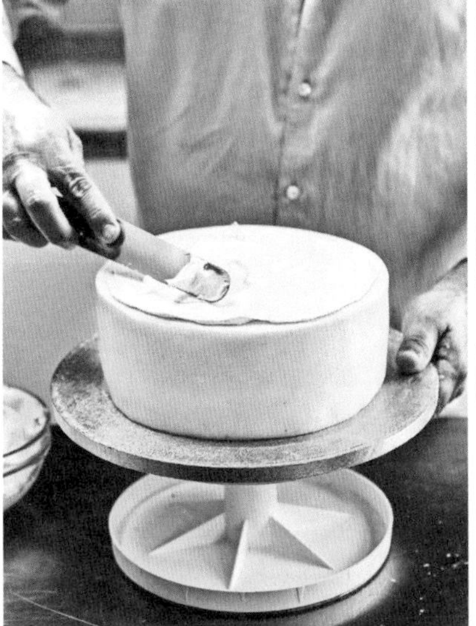

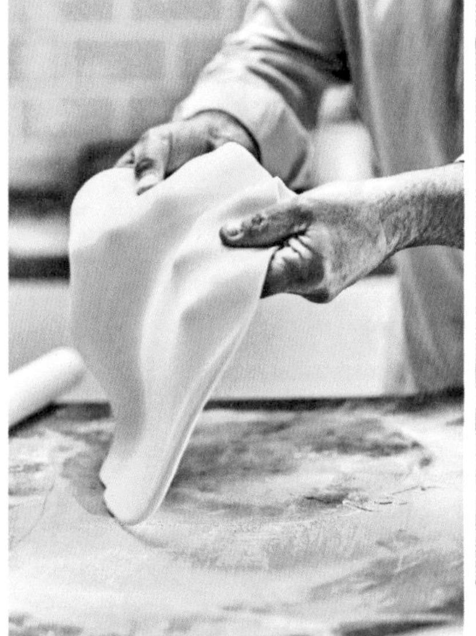

the work surface with icing sugar and roll out the sugar paste on it to a large circle, 38cm in diameter and 5mm thick, keeping the sugar paste moving. If any air bubbles appear on the surface, prick them with a needle then rub over with the smoother. Wipe the top and sides of the cake with a clean damp cloth to barely dampen the surface of the royal icing (this will enable the sugar paste to stick).

Dry your hands then lift the sugar paste and position over the cake. Starting on top, smooth out the icing then gently ease it down and around the side of the cake, using the palms of your hands to smooth it as you go. Trim the excess paste from the bottom edge of the cake.

Take your smoother and quickly but gently buff the top and sides of the cake, going back and forth (just as you would buff shoes). This will give straight sides and ease out any blemishes in the sugar paste. Trim the bottom edge as neatly and as close to the cake as possible.

Cover the smaller cake with sugar paste in the same way, using 500g sugar paste and rolling it out to a 32cm circle. Leave to set overnight.

TO ASSEMBLE AND FINISH

Take the sugar-paste covered drum board, spread a little royal icing on the centre and lift the large cake (off its board) on to this covered drum board. Spread a little royal icing on top of the large cake and position the small cake (on its card) on top. Place on the turntable.

Spread the remaining royal icing on a work surface or board to remove any air bubbles and make it smooth. Add a little colouring and stir in using a cocktail stick until it is a similar shade to the sugar paste.

Put some of the coloured icing into a small piping bag fitted with a 2mm (size 3) nozzle, being careful not to overload it as this makes it harder to control. Pipe two rows of small balls onto the icing around the side of the smaller cake. To do this, place the nozzle on the cake and squeeze the bag to form the ball, then stop squeezing and twist the bag away from the cake. You may find there is a peak on the ball. To remove this use a fine, damp paintbrush to wipe away.

Put some more coloured icing into a small piping bag fitted with a 3mm (size 5) nozzle. Angle the bag and pipe a row of balls where the small cake meets the large cake in order to cover the join.

Attach ribbon around the base of the cake, using a little icing (overlap the ends slightly). Attach ribbon around the edge of the drum board using double-sided tape. Decorate the cake with flowers if you wish.

To cut the cake, lift the smaller cake off the larger one, then use a large, serrated knife to cut each cake into small slices. Wipe the knife with a clean, damp cloth after each cut, to get clean slices without crumbs.

NUDE MERINGUE FINISH CELEBRATION CAKE

MAKES ABOUT 40 SLICES

Just as in fashion, there are trends in baking and cakes. Currently nude cakes are in vogue, where you can see the cake through the icing and the finish isn't as precise as for iced cakes. The proportions of the cake are also deeper than is traditional, usually one and a half times the depth of a cake tin. To achieve this you need to make one and a half cakes in each size and sandwich them together. For a really good finish, you'll need a turntable and a plastic scraper. This icing will last up to 2 days. Do not put the iced cake in the fridge.

For the 15cm cake
165g self-raising flour
110g caster sugar
110g soft tub margarine, plus extra for greasing
2 medium eggs
1 tbsp milk

For the 23cm cake
450g self-raising flour
400g caster sugar
400g soft tub margarine, plus extra for greasing
7 medium eggs
3 tbsp milk

For the half-depth 15cm cake
90g self-raising flour
60g caster sugar
60g soft tub margarine
1 medium egg
1½ tsp milk

For the half-depth 23cm cake
225g self-raising flour
200g caster sugar
200g soft tub margarine
3 medium eggs
2 tbsp milk

Heat your oven to 150°C/Gas 2. Grease the base and sides of two 15cm and two 23cm deep loose-based cake tins and line the bases and sides of both tins with baking parchment. (Or you can manage with one of each sized tin, re-greasing and lining to bake the half-size cakes.)

For each of the full-size cakes and the half-size 23cm cake, it is best to use a food mixer fitted with the paddle attachment. Place all the ingredients for the particular cake in the mixer and start mixing on the lowest speed to combine. Then increase the speed and mix for about 1 minute until the mixture is smooth and pale in colour. Pour into the lined tin and smooth the top to level.

For the half-size 15cm cake, place all the ingredients in a large bowl and mix together with a hand-held electric whisk, until smooth and combined. Pour into the lined tin and smooth the surface to level.

You can cook two cakes at the same time, ideally on the same shelf in the centre of the oven, but don't open the oven until near the end of the cooking time for the smaller one. Allow about 1 hour for the full-size 15cm cake and about 1¾ hours for the full-size 23cm cake. Allow 35–40 minutes for the half-size 15cm cake and 45–50 minutes for the half-size 23cm cake. The cakes should be risen, light golden and spring back when pressed gently. To test, insert a skewer into the centre: it should come out clean; if it doesn't, bake for a further 5–10 minutes.

When ready, take the cakes from the oven and leave to cool in the tin for 5 minutes, then turn out and place on a wire rack to cool completely.

Continued overleaf

For the filling
300g good-quality jam (ideally a tart flavour such as raspberry or damson)

For the meringue frosting
100ml cold water
4 tsp dried egg white powder
500g icing sugar, sifted

For the decoration
Fresh flowers and foliage

To assemble
30cm cake drum board
16cm round single-thickness card
Double-sided tape
1 metre ribbon (to go around the 30cm board)

For the meringue frosting, put the water into a bowl, add the egg white powder and whisk until dissolved to form a milky, lump-free liquid. Pour into a food mixer fitted with the paddle attachment and add half the icing sugar. Mix on a slow speed to combine, then incorporate the remaining icing sugar, a spoonful at a time, until the icing is the consistency of soft whipped cream. Increase the speed to medium and beat until the mixture doubles in volume and turns glossy; this will take about 5 minutes. Beat on the fastest setting for 2 minutes until the icing is fluffy. Transfer to a bowl and cover with a damp cloth.

Trim all the cakes level, using a serrated knife, then cut both deep cakes in half horizontally.

To assemble, spread a layer of jam on the bottom half of the deep 23cm cake and sandwich together with the other half, pressing the top down firmly. Spread with another layer of jam and place the half-size 23cm cake on top with the base uppermost, creating a three-layer cake. Place in the centre of the 30cm drum board.

Repeat the sandwiching process with the 15cm cake, using the rest of the jam. Put 1 tsp of the meringue mix in the middle of the 16cm round of card and sit the cake on top; the meringue will prevent the cake moving. Place centrally on the larger cake to check that the layers are level then lift off and position the smaller cake on the loose base of a cake tin (this is to help when moving the cake).

Use a dry pastry brush to remove any excess crumbs from the cakes. Place the 23cm cake on the turntable. Place a quarter of the meringue on top of the cake and spread it out using a palette knife, working from the centre outwards. Don't worry if the meringue goes down the sides. Try not to touch the cake with your palette knife, only the meringue. Load one side of the palette knife with more meringue and gently ease in sections over the side of the cake until all of it is covered, icing the section of the cake in front of you and rotating the turntable as you go.

Take your plastic scraper and use it to remove excess meringue from the side to give the cake an irregular finish; you should be able to see the sponge in places.

Repeat this with the smaller cake, making sure you cover the edges where the cake meets the card. Use a palette knife to lift the cake and remove the loose cake base. Sit the smaller cake on the larger cake.

Use a cook's blowtorch to brown the meringue in patches, moving the flame all the time and taking care not to burn the icing. Attach the ribbon around the drum board using double-sided tape. Decorate the cake with fresh flowers and foliage.

CHOCOLATE TRUFFLES

MAKES 20–30 (DEPENDING ON SIZE)

When you trim cakes to make the top level, you have some spare sponge that you can quickly blitz in a food processor to turn into crumbs. This recipe is inspired by one of my first jobs in a bakery, using up the off-cuts from cakes to make delicious little chocolate truffles. If you like, you can also use some crumbs to make a crisp outer coating.

150g dark chocolate (60–70% cocoa solids), cut into small pieces
75g unsalted butter
150g cake crumbs
1–2 tbsp rum, brandy, amaretto, Grand Marnier or other liqueur of your choice (optional)

For the crispy crumb coating (optional)
75g unsalted butter, melted
50g caster sugar
120g cake crumbs

Alternative coatings
About 2 tbsp sifted icing sugar, sifted cocoa powder or toasted desiccated coconut

If you want to make the crispy crumb coating, heat your oven to 200°C/Gas 6 and line a baking tray with baking parchment. Put the melted butter, sugar and cake crumbs into a bowl and mix until well combined, then spread out on a baking sheet and place in the oven for 15–20 minutes, until the crumbs are crispy and golden brown; keep a close eye to make sure they don't get too brown and become bitter. Remove from the oven and leave to cool.

Once cold, break up the crispy crumb into small breadcrumb-sized pieces, either using your fingers or by putting the mixture into a strong plastic bag and breaking it up with a rolling pin.

To make the truffles, put the chocolate and butter into a heatproof bowl and set over a pan of simmering water, making sure the bowl is not touching the water. Leave until melted, then take the bowl off the heat, add the cake crumbs and mix well. Stir in 1 tbsp liqueur, if using; taste and add up to 1 tbsp more if you want a stronger flavour. Stir well, then leave until firm enough to mould. You can speed this up by putting the bowl into the fridge once cool enough.

Set out 20–30 petit four cases on a baking tray or plate. Take heaped teaspoonfuls of the set truffle mix and roll into balls between your fingers. Roll the truffles in your choice of topping and place in the petit four cases. Store in an airtight container in a cool place and eat within 3 days.

INDEX

D

E

F

Many people have made this, my very personal book, possible.

Big thanks go to Claire Bassano for her help with recipe development, assisted by Emma Godwin and Wendy Munro.

To the whole team at Bloomsbury, thank you so much for all the guidance and support: Natalie Bellos, Xa Shaw Stewart, Lisa Pendreigh and Richard Atkinson in editorial; production manager Arlene Alexander; and Ellen Williams and Amanda Shipp in publicity and marketing.

To Hattie Ellis, a massive thank you for your patience and for skillfully turning my voice into words; and to Janet Illsley, thank you for your great project editing.

Thanks to Martin Poole and your assistant Lucia Lowther for the amazing photographs, to Rachel Jukes for propping and to Emma and Alex Smith for the fantastic design and art direction.

To the team that look after me: Geraldine Woods, Kate Cooper and, of course, Anna Bruce.

I'd also like to thank the Love Productions team, who created the television series that accompanies this book.

Last but certainly not least, a huge thanks for your constant support and love to my wife Alex and my son Joshua...